Stories
Can
Save
Us

Stories
Can
Save
Us

America's Best Narrative
Journalists Explain How

Matt Tullis

THE UNIVERSITY OF GEORGIA PRESS
Athens

Published in 2024 by the University of Georgia Press
Athens, Georgia 30602
www.ugapress.org
© 2022 by Matt Tullis
All rights reserved
Designed by Mary McKeon
Set in 11/15 Adobe Garamond Pro

Printed and bound by Sheridan Books, Inc.
The paper in this book meets the guidelines for
permanence and durability of the Committee on
Production Guidelines for Book Longevity of the
Council on Library Resources.

Most University of Georgia Press titles are
available from popular e-book vendors.

Printed in the United States of America
28 27 26 25 24 P 5 4 3 2 1

Library of Congress Cataloging-in-Publication Data
Names: Tullis, Matt, 1975–2022 author.
Title: Stories can save us : America's best narrative journalists explain how
    / Matt Tullis.
Description: Athens : The University of Georgia Press, 2024.
Identifiers: LCCN 2023056420 | ISBN 9780820366777
    (hardback) | ISBN 9780820366753 (paperback) |
    ISBN 9780820366784 (epub) | ISBN 9780820366791
    (pdf)
Subjects: LCSH: Journalism—Authorship. | Journalists—United
    States—Interviews.
Classification: LCC PN4867.2 .T85 2024 | DDC 071.3/0905—
    DC23/ENG/20240124
LC record available at https://lccn.loc.gov/2023056420

"If we tell enough stories, we can all live forever."

MATT TULLIS 1975–2022

Contents

•

**Stories
Can
Save
Us**

Introduction

In the fall of 2012, I was assembling a virtual roundtable discussion for the literary magazine *Creative Nonfiction* focused on how some journalism should be considered a form of creative writing or, more specifically, creative nonfiction. The panel consisted of Ben Montgomery, who at the time was an enterprise reporter for the *Tampa Bay Times*; Chris Jones, who was a writer-at-large for *Esquire* and a National Magazine Award winner; and Thomas Lake, who was the youngest senior writer in the history of *Sports Illustrated*. I not only wanted to discuss a certain style of journalism with these writers; I wanted to learn from them.

I was, at the time, a journalism professor at Ashland University in Ohio, the same place that gave me a faculty job even though, when I was a freshman there, I flunked English 101. I had been in that position—teaching student journalists how to report and write and, hopefully, tell stories—for four years. I had also been doing some writing on the side, for *Cleveland Magazine* and other trade publications, but I wasn't writing anything great. The biggest piece of journalism I had written at the time, at least since my days as a reporter at the *Columbus Dispatch*, was a story on Kyrie Irving and Tristan Thompson, at the time both rookies for the Cleveland Cavaliers. I struggled, and I never liked what was ultimately published. It didn't resonate the way I thought it could have. In my mind, I had failed as a reporter and a writer.

I was able to form this panel because I knew Montgomery from a trip I had taken to St. Petersburg for a Poynter seminar back in my days as a reporter for the *Dispatch*. Montgomery had become well known in literary journalism circles not only because of his award-winning work but because of how he showcased the work of others. He was the founder of the website Gangrey.com, which from about 2004 to 2014 was the hub for narrative journalists around the country. It's where the reporters and writers, both titans and college students, gathered to discuss various stories after they had been published; where they complimented, critiqued, and debated; where they learned not only about their craft but about one another, their vanities and insecurities; where they learned that despite massive shifts in technology and consumption of words, there was not only still an audience for beautifully written and deeply reported stories but a thriving and expanding audience. Gangrey ultimately introduced me to narrative journalism and helped develop my desire to interview the reporters about how they do what they do.

For the roundtable, I emailed questions to the three writers. They answered, and I forwarded those around. A discussion ensued, an amazing one—hopefully for them but definitely for me. The answers started to open my eyes about how the best narrative journalists do what they do, and I wanted to pass those lessons along. One day, I told some of my undergraduate classes several of the things from our email discussion, and after class, Glenn Battishill, one of my students, had an idea. Glenn had come to Ashland University as a freshman and, unlike me, did not flunk English 101. He immediately started writing stories for the student newspaper and had taken a lot of my classes because I was the only person who taught print reporting and writing in my department. He is currently a daily newspaper reporter at the *Delaware Gazette* in Ohio. After that class, Glenn said that I should start a podcast discussing the same conversations that I was having via email. We could record the conversations and push them out into the world. It was a brilliant idea—even though I remember asking at the time, "What's a podcast?"

Gangrey: The Podcast, a spin-off of Montgomery's website, debuted in January 2013. I am a firm believer that the best way to learn how to report and write narrative journalism is simply to talk with those who do it well and ask them questions. How do they find story ideas? How do they reach out to potential story subjects? How do they conduct interviews? What other information gathering techniques do they use? How do they come up with their amazing and enticing leads? How do they develop story structure? How does the story change in the revision process? How do they make their stories great, make them into the types of stories that people read and talk about for years?

I started asking these questions to some of the best in the business. As of June 2021, I had completed ninety-six podcast episodes, featuring seventy-nine incredible narrative journalists. I've talked with seven Pulitzer Prize winners and another three finalists. I've talked with six National Magazine Award winners and another nine who have been finalists. I've talked with fifty-three people who have written books of narrative journalism, including many who are *New York Times* best-selling authors. I've talked with reporters honored by the City and Regional Magazine Awards, the Livingston Awards, the George Polk Awards, and so many more. I've talked with reporters of all different races and backgrounds, styles and strengths, journalists who have published in the newspapers like the *New York Times*, the *Washington Post*, the *Tampa Bay Times*, and the *Los Angeles Times*, and in magazines like *Rolling Stone, GQ, Esquire, ESPN the Magazine*, the *Atlantic*, the *New Yorker*, and *Vanity Fair*.

But of course, many of these writers are not just writers. They're storytellers, whose stories have lived not only as the written word. Many of these journalists have produced, written, and been featured in documentaries and podcasts about their work. These types of stories are not going away just because the printed page is not as prominent as it once was. These stories will continue to be told through multiple platforms, drawing an audience wider and more diverse in its consumption habits.

It's been the greatest education I could imagine, and now, I want to share it with you in a form that's likely a bit easier to follow. The knowledge they have shared is invaluable for anyone who wants to report and write journalism, especially those interested in narrative or feature writing. My hope is that these conversations not only inspire you but they also help you with your own work. Once I started talking with reporters who excel at narrative journalism, my own reporting and writing took a leap. While I was doing the roundtable with Jones, Montgomery, and Lake, I reported and wrote my first piece of long-form narrative journalism. It was about the second-best horseshoe pitcher in the world, a man who was constantly having to compete with the greatest horseshoe pitcher who has ever lived, while also dealing with serious health issues. That story was ultimately noted in *Best American Sports Writing*. I followed that with a piece on an Olympian who won the women's gold and the silver medals in the one-hundred-yard dash in 1932 and 1936 respectively, only to be murdered in 1980 and to have the coroner's report say she had male sex organs. I wrote about girls' high school basketball in Amish country. I finally started writing about my own experience as a childhood leukemia survivor, a runner, and a person who couldn't stop thinking about the people I knew who didn't survive their own cancers. If I hadn't started the podcast, I never would have been able to write my reported memoir about those days and those people.

This book includes conversations with twenty-seven writers, the vast majority from my podcast. [*Publisher's note: Tullis died before he could interview some of the writers in this book. In those cases, friends of his interviewed the subjects.*] The conversations included have been abridged and cleaned up significantly; none of us talk as well as we write. I have also significantly cleaned up the questions that led into the answers, and at times, added questions that I didn't ask on the podcast. I view this book not just as a guide. I hope that it's a sequel of sorts to Robert S. Boynton's book, *The New New Journalism*. It was published in 2005, and it was full of writers who were in many ways the previous generation of great nonfiction storytellers. Jon Krakauer, Gay Talese, Ted Conover, Richard Ben Cramer, and Susan Orlean, among others, have written amazing nonfiction, but the vast majority of that work was published in the 1970s through the end of the twentieth century. This book is filled with those who were inspired by those writers and learned from them—and how, in an ever-changing media world, they might both advance and evolve the work.

My goal, of course, was not just to learn about how the greats worked, for my benefit and also for yours. It was to expand the power and potential of what amazing reporting and narrative writing can do. It can literally change a reader's mood and, possibly, a reader's life. It did with mine. My first tattoo, on my forearm, is "Stories can save us," from Tim O'Brien's *The Things They Carried*. I can only hope that these stories, and the stories behind the stories, bring you as much joy and inspiration as they did for me.

—Matt Tullis, 2021

Audra D. S. Burch

Audra Burch is an award-winning national enterprise correspondent for the New York Times specializing in sensitive and deeply reported stories exploring race, identity, and, often, trauma. These include pieces about school shootings, hate crimes, police brutality, or children who've been killed—work that requires from her weeks and occasionally months of intense emotional investment. Her job is not only to report on but to get to know the aggrieved. Such stories ask something more from a reporter than just using a pen and a notebook and a recording device, something more than weeks, or months, of interviews. Work that takes a special kind of journalist and mindset.

Before she was a Pulitzer finalist, she began as a cops reporter at the *Gary (Ind.) Post-Tribune* and then covered the "nuts and bolts" of city government along with consumer reporting for the Florida Sun-Sentinel. She was hired at the *Miami Herald* as a consumer writer on the business desk, then auditioned for a job in the features department and there established a reputation for being a stylish writer and sensitive reporter.

When she wrote about the South for the *Herald*, she was assigned to write about civil rights cold cases and a spate of churches that had burned. "And that's when I first recognized trauma reporting as I know it today," she says. "Story subjects where people were dealing with the stunning shock of a church burning with all of its symbolism, or someone killed in a decades-old hate crime. But the story where I stepped straight into that was when I wrote about the death of Sherdavia Jenkins, a nine-year-old girl killed out on her front stoop while playing with her friend. By a stray bullet. A chess champion, an A student. I practically lived with the family."

In 2017, she was recruited to the *Times* from the *Herald*. "I always wanted to be a long-form writer," she says. "But I didn't know what it was, really, just that I wanted to do it. I had seen longer pieces in newspapers, and I grew up in Atlanta, so stories in the *Atlanta Journal-Constitution*, national newspapers, and in magazines—those stories felt like I was on a journey. I was drawn to them because I liked the way they made me feel."

She was interviewed in 2023.

You write about race and identity for the largest media outlet in the world. Do people want to talk to you about race at all? What is that like to try and get them, particularly white Americans, to go there?

Some of my most difficult stories have been about race and racism, how identity plays a role in how people relate to the larger world. People are uncomfortable talking about race and considering the notion of systemic racism. I wrote a story in Newnan, Georgia, [in the story the town prided itself on its "quiet charm"] essentially about an ambitious art installation, seventeen portraits in various locations in town celebrating the types of regular citizens who live there. But when I was interviewing some people for the piece, it became clear that what I was writing about was, in part, fear and belonging. Fear of demographic changes [the portraits in the story included African American citizens and two sisters wearing hijabs]. Some of the townspeople interviewed said things like, "I feel like Islam is a threat to the American way of life. . . . There should be no positive portrayals of it," but were insistent that this wasn't about the Muslim girls in the art themselves. The more people talked, the more it became clear this was about some who welcomed change and others who feared it. There were points in the conversations I could tell people were hesitant. It was obvious it started as a story about art, but it became a story about race and ethnicity and people who looked different.

You also write about trauma. What is trauma reporting, and what does it take as a journalist to do it? In particular a recent story in the *Times* about the family of one of the students who was shot and killed

at Parkland High School—the Hoyer family, still trying to deal with the loss of their youngest son while preparing for the sentencing trial of the shooter.

I would say a lot of what I write about comes about in really uncomfortable conversations, trying to get to the heart of how people are understanding something difficult that has happened in their life. How they're processing it and what to do with some really hard questions. A lot of the questions that I ask are in service of getting people to talk about the really hard thing that they're facing. In some ways, it's heartbreaking because you're asking someone to relive it. And you have to weigh the odds. Is this worth it? You don't want to torture someone in service of the story. I do think what I try to give people I'm writing about, in exchange, is just honesty. [In the Parkland story] I was asking how they were feeling at every point of the interview. Sometimes during the interview you don't know what to do with yourself. I know with those first couple conversations, I remember welling up. I remember I excused myself and went to the restroom and tried to center myself. I try to be brutally honest about the journey we're about to go on.

How do you deal with asking people so often to relive, to be vulnerable? And how do you make the decision to pursue the story and what it might take both out of you and the subject? To weigh the odds, to say, is this worth it?

I think one of the first questions I ask myself is what is to be gained by asking a person to relive something that has been decidedly traumatic for them. And often, the answer is that other people can see themselves in the tragedy or empathize with the victims. It helps people to understand how we process death and loss and what is actually at stake. Particularly when we talk about death and violence or death at the hands of violence. While I try to treat these stories as what they are, intimate moments that people are navigating, I think there's a way to see the universe and light in them. And by light, I mean, a way to see that pain, while it's individual, it's also universal.

There are different types of reporting, obviously, many talked about in this book: getting documents, using data, the art of interviewing strangers on the phone, et cetera. But there's a true sublimity to being able to acclimate into the lives of the shattered and get them to speak, the Hoyer family, for instance. This type of journalism calls for something beyond regular "reporting." It requires being present, being vulnerable, that it's okay to comfort people.

I think it requires that you share something of yourself. I think the act of sharing is almost radical when we think about it in terms of what journalists do. I think what you share has to be authentic; I don't mean performative. I think you have to truly share something of yourself. I also believe that, when people are opening up and sharing with you their deepest emotions, it's a gift. It has to be respected as such. I think that there's natural tension, and a lot of the ways I try to get at that is asking people how they've reconciled something. What I tend to find is that people aren't as sure as you might think they are. I often find that one of the richest details you can add to any story, and particularly with trauma, is asking people to share their inner debates. Particularly if they have changed their mind about something. Getting them to walk you through how they think about something and how they got there. And nine times out of ten, how they got there will tell you something about who they are. One of the things I feel like has been consistent in those stories is that I'm trying to provoke a sense of humanity, whether it's on deadline or I have months to consider. I think the facts generally speak for themselves, but what readers often gravitate towards is a voice, the description of the voice or the expression or a sentiment or if they feel themselves in the words. And so a lot of what I'm doing is trying to connect the reader with this one person or authority—a voice in the story. I have a particular style like a lot of writers, but I feel like I have not done right by a story if you walk away hearing my voice more than people in the story. And so it's important for me, that I am not just writing but listening for how I'm crafting a story and trying to remove ego from it.

When you meet someone you interview, when they let you into their lives to talk about any of this, how do you start?

If I have time, I almost never talk about the story in the first part of the interview. I talk a little about myself, who I am, where I grew up, things that I find are natural connectors. And I ask them some of the same things; I ask them things that may end up in the story, but not formally, like, what's your favorite childhood memory? The idea is to build a rapport. And hopefully they become comfortable talking to a stranger that's been sitting in their living room. I think in these types of stories we owe the people a longer runway. To connect with them. A lot of times the air is already charged during the interview. You want to settle the air down a little bit. Settle everything around you to feel calmer. And so sometimes, somebody listening to your voice versus their own is helpful. The other thing, I do try to offer clarity about what this process is. Generally, how much contact we might have, what the process is for writing a story, what the fact-checking is like. Even though people are knowingly talking to a reporter, there are still some mysteries for them. Talking about the process helps demystify what we do. Particularly if we do something different than what might have been their experiences with the media already. If they've seen news stories on tv or blurbs in the paper, that's a much different kind of reporting than what we're doing here. I'm having that conversation throughout the reporting process: here is what I'm thinking about.

Why do you gravitate to these types of stories?

I've always been drawn to stories about loss. So much of who we are is revealed in loss. I really enjoy getting to know someone even when the circumstances are difficult. And getting to know them enough to write with some sort of authority. And then, it's just the humanity those kinds of stories lend themselves to. Is there anything more human than love and loss? Doesn't every story we write in its own way tell us something about how people live or die?

What is it like to try and write such a story?

I don't think that trauma as I know it was a part of my career in a recognizable way until I was covering the American South for the *Miami Herald.* That would've been early to mid-2000s. I think in those early days I was still learning how to talk to people about loss in a way that was respectful but probing. I wanted answers that would truly capture the emotion. What does emptiness feel like, walking into a house and a child is missing? What does it physically feel like? I couldn't imagine it. I didn't have children. Every day I would go to the home of Sherdavia Jenkins, early in the morning, and I would literally be there all day. A lot of the time I was just quietly observing. I remember one day we were sitting in the living room, and the phone rang, and it was a conversation about Sherdavia's gravesite. I knew instantly this was part of the story. The simplicity of the mother's voice. She was on the phone with the father, and he was telling her what the headstone would say, making sure they got the year right. Looking back, I knew those words, the conversation, as simple as it was, would connect with people. I think that was my first true narrative piece. I think it was also the first time I can recall that I employed dialogue. I remember very specifically looking in my notebook at the end of that day, at that exchange, and sharing it with my editor. I don't remember which of us said, "We have to write it just like they said it." We needed that exchange in the story just like it happened. And that was the very first time I remember including dialogue, but that has come to be part of my writing when I can find the occasion to do it. That was the story that felt different. I don't know if I knew the right words to describe it, but I knew that's what I wanted to do.

In the Parkland story, Mrs. Hoyer is sitting on the unmade bed of her son, his prescription glasses on the nightstand. Are you taking notes simultaneously while listening to people? Capturing how they move, what they look like, et cetera, while interviewing them?

I try to see stories through multiple lenses. One of the lenses is motion. What is moving from A to B? That could be someone physically going up the stairs, as was the case with Mrs. Hoyer or it could be someone's personality shifting from one emotion to another. Any kind of movement is something I try to take note of, along with the built environment. It tells us something about people. Where they live, how they live, where they choose to call home. From a technical standpoint, I record in one hand (or place near the people I am interviewing), but I'm jotting notes in the other. The things I'm jotting down are the things that strike me. I don't rely exclusively on a recorder anymore. If someone is saying something that rings in my ear, I jot that down in the notebook. I'm also jotting down what I'm seeing: The room is beige. The glasses are prescription. The other thing I do is take pictures, if I'm given permission, to help me remember so I can go back and make sure my notes are accurate. When you're doing a trauma story, you ask people to be very vulnerable. At some point you have to go back to them. What I don't want to do is go back to them and ask them minor questions, especially since I know I'm going to have to go over much more serious things.

You've written about children, too, in the most heartbreaking circumstances imaginable; children being suffocated, mutilated, and murdered in a story series called Innocents Lost for the *Herald*. Very important, but very hard to read, though much less [than], I imagine, to painstakingly report and describe.

For Innocents Lost, my reporting partner and I felt the way to make these stories really, really resonate was that we had to tell them with as much humanity and detail as possible. I traveled across Florida speaking with families whose children had died of abuse or neglect after falling through the state's child welfare safety net. Fairly early in the reporting phase, I was at a woman's house in central Florida where she was talking about her young granddaughter who died after taking a mix of pills while at the home of a friend of her mother's. I felt like when she talked about her granddaughter, it was almost in a clinical way, a wooden way. I looked across the living room and saw a photo album. I took a chance and asked if there were any pictures of her granddaughter in there, and she let me see the book. I asked her to share with me her memories based on the pictures, and that unlocked the emotional attachment to her granddaughter. And that became something that I used as a literary device throughout the project: when parents or grandparents struggled to talk about their children, pictures can do the heavy lifting. What was most important is that this was a series about innocent children that had died. My job was to figure out how they lived. Who they were. Even if they were just alive for a year. We also used the power of repetition as a way to really shake the reader and say, look at this, these are all the ways babies died. And if you can't get through this, well, we knew going in how hard this was going to be to read. And so we said, we gotta make people read it. They have to finish this. And as you probably know, that series resulted in the most sweeping child welfare reform in Florida's history.

Reporting these types of pieces isn't something that's learned overnight, in an internship or even in a first job. How did you learn to become a reporter that can really do this?

One of the things about police reporting is that it really forces you to ask a lot of questions. But there has to be a kind of economy to those questions. It wasn't until much later that I learned how to ask a question that solicits a longer answer. You know, how to ask an open-ended question that makes people think beyond a sort of standard, superficial, surface answer. I didn't know how to do that early on. I would go back to write a news story, one that I was trying to make into something longer, and I didn't have enough reporting. When I went into my notebook, there just wasn't enough stuff in there, which told me that I was either not asking the right questions or not asking enough questions. The empty notebook was the hardest lesson that I learned. There's no amount of writing that can fix it when you open the notebook and there's not enough there. It requires more reporting. I don't know when it happened, but later, I started writing or framing the story in my head even as I was doing interviews. That helped me know what direction I was going in but also when to probe deeper, to ask more and/or better follow-up questions. You know, journalists in some ways are like musicians. You have to be able to hear. And when you hear the right note, it tells you to go further, to keep going, to try and get more answers. And the notes create the song.

Part of your job is timing a longer story to the actual news. What does it take to time an ambitious story to a single day's events?

Part of it is planning. For the Parkland story, we knew we wanted enterprise pieces in addition to our daily trial stories that were going to ask big, hard questions. That story asks, "What is justice?" It's not an uncommon question. But what was interesting to me was how the family wrestled with the answer. The story was about the journey. From the time I began talking to them months before it ran, what I found, and I think there's a line in the story, is that their thinking changed a bit. The line in the story is "justice shapeshifts with the tides of mourning." I saw the family more than a half dozen times. I was very deliberate in wanting to meet them first in their home, which is where people find comfort. A place that feels safe. But I knew there were other places that helped form the arc of their son's story. It made sense to go to the cemetery while they visited his grave. But when I went there, I did not run up on them. At one point they were standing in front of their son's memorial, and I stood back for a minute. That, to me, felt private. Their words to him were private. When it appeared they had finished, then I approached them. I also met them at the courthouse. I didn't sit with them (they were with other families), and I didn't approach them afterwards. One of the things that doing this for a while teaches you is restraint. I don't know if it comes naturally to me. It's a learned art. I think that people tend to be more giving when they have space: personal space, space to think.

When you come out of one of these stories, or during it, how do you self-care? These stories are not just hard on people and families— but on journalists too.

I have come to be a big believer in doing a bit of rebuilding, or re-centering, after traumatic stories. Sometimes I do look for ways to do easy activities, like walking. Just a walk to the beach or the lake, to clear my head. And when I'm watching TV, I'm very specific about watching things that are not violent or upsetting to me. Stuff that is light, funny, hopeful.

Brin-Jonathan Butler

Brin-Jonathan Butler is a freelance writer, documentary filmmaker, podcaster, boxing trainer, and author of two books including one focused on chess great Magnus Carlsen and the World Chess Championship in November 2016. Butler has been published by *ESPN the Magazine*, sb Nation Longform, Vice, Salon, Al Jazeera, *Harper's*, the Daily Beast, and many other publications. He is currently working on a documentary titled *Split-Decision*, which examines Cuban-American relations, something Butler has extensive knowledge of. His first book, *Domino Diaries*, was a memoir about his ties to boxing and time he spent in Cuba.

Butler's book on Carlsen and the game of chess came about in a way writers dream of. An editor from Simon and Schuster contacted Butler, offered him a deal to write a book about the World Chess Championship. "It was preposterous. I've never had an editor throw an idea at me to write anything before," Butler says. "Normally, we're pitching endless ideas; they're shooting them down. It's the rat race we're in. . . . I thought it was a Nigerian prince email scam."

Carlsen refused to talk to Butler, so Butler covered the championship and talked to people all over the world about chess, including literary journalism legend Gay Talese. He sought a wide array of people who could help speculate about what was going on in Carlsen's head, from great chess players to great chess writers, from people obsessed with other things to exploring mental illness and what it means to be a prodigy.

As a writer, Butler pretty much will only cover things he is incredibly interested in. The vast majority of his magazine publications have focused on boxing and boxers. Butler is a member of the Boxing Writers Association of America. His memoir, *Domino Diaries*, is about his boxing career, his obsession with Cuban boxers, and his chasing of

Ernest Hemingway's ghost on the island. Butler spent a decade in Havana trying to understand the culture there. During this time, he became romantically entangled with one of Fidel Castro's granddaughters and ended up in Mike Tyson's mansion for an interview. "I haven't had a tremendously lucrative literary career, but there's not much that separates my personal obsessions from my professional," Butler says. "I only pursue the things I'm obsessive about, because I don't have casual interests. It is an obsession."

I spoke with Butler in October 2018. We talked primarily about *The Grandmaster* but also his memoir and his writing in general.

Your second book is titled *The Grandmaster*. What's it about?

The Grandmaster began in 2016. I was asked by Simon and Schuster to cover the World Chess Championship here in New York between Magnus Carlsen and Sergey Karjakin. Donald Trump had been elected thirty-six hours before, so the backdrop was literally pinatas of Trump being beaten outside Trump Towers, at the bottom of Central Park. It was a wild scene, it felt like New York was in a collective nervous breakdown. Pretty much the only place where people weren't talking about politics was the World Chess Championship. It was a surreal, bizarre thing to cover.

I didn't know book publishers reached out to writers and said, hey, can you write this book for us?

It was preposterous. I've never had an editor throw an idea at me to write anything before. Normally, we're pitching endless ideas, they're shooting them down. It's the rat race that we're in. To have an editor reach out to say, "I saw you had a profile photo on Twitter where you're playing chess. I'm sure you know that the World Chess Championships are going on a few miles south of where you live." I thought it was a Nigerian prince email scam.

I followed up immediately, and still, talking to the guy on the phone, I'm waiting for the scam because this can't be real. Within three days from that initial email, I switched agents, signed a contract, and was the only journalist covering it given vip access.

Did you have any expertise in chess?

I have a background of playing a little bit. One of my first jobs as a kid was hustling chess outside the Art Gallery in Vancouver, which was Vancouver's answer to Washington Square Park, where Stanley Kubrick and Bobby Fischer and many chess players were coming up in New York, that's where they would play and hustle speed chess.

Once I had the contract, I bought forty chess books. I had to cram and immerse into as many different angles as I could find.

Originally, the goal of the book was for you to have access to Magnus Carlsen and try to understand who he was. That didn't happen.

I didn't exchange one word with Magnus Carlsen, or his opponent for this entire book, so that's a big challenge, but I thought maybe there's some fun ways to read into him through this intimate corridor of spending six hours ten feet away from him behind glass, staring at his face, doing such an immersive thing. I can't think of a more preoccupied person on the planet than a World Champion Chess player. It was an interesting thing to allow yourself to meditate on somebody's process, who on the one hand is close to you, physically, but on the other more distant to you than just about anybody I've been around in my entire life.

I sought a wide array of people to help speculate about what was going on with him, from great chess players, great chess writers, other fields of obsessions, exploring mental illness, what it is to be a prodigy, the tender bond between genius and madness that certainly chess bears out with a lot of its greatest practitioners, then obsession in a lot of other fields of creative endeavors. I've been a massive fan of obsessive geniuses all my life, so I saw elements of Bobby Fischer in Magnus Carlsen, which he confirmed in some interviews.

There are a lot of things to work with there that seemed like moving targets. I was concerned putting this together that it have a kind of coherent narrative that would be compelling, as opposed to some totally nebulous mosaic that people would say, "What in God's name is this?" I had a lot of concerns but at the same time was having a lot of fun gathering stuff.

For so much of your life you've been writing about boxing and bullfighting. Did that background help you when you sat down to write this book?

I don't think with boxing I've ever written much about the actual combat. It's the backstories of fighters; it's the backstories of people living at extremes. I think there's something about what's going on behind their forehead as they're processing an event where they're half-naked, exposing themselves to millions, or tens of millions, of eyes around the world, doing something most of us spend our entire lives to some degree in terror of.

At the same time, if they get really good at these specialized areas of endeavor with incredible amounts of competition, you're going to find it's not virtue that drives them, it's their demons. In that way, it was easy to find connective tissue between boxers and chess players, or bullfighters, or any endeavor that is seeking the world stage.

Nobody needed to prod Bobby Fischer to play chess or Glenn Gould to play the piano or Beethoven to compose. If anything you have to try to restrain them from doing it because they're so obsessively driven. In the realm of chess, this Gladwellian idea of ten thousand hours to become a genius is preposterous. These guys do ten thousand hours before they're twelve years old.

That's been a common troupe of elite athletes. The level of sadism they have is off the charts, but we spin a different narrative to say it's something virtuous. But no, it's a demon that's in their heart driving them towards this. Magnus Carlsen was a[n] [un]mercifully picked-on kid; this is an area where he can exact revenge. Maybe he can do it better than anybody who's ever been born, and he takes immense pleasure in that. There's something to that with chess I found darkly compelling.

How do you decide what you want to write about?

I haven't had a tremendously lucrative literary career, but there's not much that separates my personal obsessions from my professional. I only pursue things I'm obsessive about, because I don't have casual interests. It is an obsession. Chess was always something I was obsessed with. It began when I could put a face on it early with Bobby Fischer, trying to figure out what made him tick, what made him so compelling.

I'd say 99 percent of what I've written about is stuff that I'd be writing about even if I wasn't paid for it. It's collateral damage of people who are around these things I'm obsessed with. I'm desperate to find a new take, a new little gem, and often laymen think for themselves in assessing and observing what they're looking at. It's a much more interesting take than even people that have given their lives to it, and I love the feeling of being taken somewhere new with something that I've been looking at for a long time, or all my life.

You're good at having conversations with complete strangers. This shows in your first book, *Domino Diaries*, as well as in *The Grandmaster*. Has that always been easy for you?

As you see in the book, I'm interviewing little kids; some of them are chess prodigies themselves; some of them are little kids who showed up; some people are riding up the escalator who say, "I couldn't deal with chess. It was too stressful, so I turned to doing open heart surgery."

I'm desperate for those kinds of moments, and having four hours to interview Errol Morris, who's one of my favorite living artists, was the same for him. All the stories he wanted to tell were weird things, and nothing is more fun than somebody stamping their own idiosyncratic, unique take on being crazy. I think basically everybody's crazy if you let them have ten minutes to talk about anything they're passionate about.

What was it like to talk with Gay Talese?

I left a lot out of that interview because most of what he wanted to talk about was actually giving me relationship advice; I didn't ask him for any. I wasn't saying, "Talese, let's have a conversation about how I'm in a shitty relationship." I'd say 90 percent of what he actually talked about was, "Brin, you just got your advance; this girl is thirty years old. What are you doing? You're not going to marry her. You need to get out of that. You need to extricate yourself out of that. I'm not going to give you any money to do it. I'm not going to help you." I didn't ask, "What are we talking about? I'm here to talk to you about Bobby Fischer, and you seeing him when he was thirteen years old." How did we get to my setup, but he was into his obsessiveness with solving my entire life in forty-five minutes.

You start the book off with some of your own life and its relationship to chess. Why did you do that?

I was fascinated with chess. I was introduced to it early; I was about three or four years old. My father had major financial problems. There was a huge real estate crash in Vancouver, so the first house he bought after he became a child protection lawyer, he was paying something like 25 percent interest. We lost the house, and my mother went to work at a little antique furniture shop. When I went in to see her at work, it was the first time I had ever been to an antique shop. I was looking at all these incredible objects having no idea about their history.

I saw my mother playing chess with the guy who owned the shop.

When I was looking at the chessboard, I immediately responded that this was the object I found the most fascinating in the store. He offered to teach me to play, and I said I'd love to learn how. I was playing board games at the time. I always loved board games, and he gave me this warning that said, "Be careful, because if you play this game, it might never let go."

I stayed away from chess a long time. When it came back into my life years later, I was turning nineteen years old and meeting my uncle and family in Budapest for the first time; I turned to it, became addicted for a couple years, and found I couldn't write if I was playing chess. It seemed to draw from the same well creatively [that] writing did, and I was an obsessive writer at that time, writing a pile of unpublishable stuff.

I wanted to get that across to readers. I had a sense of this duende that chess had, that made it mystical, made it like a cursed pursuit. I found it on one hand enticing and on the other frightening. How does a board game have an undertow or a riptide emotionally?

There are a lot of prodigies I met that were great math prodigies, and the moment they played chess, they gave up math. Of course, nobody can make money playing chess, so it becomes as much a struggle, not with the game, an unfathomable game, but with the cold hard reality that chess might be the only thing that capitalism looks at where 600 million people are doing it, and it has no idea how to cash in on it.

I noticed that one of the people you dedicated the book to was Glenn Stout. We both wrote for him at sb Nation Longform. What has he meant to you as an editor?

I think the spirit of Glenn is to be in the corner of everybody. He's the best editor I've worked with. I might be able to help other writers get closer to their potential, but I wouldn't have a clue how to help them reach beyond their potential with the things they most want to do in the world. Here's the easiest way to distill him for me: When anybody wrote to me after reading a story, they would say "I'd love to submit something to Glenn Stout. Do you think you could put in a good word for me?" I'd say there's no point. He doesn't give a shit who sends something in. If he likes it, if it's a good idea, he'll run with it. He doesn't care where you come from. He doesn't care where you went to school. There's no elite aesthetic. He does root for underdogs. He does root for misfits. He's pulling for you to make it, and he's not pulling for you to make it so he can then gain credit for helping you make it. He's a real supporter. I don't know of anybody who was a bigger advocate.

Look at the books he's written. I don't think any writer out there has written more female protagonists than he has. He was a huge advocate for pushing for women to break into the industry and minorities to break into the industry. I had so much fun working on stuff; I had so much fun seeing what he was offering other people.

Your first book was *Domino Diaries*, which is a memoir. How did that book come about?

I started writing fiction, wrote probably a million words before I was paid for one, and still haven't been paid for any of those words of fiction, because maybe they weren't any good. But behind the scenes, I was working some weird, odd jobs. All the money I had was put towards going to Cuba and being trained by Olympic champions and indulging in my fascination with what Cuba was from the first time I went in 2000, until what I thought was the last time I'd be able to go, which was when Bin Laden was killed in 2011.

At some point, about 2006 or 2007, I jotted down notes as an exercise about what I was seeing in Cuba while I was wandering around Havana and posting them on social media to friends because internet was expensive there, so I didn't have time to individually email people. I'd get up at four o'clock in the morning, walk to a hotel where there was internet access, ten bucks an hour, and for that hour do nothing but write and post. All of these people said, "Why on earth are you writing anything else but this? This is crazy that you would write about anything other than what's going on in Cuba right now. Don't you see that?"

I didn't see that, because what's interesting about some kid who's not an important boxer, learning to box, trying to figure out this bizarre island ninety miles away from the United States, and I'm not doing anything special there; I'm just observing and talking to people. That's not a worthy memoir.

So what happened?

I published something in Salon, which they don't pay for. There was an editor who reached out to me and he said, "Is there a book here?"

I said, "Well, I don't know. What are you looking for?"

In the end, another offer came from Random House to do a biography about one of the boxers that I was writing about, and that Peter Horoszko from Picador got into a conference call where there was, not a bidding war, but a discussion from different publishers about if there was interest in this book, and my agent at the time said, "I need to let you know, the only thing anybody's going to be interested in is this Cuban boxer who defected, who Fidel Castro said was a traitor, and all that. Nobody is going to give a flying fuck about you in the story, so don't take it personally, but it's not a memoir that anybody's going to want here."

The first person who got on the line was Peter, and he said, "We at Picador don't know anything about Cuba, and we don't know anything about boxing. The only thing we're interested in is why some kid from Vancouver would go to Cuba and take this incredibly bizarre journey. If you want to write that book, we're in, but if you want to do the boxing thing, or a biography of some boxer, we don't know anything about that." The agent laughed, and off he went. That was the perfect kind of setup. Unfortunately, it was marketed as a boxing book, but there's no boxing in the book.

There are characters who are boxers, but you're not hearing about any boxing history, you're not hearing about the records of people or important fights. The central question of Cuba for me was, how does a place like this exist? This should never exist. How do so many of these people wish to remain, despite living lives where happiness cannot be defined in a materialistic way?

I saw a lot of pain; I saw a lot of joy; I saw this whole spectrum from a human perspective of the most alive place I'd ever seen. All I'd been warned about was how much incredible poverty I'd see; what I saw was true in the financial sense. Everywhere else, it was the richest place I'd seen in my life, infinitely more so than where I came from.

Pamela Colloff

Pamela Colloff is a staff writer at the *New York Times Magazine* and a reporter at ProPublica. She has won two National Magazine Awards. Colloff's two-part, twenty-nine-thousand-word series, Innocent Man, won the National Magazine Award for feature writing with *Texas Monthly* in 2012. It chronicled the story of Michael Morton, who spent twenty-five years in prison for murdering his wife—a crime he didn't commit. Colloff's work showcases her ability to bring complex criminal justice issues—including the wrongfully imprisoned—to light in compelling narrative fashion. "Covering the criminal justice system has shown me how it perpetuates larger inequities in our society, which made me want to illuminate the many problems within the system," Colloff wrote to me. In 2017, Colloff joined ProPublica and the *New York Times Magazine*. Her first piece for those publications was "Blood Will Tell," a two-part series focused on Joe Bryan, a former high school principal convicted of murdering his wife in 1985. Bryan's conviction largely hinged on the testimony of a bloodstain pattern analyst. Colloff enrolled in the same forty-hour course offered around the country for bloodstain pattern analyst certification, revealing some shortcomings in forensic science.

"I realized it would be possible to tell a story from so long ago in a vivid way because people had written statements within hours of things that had happened," she says of the Bryan case records. "Blood Will Tell" won the Scripps Howard National Journalism Award and paved the way for Bryan's release from prison in April 2020.

I talked with Colloff in January 2013, shortly after Innocent Man ran, and again in June 2018 about "Blood Will Tell."

Can you tell me about the Innocent Man?

This is the story of a man named Michael Morton—an ordinary guy, middle class, a grocery store manager living in north Austin in the mid-1980s with his wife and three-year-old son. His wife was murdered one morning when Michael wasn't home. He was at work or on his way into work. Law enforcement quickly narrowed in on and assumed it was him and never looked back. He spent twenty-five years in prison, having not committed this crime, separated from his son, who was four when he went to prison.

He was much later exonerated when DNA evidence was finally tested over the vociferous objections of the Williamson County district attorney's office. Those DNA results not only revealed that Michael wasn't the killer but pointed to the identity of another man, who is standing trial this spring for the murder of Christine Morton.

How did you find out about the story? How did you decide you wanted to write about it?

I live in Austin, and this was a huge story when these DNA results broke. I've been writing about wrongful convictions for a while, and, unfortunately, we have a lot to write about here in Texas. Even though the case was garnering a lot of media attention, to me there was so much more narratively that needed to be told.

I hope it—and from the reader response, I think it does—personalized the issue of wrongful convictions. Anybody can relate. You're just an ordinary person, married, doing your job. Then all of a sudden—I mean by the time Michael went to jail, even his friends were convinced that he had done this. Hopefully that reaches a broader audience than some of these cases usually do.

How did you start your writing and reporting process?

What was strange about this story is the people who usually would be eager to talk—the defendant's lawyers and hopefully the defendant himself—I didn't have access to for a while. Michael had agreed from the moment he walked out of prison to an exclusive with *60 Minutes*, and he couldn't talk to the media until the piece aired—six months [after] he got out. His attorneys wouldn't talk during that time either.

I spent that time getting up to speed on the case and reading the trial transcript. In a weird way, it was good; by the time I finally sat down with him, I knew the case, and I had talked to a lot of people already.

Was it hard to get people to talk to you?

Incredibly. I hope this doesn't come across in the story, but access was a recurring problem. When I would contact old friends of his or neighbors, almost uniformly, people were reluctant to talk. Some, who still believed he had done this, were afraid of him, didn't trust the results, or felt the evidence had been too overwhelming against him.

I'd say the other group of people who were reluctant were simply embarrassed. Everyone had abandoned him, except for one friend, and it was hard for people to deal with that. The people who did agree to talk I had to aggressively court. Through the reporting, some of those people got back in touch with Michael.

How many documents did you gather to report this story, and how did you get them?

It was staggering: a twenty-five-year-long case with multiple appeals filed and a case file thousands of pages long. But you know, that's a good problem. I'd always rather have that problem than too little. I've never read a boring trial transcript and always start there—especially in wrongful conviction cases. You can see why the person was convicted: Things that aren't explained to the jury, the way that the truth is shaded, or what people believed at that time.

I started there, worked my way through the appeals, and eventually got to the case file. It was almost like going back in a time capsule because this was eighty-six, eighty-seven that the investigation was taking place. That part of Texas was a different world then, rural. Now it's cosmopolitan and close to where I live. It was interesting to go back to that time. It took the better part of nine months [to report].

I'm curious about how you pitched this story. Did you say, "It's going to be about thirty thousand words"?

I did not. I probably would not have undertaken it if I'd realized what it was going to metastasize into. I was on maternity leave with my second child when this DNA stuff exploded here in central Texas, on the front page of the paper many days in a row. For weeks, I was sending my editor emails, "Please don't give this story away while I'm gone. I'll be back soon."

We talked initially about doing something smaller, like a profile of the district attorney in the middle of this or a profile of Michael. As soon as I read the trial transcript I said, no—that this was big. I had written a fifteen-thousand-word story before; I thought it was big like that. It wasn't until I got into all the stuff with what happened to get him out, which was so involved. Most people read in the papers that there's this DNA test and it's not him, so he gets out . . . but it was this incredibly complicated, but fascinating, legal story. When we went to press on the first part, I was still writing the second part.

How did you report on something like this and not become depressed?

I'm used to it. And actually, this one has a happy-ish ending in Michael getting out and this reunion between father and son. There's a story I wrote that was published in 2012 where I believe this woman was wrongfully convicted. The story comes out, and people are outraged . . . and then she's still there. Those are the ones that are difficult.

The ending is powerful. You've said you knew it was going to be the ending from the moment you started the story.

Not when I started reporting but when I started writing. The last thing I did before I started writing was interview the son, Eric. I hadn't planned it that way; it had taken that long to get him to talk. I think my emails were sounding increasingly desperate as my deadlines got closer.

When I went to interview him, I knew that his daughter was named Christine and thought that was beautiful. I definitely wanted to mention that at the end of the story because that's a tribute to his mother, who he has no memory of. When we talked, there was this interruption in the middle of our interview, when Christine woke up from her nap. Eric's wife brought her into the living room, and there was something about, for lack of a better word, her innocence to what had been going on, all of the sadness and tragedy of what had happened in her family. There was this new beginning.

I was so moved that Eric was now a parent and could understand what his father had felt for him, even though they had been disconnected for so many years. I ended the story with Christine because the whole story is about Michael, and there's some about Eric, but I didn't want the victim of the crime to be forgotten either. We end remembering her. That seemed to me the right way to do it.

I wondered when I read "Blood Will Tell" if this was a case you knew about before you made the jump from *Texas Monthly* to ProPublica and the *New York Times Magazine*?

No. Interestingly enough, the only overlap was my interest in bloodstain pattern analysis—the type of forensic science used to win two convictions against Joe. I was interested in finding a story that illustrated some of the potential problems of this type of forensic science and of forensic science in general. There's a group in Austin called the Texas Forensic Science Commission that meets quarterly. They're a state body that looks at various cases where there may have been forensic science used to win questionable convictions. I saw the commission was looking at Joe's case, started reading about it, and was immediately hooked.

What is it about these types of stories that grab your attention?

I've tried to find the through line in a lot of the work I've done in the past ten years. I don't know that there is one, but I'm interested in what ordinary people in extraordinary circumstances do. I was interested in that in Joe's case, where there are interesting characters and a sense of place. That provided a good way of looking at some science-y stuff that I thought readers otherwise might not be that interested in.

When you decided you were going to work on this, what was the first thing you did as a reporter?

So many things. First of all, it's a thirty-three-year-old case, so you can imagine the challenges. The first thing I was trying to figure out was who was alive; many of the main players had either passed or would not talk to me. As an example, at his trials, there were two prosecutors and two defense attorneys. Of those four attorneys, only one is still living. I made a giant list of the people I would love to talk to and went about trying to track those people down. That was combined with trying to find all the different pieces of the case file, which was challenging, but once I did, I was able to look at the police investigation through different police reports. It quickly became apparent that, at the very least, something was not good about the investigation.

You utilize public records a lot in your reporting. What's that process like for you as a reporter in Texas? Once that big package of material shows up in your office, what goes through your mind?

It's like Christmas when you get all the documents. Because I've worked in Texas almost exclusively for so long, I don't feel like I'd be an authority to speak about what it's like in comparison to other states, but generally, I've had pretty good luck getting the things that I needed. One of the most important things is that Texas allows reporters to go interview inmates in person—though they have greatly restricted that in the past couple of years. I was able, for example, to correspond as much as I wanted to with Joe Bryan and was able to visit him every three months.

As far as finding everything, I had to figure out where everything was. When I finally figured out that everything was in this little town called Comanche at the county courthouse—where Joe's retrial in 1989 took place—it was just a matter of getting to it. Then there's this dance that I've done a million times with the district clerk at courthouses: I'm a reporter, and I want to look at facts. Luckily, this district clerk let me spend the day looking through things.

I realized it would be possible to tell a story from so long ago in a vivid way because people had written statements within hours of things that had happened. Honestly, the statements were so good in some cases, I thought that it might be at least as helpful as interviewing someone three decades later about what they remembered.

How long does it take to read through a court file and find the type of information you are able to use to bring stories to life?

One of the things that's interesting about reading through the trial transcript or looking through a case file is things that don't mean anything to you on the first, second, or even third pass that, once you've understood the case, you start making connections that you wouldn't have otherwise. Each of the trial transcripts is two thousand pages; I needed to read those. I generally give all of that a quick read the first time and, when I know more and when I've talked to people, go back and give it several more read throughs. That took time. Then there was material that was hard to get despite everything. The biggest public records battle I had, interestingly enough, was on photos of the blood-spattered flashlight at the center of this case.

I didn't say this in the story, but we were able to publish photos of the flashlight. The district attorney's office in this case didn't want us to have those and went to the state attorney general to block our access. I thought that was peculiar. Why is it that this da's office that's had this case for over thirty years is both blocking DNA testing and doesn't want the public to see the key piece of evidence? I don't have the answer, but I thought it was odd.

Do you remember when you decided you would attempt this story?

I learned about it early last year and think I got the go-ahead in late spring of last year. I was starting a new job, so there was a lot of stuff to learn all at once. My editor at ProPublica is this amazing, modest woman named Tracy Weber who, before becoming an incredible editor, was a reporter at the *LA Times*, won a Pulitzer, and was a finalist for another. She's rigorous while being extremely kind and encouraging. That combination helped my reporting and led it to stronger places.

How many times did you visit Joe Bryan in prison?

I saw him a total of three times. Keep in mind that you're officially limited to an hour there. Sometimes the guards were more vigilant than others, so sometimes I got a little more time.

What were your interviews like?

The first time I interviewed Joe was similar to several other first inmate interviews, in that the first was kind of a wash because the person had bottled up so much for so long. It wasn't really an interview as much as someone spilling their guts, so to speak. When that happened, I was able to recognize that there's not much, if anything, that I can use from [the first] interview, but I've been able to see what he's like and established some rapport. That was helpful. As the story says, his presence there is so incongruous, and it's true when you meet him. He's [this] soft-spoken, gentle-seeming old man. I've interviewed people who have seemed quite lovely who have done terrible things. That doesn't mean anything, but it confirmed what many had told me about Joe.

What is it like to interview someone in prison?

Awkward. Sometimes you're talking through a phone, sometimes through glass or plexiglass. Prisons are so noisy, so the mechanics are difficult. I've interviewed plenty of people who I was not writing about their innocence—so, regardless of the content of the interview, whenever I've left prison, I have this heavy feeling. When you take that first step outside after a couple hours, it's a relief.

When you're interviewing in a prison, are you able to record or do you have to rely on note-taking? Did you have glass between you and Joe?

One time, they seated us in this other area with bars between him and me. I've usually been able to record. It's tricky when you're talking through those phones because I have this whole rig I use. It looks like an earbud in my ear that goes to my recorder, and then I put my ear up to the phone, and I hope that that picks up enough. Unlike a regular phone, the prison phone's sound is terrible. A lot of times I don't know what I have until I walk out, so I take a lot of notes. Other times, and this was true of Joe, there's glass and then there's like a little metal mesh band at the bottom, and so your voice carries through those little holes.

You chose to do something incredibly interesting, which shows up in the first half of part two of your story: you signed up for a class in bloodstain pattern analysis. Why?

I had a lot of questions as a layperson about this type of forensic science. There were things, to me, that didn't make sense about it. I hadn't taken science since high school, so it had been a long time. I read the main textbook that a lot of people who do bloodstain pattern analysis have used, and I still wasn't grasping these issues. I thought maybe the training, only a week out of my life, would be helpful. That seemed doable, but it also connected directly to the story; the expert witness in Joe's case was a police officer who received close to the training that I had. It was a week-long class at a police department, just like I took. I signed up for a class taught by the consulting firm of the man who taught the expert in Joe's case and spent a week at the Yukon police department in Oklahoma learning how to analyze bloodstains.

I read that you were honest when you applied for the class and said that you were a reporter. Were you the only non-police officer there?

I identified myself as a reporter when I first emailed the consulting firm that teaches these classes, used my ProPublica email address and obviously my real name. I also identified myself as a reporter when the class started and was the only non–law enforcement/forensic scientist in the room. To the credit of the people in my class, no one cared. It wasn't a source of conversation or a lot of questions. I'm in a room of investigators; if they did Google me, they didn't share that.

I felt like I had a good view of how police officers are trained in this discipline. One of the things that interested me is, in the course of researching this, I found that the expert in Joe's case who qualified to testify, who only had a week of training, was not an outlier. There actually have been police officers all over the country who testified as expert witnesses in criminal cases, who've had forty hours of training in this complicated discipline that involves physics and trigonometry. I was going with the intent of: Is it possible? Can you really spend five days in a classroom, walk out, and be able to say, when someone's life is on the line, "Yes, I know it happened at this crime scene."

Structurally, the story comes in two parts. Was that always the goal or was there talk of making it three or four or seven? Or one big, super long story?

Jake Silverstein, the editor-in-chief of the [New York] *Times Magazine* now, was my editor and boss at *Texas Monthly* when I was there. We worked on the Innocent Man together, the story I wrote in 2012 that was twenty-nine-thousand words. Jake ran it across two issues, which meant there was a month delay between each part, which is so different than how things work now. In the back of my head, I wasn't worried about length. I kept writing because it's so much story. I wrote much more than what ran, and there were many iterations of the story.

What was it like to work on a story that was going to be published by two different, excellent publications?

Going from a wonderful regional publication to two national powerhouse publications was exciting. I've got a big megaphone right now, so how am I going to use this? I need to figure out what I want to write about next. Negotiating that partnership and making sure everybody got what they wanted out of it, it all came together. We hadn't all worked together before, so everything was new, but everyone was smart and into this. I felt lucky to have this team working toward this.

John Woodrow Cox

John Woodrow Cox is an enterprise reporter at the *Washington Post* and the author of *Children Under Fire: An American Crisis*, for which he was a finalist for the Pulitzer Prize in feature writing. The book is an expansion of a 2018 series focused on the impact of gun violence on children in America. Cox has won Scripps Howard's Ernie Pyle Award for Human Interest Storytelling, the Dart Award for Excellence in Coverage of Trauma, Columbia Journalism School's Meyer "Mike" Berger award for human-interest reporting, and the Education Writers Association's Hechinger Grand Prize for Distinguished Education Reporting.

Cox says his days as a cops reporter at the *Tampa Bay Times* played a huge role in his learning how to write narrative journalism. In those days, he was writing on deadline because crime stories have to be told in a timely manner. He didn't refer to his notebook until after he'd written a first draft, and even though he no longer has to turn stories around quickly, these are practices that have stuck with him.

Humanity, he says, comes before journalism.

"The first thing I always tell people who have suffered traumas is that I'm sorry for what they've gone through," Cox says, "and I tell him that they're in charge."

His goal with the stories he writes about children whose lives have been changed because of active shooters in their schools and parents whose children have been killed is to try and sponge up as much of their lived experiences as possible. But he also knows he will never completely understand.

"I try to get as close to that as I can, to immerse myself so I can then put it on the page," Cox says. "I think that starts with empathy."

I've spoken with Cox twice. In October 2013, we talked about the micronarratives he was writing about ordinary people in Tampa. In

October 2020, we talked about his story on the Marquez-Greene family, whose daughter was killed at Sandy Hook.

When you were at the *Tampa Bay Times*, you did a series called Dispatches. They were fascinating short narratives about regular people. How did they come about?

They began, I think as all good stories begin, over beer and bowling in St. Petersburg. Melissa Lyttle, the brilliant photographer who shoots all the art for these, and I were brainstorming some ideas for the new *Floridian Magazine*. The original idea was to find people in neighborhoods who represented that area and to show how different Tampa Bay was.

The problem was that it steered us to cliché subjects in that area. We were looking for the most representative person, which was the opposite of what we should have been doing. Through some further conversation with Bill Duryea, who's the editor, we came up with something more general. We wanted to find regular people who had some extraordinary aspect to their life.

Was there any reason why you decided on such a short length?

It's funny, actually, that I ended up doing these because I tend to write long. I've loved this process because I like having such emphasis on every word. Every detail has to count. It doesn't matter how good they are; it's how close they are to the thread. It's gotten easier for me to do this, but that's the test. None of these can go down any rabbit holes. They have to stay right on the arc that we envisioned.

Do you feel like you're getting the hang of reporting and writing these stories yet?

I've learned that pre-reporting is a big part of it. I spend a lot of time interviewing these people and getting to know them. I go into the moments with some hypothesis of what I think the story will be about. Sometimes that changes. Some of them, the outline comes to me immediately. I know exactly what the story will be as soon as I'm done reporting. Some of them, I have some difficult conversations with my editor to brainstorm what the story is and where it's going.

How much time do you typically spend reporting these stories?

That varies. The last one we did with the fisherman in Madeira, I reported that one for nine months, six notebooks. I spent a ton of time with her, and it was a tough one to report, partly because of the nature of the character. She was somebody who was in and out of jail a lot. She would have a cell phone for a while and then lose it. She'd get fired from boats. So we felt like with her we had to wait. Some of them weren't that long. Some of them have been a few weeks, but I would say that I do at least two interviews that are several hours each before I get to the moment, whatever we think the moment is, when I spend a day with the person.

You've also covered crime as a reporter. For me, covering crime was a good training ground to do narrative. What effect has it had on you as a reporter and as a writer?

I think that's where I learned narrative, especially narrative on deadline, because the nature of crime stories, you've got to turn them around in a day. One thing that forces you to do is, when I'm going through my first draft, I don't tend to refer to my notebook a lot until I've written it. The best details tend to stick out to you. You remember them and normally if you have two hours to write something or an hour or if you're on deadline, that's all that comes to you. I think another thing about crime is that there's a built-in narrative there. There's always a built-in story, and it's about collecting the details that matter. I covered crime for the *Times* for about the first year and a half or so, and that was my training ground.

You wrote a story in March 2012 about a nine-month-old who drowned after falling into a swimming pool, and I think that's probably one of the most haunting cop stories I've ever read.

That was a rough day. Earlier that week, I had covered another crime story about a guy who shot his wife in the back of the head. That story was about her son who had actually cleaned up the blood in the bathroom because he didn't want his family to remember his mother that way. I was emotionally exhausted from that. I had gone into the bathroom with this guy, and the bucket was still there. It was a wrenching experience.

Two days later, we heard on the scanner that a baby had been pulled out of a pool and was unresponsive, and there was an address. I didn't want to go, but we got in the car and we went, and we were getting there right after they had loaded the child in the ambulance. The mother pulled up just after we got there. She started to get back in her car to follow the ambulance, and the deputy stopped her. We knew just a few minutes later that the child had died. That was a huge challenge for reporting. I knew what was coming, but the parents didn't know.

Inside the house was the father, and he had been home alone. These were, by all accounts, tremendous parents. They worked opposite shifts so that somebody could be home with the kids all the time. The father was inside, and they wouldn't let his wife in the house. This was a detail that didn't appear in the story thanks to [editor] Mike Wilson, who is so good at being sensitive. Inside the house the father was vomiting. He was so overwhelmed, and they wouldn't let his wife inside.

I didn't interview anybody. I stood there in the street at a safe distance and watched the wife. She was pacing in this gravel driveway next door, smoking cigarettes, talking to herself, and yelling at the cops because she wanted to get in the house. Then finally they let her in the house, and it was like slow motion because I knew what was coming. We were like, okay, we know they're about to tell these people that their child has died.

I'll never forget the scream from this father, and he comes exploding out of this house and collapses onto his knees, and he's screaming. I think the only place in that story where I do anything "writerly" is when I'm describing how the scream sounded because I couldn't put an adjective or an adverb to describe it, but I did see these deputies who I know had been with the sheriff's office for thirty years, they turned away. That was the way to describe it, the way the reader could understand how awful it was.

Was there any feedback on the story? I know that on Gangrey.com, there was some debate about the ethics of being there in that moment. What did regular readers say?

I expected there to be more criticism than there ended up being. There was a healthy debate on Gangrey, and I felt a little bit guilty, not because I felt like I'd done anything wrong at all, because I felt like I didn't. I gave these people a lot of space. I didn't approach them, and I felt like we were sensitive, as sensitive as we could be. There were details that we took out of that story to protect that family. One thing I felt compelled to do was to go back and face them, and if they were angry at me, give them the chance to tell me that, tell me what a terrible thing I had done.

A few days later, we went back to their house, and we knocked on the door and a part of me didn't want them to answer, but they did. We told them who we were and told them how sorry we were for what they'd gone through and that if they wanted to tell their story they could. They never ended up calling me, but they were thankful that we came, and it was a good lesson.

In 2020, in the midst of the pandemic, you wrote a story that was focused on the Marquez-Greene family from Newtown, and it was incredibly impactful. What was this story about?

This year, I'm doing a series on how the pandemic is impacting children in America. I've known Nelba [Marquez-Greene] for years. She confided that she was struggling with the idea of allowing her son to go back to school. Her daughter was killed in the Sandy Hook shooting. At the time in 2012, her son was in third grade, so he was in school that day as well but survived. And now, she and her husband Jimmy were wrestling with this idea of, can we let our surviving child go back to school, in the middle of a pandemic. I followed them over the course of about two months as they wrestled with that decision and then, ultimately, when he went back to school.

Given the pandemic, how did you report this story? Did you make trips to Connecticut?

I went there twice. The Marquez-Greene family takes this seriously. Jimmy, the dad, is asthmatic, so they had real concerns. I never did go into their home. Anytime I'm reporting, I'm wearing an N95 mask, taking every precaution that I can. I spent about fifteen hours interviewing the three of them. Those were all mostly through Zoom. And then I went up there to see Isaiah practice hockey. I did a socially distant interview with Nelba in the backyard, and I came up with some creative ways to get other scenes, because I didn't want this to be a story that was entirely reconstructed. They were going on these driving practices every day. Every afternoon, Isaiah would go drive, and Nelba would go with him. I asked her, at some point, when she was doing that, to FaceTime me. There's a beginning of one section that is just the description of them driving. She turned on her phone and set it to the side, and I sat there for a half hour as they practiced driving. I was able to get dialogue and a real scene that way.

I was there the week he was going back to school, and the final section is all live scene. I was with them as they were packing the car up. I asked them if I could put a recorder in the car when Isaiah was driving with his mom to the school, so I ended up getting compelling dialogue from that as well.

The use of dialogue in the story struck me. There are few straight quotes.

I almost never use quotes. In terms of relying on people's recall for dialogue, I never trust more than a few words. That whole first section is reconstructed, but the dialogue I use, some of it is clearly what Isaiah remembered thinking at the time, and then a little bit of dialogue back and forth between Isaiah and his mom; it's never more than three or four or five words. If you have two people telling you, this is what he said, this is what she said, this is what I clearly remember, it lines up, then, in those situations, I'll use short quotes or short bits of dialogue.

That first scene opens up with Isaiah sitting on the couch and getting the email that his school is going to open. Did you know early on that that was where you wanted to start the story?

Yeah. The structure of the story is a classic narrative. Here's a question, and the reader is going to wait to see how the question is answered. Now, there was a lot weaved into that, but the question was, will he go back to school? That was the moment the question was asked, and even Isaiah himself, he gets this news, he's excited about it, and immediately the question comes into his own mind: Will I go back?

One of the first interviews I did with Isaiah through Zoom was having him reconstruct that day from his point of view. His mother didn't know until I interviewed him that he thought that she was not going to let him go, based on her reaction that day. That was news to her because she thought she had kept her poker face on and that she hadn't given him any sense that she was in fear. But he told me, "When I looked into her eyes, I saw her fear, and I didn't think there was any way she would let me go."

What was it like to talk with Isaiah?

He's this incredibly intelligent, thoughtful young man, but he's also a sixteen-year-old boy. I've been writing for years about childhood trauma, and that is pretty much the most difficult demographic to interview, the boy who is sixteen, because there's an awareness of wanting to look cool. That's true for all of them. They're aware of how their words sound. It took some time, but then I hit it off on that first interview. We talked a lot about sports. I'd met him before because I had wanted to do a story about his family back in 2017, but it didn't work out. So we had a little bit of history. It just took time.

I'm never trying to make people emotional. I'm trying to understand where people's heads were, in a moment. The question I asked most often is "what happened next?" If I was trying to evoke a lot of emotion out of him, that would have been a much more difficult task.

I met Nelba days after I read this piece. I told her how much I enjoyed the story. She had what I think is the greatest compliment that any story source can give a reporter when she said that you were compassionate.

I always say that we have to be human first. We're humans before journalists. I think people can sense that. I learned that when I was a cops reporter in Florida, knocking on doors of people who had just lost loved ones or whose loved ones had been accused of some heinous crime. The first thing I always tell people who have suffered traumas is that I'm sorry for what they've gone through. That's the way I always begin, especially when I'm interviewing kids. And I tell him that they're in charge. I do a lot of pre-reporting to find out if the kids have triggers, if there's things that I should avoid talking about, because I never want to do additional harm to somebody.

If you don't have empathy, you cannot tell these stories, because the heart of what I do is bathe in people's lived experiences. I try to sponge up as much as I can. I'll never understand their feelings of what they've been through, but I try to get as close to that as I can, to immerse myself so I can then put it on the page. I think that starts with empathy. If you are not an empathetic person, you can maybe do other types of journalism, but deep narrative on people suffering? I don't think you can do it if you aren't someone who is capable of empathy.

In many ways, the story about Isaiah and the Marquez-Greene family fits the type of stories that were included in your Pulitzer finalist series because they are survivors of gun violence. How did the gun violence series get started?

The genesis of what's become this season of my career began in 2015, when I wrote a story in my first full year at the *Post* about a girl who was born with hiv and who was going through the process of learning that that's what she had. She didn't know that she had hiv. I followed her for six months and was in the room when the doctor delivered this news. That story reached a big audience and my editor, Lynda Robinson, thought that I had this natural ability to write about children. She had mentioned this idea about a project on children and violence—broadly at that stage, it wasn't even gun violence. She thought it was this undiscovered area. Quickly it became clear that it needed to be focused on gun violence.

I did six stories over the course of that year, exploring from all these different lenses how the epidemic of gun violence impacts children in America. The first piece was about a boy in southeast Washington, D.C., whose father had been shot to death in the middle of the day, right outside of his school. He was in second grade at the time. I actually met him at the vigil before the funeral. I sat next to him at the funeral and followed him on the first day he went back to school and that was the first piece in the series. The second piece was about a shooting at an elementary school in South Carolina that no one remembered because only one child died. It was a group of first graders on the playground, and a teenager pulled up and opened fire and his gun jammed, and that's why he only killed one kid. Those two stories ended up being the foundation for this book that I have since written.

That year, I went everywhere. I went to Cleveland, for a road rage incident where a four-year-old had been shot in the head and survived, and I went to Las Vegas for a couple of weeks following a group of teenage girls who'd been at the concert [where sixty people were killed in a mass shooting]. I went to Chicago for a story there. And then I did a story about a shooting in Virginia. The idea was to turn the lens and try to show people what that experience is like for children who go through these things.

Considering you're dealing with so many people who've been through so many traumatic events, what's that like for you, for your own mental health?

It's draining. It definitely takes a toll. I'm pretty good at compartmentalizing and setting things aside to some degree. I'm pretty good at moving on. In some ways, it's gotten a lot harder during the pandemic, because the way that I would deal with these things is to take a trip with my wife. I always found that to be therapeutic and would help me clear out all the secondary trauma that I was dealing with. That's all gone now. All the travel I'm doing now is for work. Many of us are covering dark subjects right now. It was always hard, but it's definitely gotten harder, and I haven't entirely figured out the best way to manage it. I don't see a counselor, I don't see a therapist, but I am certainly a big proponent of therapy and counseling. If I felt like I needed to, I would not hesitate to see one.

I will say that I feel like it's a real privilege for me to get to tell these stories. I feel like this is what I am meant to do, what I am called to do at this moment in my life. I don't think I'll do this forever; it's not sustainable. But for right now, I feel like this is what I'm meant to do.

Kim Cross

Kim Cross is the author of the *New York Times* best-selling *What Stands in a Storm*, a book about the worst tornado outbreak on record. The book was a GoodReads Choice Awards finalist and one of Amazon's Best Books of 2015. As a freelance writer, Cross's work has been anthologized in *The Best American Sports Writing*.

Cross's journalism exists because of her remarkable and tenacious reporting abilities. Her stories often feature extensive, to-the-minute accurate timelines that she's built using everything from GPS data to archived news segments.

Cross was a senior editor at *Southern Living* when tornadoes carved up the South in April 2011. When that happened, editor Lindsay Bierman said the magazine, which didn't typically cover news, needed to do something because it happened in their backyard. Previously, Cross worked at the New Orleans *Times-Picayune* and the *St. Petersburg Times* (now named the *Tampa Bay Times*), and so she led the coverage.

The focus of the series was how people coped with the devastation, focusing on faith, food, and fellowship. Readers loved the package, and it generated hundreds of reader emails and letters thanking the magazine.

Cross has written for *Bicycling* magazine, *Southern Living*, *Outside*, SB Nation, and ESPN, among other publications.

I spoke with her twice. We talked about her book *What Stands in a Storm* in September 2015. We talked again four years later about her *Bicycling* magazine story "NOEL + LEON."

What is your book *What Stands in a Storm* about?

The book is a literary nonfiction account of the biggest tornado outbreak in recorded history, and I wanted to take you through the storm from the perspective of the people who lived it.

What made you want to write this book?

It happened in my backyard. I live in Birmingham. Everyone here either was personally affected or knew someone who was. Sixty-two tornadoes hit my state in one day and a lot of them were the biggest variety, the EF-4 and the EF-5, that can wipe a town off the earth. I was sitting at home on my couch with my husband and my four-year-old son when the EF-4 was coming through Tuscaloosa. I had lived in Tuscaloosa twice, first as an undergrad and second after working for a few years in San Francisco. I moved back with my husband and went to grad school.

We were looking at it on TV as it was being captured by the live SkyCam coming through what was formerly our hometown. It was like that moment, watching the Towers fall on 9/11 and you think: Can this be real? Is this really happening? The tornado continued coming toward Birmingham, and for a little while, it looked like it was on track to hit our house. At some point the power failed, and we got in our laundry room and put bike helmets on and had the moment that everyone who's ever been through this has experienced where you have time to think, "Wow, we could die." There aren't many times in your life when you can contemplate that.

I felt like this was such a shared experience for everyone in our state and anyone who's ever been through a storm and wanted to capture it.

Why did you structure the book the way you did?

I wanted to give you the sense of urgency and chaos and uncertainty that was the hallmark of that day for everyone from the meteorologists to the people who were going through it to the families who were searching for people they didn't hear from.

I felt like that was the emotion that you needed as a reader to empathize with the characters. What made that possible was a strict timeline, or basically five timelines laid one upon the other that allowed me to capture that. I started with the broadcast of James Spann, who was the meteorologist that everyone turned to on that day.

Basically, he does wall-to-wall coverage during major outbreaks, which means that there are no commercials from the minute the first warning goes on the air to the expiration of the last warning of the day. No commercials, no shows, no interruptions. Someone posted that on YouTube in a few minute increments. . . . I sat myself down in front of the computer for several days and transcribed thirteen hours of broadcast coverage.

How did you find people to talk to for the book?

I had to approach it with almost a canvassing casting call, where I looked at all of the towns hit in Alabama. There were lists of victims, and I looked at almost all of them to see who these people were, what had happened to them, how they'd died, who they left behind, and then I started winnowing down to, who do I want to focus on? There were too many towns hit and too many tornadoes to include them all, so I had to narrow it down to a reasonably small cast of characters so that you wouldn't, as a reader, get lost in all of the people. I narrowed it down to two towns that I thought would be representative of a lot of the towns. One was Tuscaloosa, which is the home of the University of Alabama and the Crimson Tide football team, and I figured that most people can relate to a college town and it was the biggest population center that was hit by a big one that day.

Then I also chose Cordova, which was a little town about an hour northwest of Birmingham, because Cordova, unlike Tuscaloosa, had a volunteer fire department. They didn't have professionals; they had people who are unpaid and go out on search and rescue because they love it. They have considerably fewer resources than a town like Tuscaloosa. I wanted to show what the little towns were going through and how that was different from the big cities because most of the firefighters in our country are volunteer firefighters. I thought that was an important perspective to convey.

Then within those towns, I looked for characters that I thought would be relatable and who would remind you of someone that you know so that you could paint a familiar face on them and care about them.

You've mentioned before that when you were reporting, you thought like a fiction writer, how did that help you later, when you started writing the story?

This is something new for me because I've always been steeped in journalism and nonfiction and you never make anything up. You're not supposed to imagine anything. You go with what the source says and you fact-check it. When I was roughing out some of the scenes, I started noticing that the details felt a little bit thin. I'm in the house, but I don't know exactly what the house looks like, and the house no longer exists. So I imagined myself as the character. If I'm hiding here and I turn my head to the right, what would I see? That would guide my questioning. It would inform the details that I would look for.

There's a scene where a character is driving from Mississippi to Tuscaloosa to look for her sister, who has not responded to calls or texts and is feared missing or dead. She has made missing person fliers, and she's riding in the car with her fiancé.

On Google Earth Pro, I looked up the road they would have been driving. If she's looking out the window, what is she looking at? She has these fliers. Are they in her lap? Is she clutching them? Are they in the backseat? These were the details I needed to flesh out a scene and make it come alive. You have to imagine what you need to see in a scene to know what questions to ask. There's nothing that's made up, nothing fictional, but you almost have to make assumptions and then fact-check them with the source in order to get that level of detail. Most of the time, it doesn't occur to sources to tell you these little details, which make a scene cinematic. You have to tease them out that way by imagining what it might look like and then asking them, "Does this feel true?"

Nonfiction books aren't often fact-checked, but I know you did. How did you go about fact-checking your book manuscript?

I obsess about the facts. I lost sleep over a number of things in this book and one was that I wanted to "John McPhee" the weather. The way he wrote about geology was my gold standard for writing about meteorology. I wanted to make it understandable and relatable to a lay audience, to nonscientists, without getting so overboard with metaphors that meteorologists would find flaws in it or roll their eyes. Secondly, I wanted to make sure that in all of my distilling of what people told me into scenes that aren't attributed in the traditional journalistic sense, I wanted to make sure I didn't make assumptions that were incorrect.

In doing that, to fact-check it, I recruited a number of meteorologists to help me as I was writing it, to review scenes, and also to read it before it went to press. I reached out early to Chuck Doswell, who is one of the most experienced tornado researchers in the country. He spent his entire career researching tornadoes, and he's also one of the biggest critics of books about meteorology, especially those by laypeople, because they tend to get the science wrong.

He told me that he didn't do interviews anymore because he'd been misquoted so many times. He would correspond only in writing so he had a record of what was said. I said, "I'm good with that." As I wrote, I would send him passages and say, "Chuck, did I get this right?" He's pretty cantankerous and would say, "Some of your concepts are seriously flawed." I'd be like, "Great, tell me which ones and tell me how to make them right." He read it as we went along, and then at the end, I asked him to read it and look hard at any of the science that was incorrect. He identified some serious errors that only a scientist would notice.

Did you reach out to anyone else?

I reached out to David Quammen and asked him who fact-checks his books, and that's how I found Emily Krieger. I realized that although magazines have a staff of fact-checkers who go behind you and check your facts, book publishers don't. It was on me to hire one. Emily Krieger was a fact-checker at *National Geographic* for years. I thought okay, she is gonna be great with the science. She was expensive, and I sold my mountain bike to pay for her fees. I had her check my science exposition carefully.

But I also knew there were things like scenes and assumptions and details that only the characters and the families would notice were not right. One of my last duties before the book went to print was to sit down for a private reading with each of the three families who had lost a child in the storm. I sat down with them separately, and I read every chapter in which their kid appeared. It was a really important part of the process for me as a person, as well as a journalist. When a source is trusting me with the most sensitive and emotional story of their lives, I have to get it right.

What was the story "NOEL + LEON" you wrote for *Bicycling* magazine about?

The story is about these two guys, an American and a Brit, who set out to ride across the world's largest landmass, Eurasia, on a bicycle. They're complete strangers. One is riding east and the other's riding west. And by a stroke of crazy chance, they meet smack dab in the middle, like right near the Caspian Sea, which is the dividing point between Europe and Asia.

They're opposite in nature. Noel is an American, and he believes the world is a safe place and that people are nice. He sets out and isn't too worried about things, and the real world proves him right. Leon, who is the Brit, loves misadventure, and he sets out thinking the world is this sketchy place and what he's doing is dangerous and there are dodgy people out there. The universe also proves him right.

How did you learn about this story?

I learned about it more than five years ago because my local bike shop owner told me about it. Barb Malki of Cahaba Cycles sells Trek bikes, which are based in Wisconsin. Noel's family owns a Trek dealership called Wheel & Sprocket in Wisconsin. They met at some bike-industry event. Noel didn't talk frequently about his epic trip, but he must've shared it over dinner. When Barb told me this, I thought, "You must be mistaken. This couldn't possibly be true." It sounded too good to be true, like an urban legend. I set out to fact-check it. Barb gave me Noel's phone number, and I called him up and talked to him, and he verified the story. So I said, "Do you think you could put me in touch with Leon?"

He said, "We're not really close friends or anything, but I think we're friends on Facebook." He reached out to Leon on Facebook and got his email. Leon was living in China at the time, and so I Skyped with him. I couldn't believe it to be true.

What was some of the information that you used to nail down exactly what they had done?

At the time that I interviewed both of them, five years had passed since the trip. Memories are perishable, so you lose a lot of detail when that much time passes. But Leon kept a day-by-day blog. And this was back in the day when you had to go to an internet cafe to post an update. So he must have kept a notebook or something. Almost every day on his trip, he described exactly what happened that day and uploaded photos. He even tracked his mileage. This documented details that he could not have remembered five years later.

Noel also kept a blog, but his had been corrupted. But he did have a Flickr photo stream that had thousands of pictures with captions. And the photos were time-stamped. When you take a digital photo, the date and time are preserved in the EXIF tags. I was able to verify what date a photo was taken in a specific place. He also had a bike computer with GPS. It didn't help him navigate, but it actually tracked his path, and he had uploaded all of these GPS tracks, day by day, onto a website. I downloaded them and uploaded them into Google Earth, and then I tracked Leon's progress by inputting it into Google Earth. I was able to see how much they paralleled and where their paths crossed, and I could actually zoom in on Google Earth to the little tea house in the middle of the desert where they met, which is kind of crazy.

You heard about this five years ago. What made you keep pushing until you found a home for its publication?

There was something magical about it, and something so improbable. I fell in love with it. The other thing that was interesting is their names are reversed. If you spelled Leon backwards, it's Noel. And so their names together form a palindrome. I was so tickled by that. I was also delighted by the fact that neither Noel or Leon found it as interesting as the people they told about it casually. I was also shocked that it hadn't been told. I loved the idea of retracing this, the many decisions and coincidences and things that had to go wrong in just the right way for them to meet exactly when they did, exactly where they did, at the moment when they needed to meet. It struck me as almost a true fable. I kept thinking of Paulo Coelho's book *The Alchemist*, which I read when I was in high school and fell in love with, and it had this quality of being like a fable. I wanted so badly to tell it.

When we first started emailing about this story, one of the first things that you mentioned was the number of palindromes in the piece. Why was that important to you?

From the beginning, when I was originally talking about the story with my friend Glenn Stout, we talked about how this story wouldn't be as interesting if their names weren't what they are. Leon and Noel are the same name in reverse, and they were doing essentially the same journey in reverse. And the fact they met in the middle, it screamed to me that this whole thing was a palindrome.

I wanted to try something experimental, something I'd never seen before in terms of structure. I love story structure and I obsess about it, and I had never seen a story that was structured as a palindrome. I set out with that challenge, while also knowing that sometimes, when you swing for the fences, you strike out. I was like, I want to be able to try this, but I also have to realize that if it doesn't work, if it confuses the reader, then I'm going to have to be willing to let it go. But I won't know if it works until I try it. To my editors' great credit—I have to give props to Matt Allyn, who was my original editor at *Bicycling*, and then he went on paternity leave, and Leah Flickinger stepped in, and the two of them came back and helped me get the final revision together—they were willing to let me give this a shot. I don't think I would've been happy if I couldn't have at least tried that.

Bronwen Dickey

Bronwen Dickey is a contributing writer at *Oxford American*, author of *Pit Bull: The Battle Over an American Icon*. A National Magazine Award finalist for feature writing in 2011, she's won several reporting awards and published stories in *Popular Mechanics, Esquire, Slate, Garden and Gun*, and *Outside*.

In 2019 she wrote a story for *Esquire*, "The Remains," about a young man who came to the United States with his family, grew up in east Texas, but was deported after a strange series of events. In an attempt to return to the United States, he died in the south Texas desert. The piece was also about forensic anthropologists who worked to identify his remains and contact his family. One challenge to reporting this story was learning his history. Dickey found out who he was but didn't want to put his family in harm's way; they were undocumented immigrants. Ultimately, a member of the family was willing to talk with her. "My main priority was not writing anything to endanger or jeopardize family members . . . who . . . didn't want to speak," she says. "I realized every story . . . has human consequences or can have serious ones. We get to walk away from the story, start another, but people in our stories don't get to walk away. They are living with that forever."

Dickey was a National Magazine Award finalist for "Climb Aboard, Ye Who Seek the Truth," published by *Popular Mechanics*. It was about a cruise ship full of the biggest conspiracy theorists in the world. On top of the National Magazine Award recognition, it won the Hearst Editorial Excellence Award in Reporting and an honorable mention in the Lowell Thomas Travel Journalism Award and was noted in *The Best American Travel Writing*.

I spoke with Dickey in January 2020.

You have a story in the October 2019 *Esquire* titled "The Remains." What is that about?

A young man named Cristian Gonzalez, who came to this country with his family. He grew up in east Texas, considered himself, as did his friends and family, American. He was deported, after a weird conflagration of events, to Mexico, a country he didn't know, and felt lonely there. He tried to get back into the United States but died in the south Texas desert. There's a team of scientists and researchers at Texas State University who have gone into south Texas, found remains of hundreds of migrants in new municipal cemeteries. They're doing DNA testing on remains to get migrants back to their families.

How did you learn about the group doing that, as well as the Gonzalez case?

The story started because my editor, Ryan D'Agostino, approached me, asked if I wanted to do something on forensic anthropology. He was thinking about forensic anthropology research facilities, known as body farms. I said I'll certainly write about that. We tried to figure out how to make it relevant to what was happening in the country. I found this team of forensic anthropologists working on issues related to border deaths. There was much going on about the ongoing humanitarian crisis at the border, people being turned away and all these things going on politically; that seemed a good place to dive in. I reached out to the head anthropologist at Texas State, who runs the Operation Identification project. She told me the story of Christian. It was the only time remains they found and tested belonged to someone who grew up in the United States.

The section you start the story with is an incredibly well-done scene. How did you go about re-creating that?

It's difficult, though interestingly enough re-creation is one of the parts of writing I enjoy most. It's going on a historical scavenger hunt, trying to find details that will fit into the puzzle, the picture you're trying to build.

This project was extremely well documented. It involved several different universities coming together to collaborate. I spoke with the head of the anthropology team on scene in 2012, spearheading this project. I spoke with one of her colleagues, one of the students who was there. I was asking them to tell me everything they remember, every detail. What was the air like, the weather? What were you feeling? What were the challenges, things that surprised you? I was trying to get granular, to get those little things people might not know they remember. It's hard to explain; I wasn't able to get a ton because years had passed, but one anthropologist remembered the sweat. There was a soft breeze but oppressive heat in south Texas, an overcast day. I'm always trying to get things like that. I looked at weather reports, weather patterns in south Texas over a period of months. I was looking at photos and documents they took: anthropologists' and archaeologists' map[s], grid[s], photograph[s], everything; I had photos. I went to this site, watched the cemetery, tried to get a feel for what that was. In succeeding years there was a lot to draw from, how people were feeling about it, lots of people working there; I was going from collective memory.

Asking superspecific questions can be strange. Do you give subjects a heads-up, say, I'm going to ask you weird questions?

I say there are going to be many questions. It's going to seem absurd. It's going to be about stuff you probably think insignificant. I'm trying to create a picture of what someone would see watching a documentary. Little details about the room you were sitting in, ways you were gesturing, what someone was eating; all things that don't seem important to the story in your mind are important to the story in mine because they help people feel they're there. I give them a warning, say this is going to sound absurd. I hope it doesn't feel intrusive, but that's the way it's going to be.

I can't remember who I was talking to recently who said, "Imagine I'm on your shoulder; you're wearing a GoPro. Tell me what I'm seeing." That was a good approach.

You mentioned in your story a process of cleaning a skeleton, it can take some time getting used to. Did you witness that?

I didn't. I saw various things done: the things students and scientists were doing, cataloging personal effects, photographing those. The head anthropologist of Op-ID, Kate Bradley, walked me through the facility, showed me how every part happens. Even if she wasn't doing it, she was describing it in detail. I went into the room where steam jacketed kettles are; there were remains in the kettles. They didn't pop them out for me to see. There was a body bag on the floor with remains. It's all in a state of progress. She described how the process happens. It takes a lot of getting used to; that's usually when people know they can handle it or not. A number of students had to leave because it violates what we tend to believe about the sanctity of our species, even though it's in the name of science.

Christian doesn't start out in the story as Christian. He starts out as No. 0383. About a third of the way through is when we learn who he is. It was impactful to move from a number to the story of a man who was alive.

That's kind of you. When I look back at this story the way I look back on almost everything I write, I see missed opportunities, things I wish I'd done better. To me this story reads like it's a third of where I wanted it to be.

When you're working on deadline, you sometimes have to abandon the thing when it has to ship. The way I conceived of it is, because so much of the story is about burial, and I don't want to be too heavy-handed in resurrection, but so much is the significance of burial in the unmarked grave versus actual burial and a funeral, the significance of remains, what we do with them. In the beginning he's an anonymous number; [in] the end we get to know him a little. He's going back into the ground as Christian Gonzalez with a family in his hometown, Palestine, Texas.

You've mentioned you were heartbroken over the end of this piece because you felt it didn't go where you hoped.

There was so much emotional gravity to it, and what had happened had devastated the family so much. I wanted to give this piece the best I could do, but deadlines are deadlines. You can only do so much in the time they're giving any of us. This was also a complicated piece. It was assigned for one magazine, and then it was switched to another, so the focus shifted, and there was a lot going on behind the scenes. To me, it felt a little rushed, but every journalist feels they don't have enough time.

What was it like when you reached out to Christian's family? Was this something they wanted to talk about?

Very difficult. I had to navigate things that I had never had to navigate before in terms of writing about people who are undocumented. So Kate Spradley at Texas State gave me Zaira Gonzalez's email address. I emailed her and asked if she would be willing to talk, and she said she would be fine with that. She had spoken to their local paper about it, and I think a forensics magazine had done a small feature. Part of it for her was she wanted people to know what had happened to her brother, and she wanted people to know about this project, and she wanted to help other families of people who had died crossing the border and get the information out there.

I tried to be, as I always am, as sensitive as possible, realizing that this was one of the worst things that ever happened to their family.

He had gone missing, and they had no idea what happened to him for five years, which was excruciating. She was receptive about it, but I wanted to be as respectful and accommodating as possible.

Aside from having to work quickly, what were other challenges you faced when reporting and writing the piece?

Zaira was the only member of the family who wanted to put the story out there publicly, be interviewed, because the issue of being undocumented was sensitive. I understood that. My main priority was not writing anything to endanger or jeopardize the safety of family members who were undocumented and didn't want to speak. For instance, names of parents aren't in the piece, even though I know their names, lots more about them. I didn't want to put in anything to jeopardize their safety given the political climate, ice raids and things that were happening making them more frightened. The challenge was honoring the facts, and doing the job I was there to do.

I realized every story any of us do has human consequences or can have serious ones. We get to walk away from the story, start another, but people in our stories don't get to walk away. They are living with that forever.

You wrote a story about a conspiracy theorist convention that took place on a cruise ship. That ran in *Popular Mechanics*, was a finalist for a National Magazine Award.

That's another story I did for Ryan. We were looking at a number of options that hadn't panned out. On some blog I saw there was going to be a cruise for conspiracy theorists. I was working on my book, researching science denialism and conspiracy theories, the psychological ideation that makes people buy into them. I was interested in it.

You say the story will write itself—it never does, but it seemed something that would make an incredible narrative: an absurd location, a confined space, bracketed by dates. You have this community of people who believe different things in one space. I approached him, said, "Are you sending anyone on this?" It didn't occur to me he might send me. I was shy about asking for things or pitching back then. He said go.

It didn't pan out the way we thought it would.

This is one of those stories where you go in as a reporter thinking it's going to turn out a certain way, then the tables are turned. How did you handle that?

I conceived of it as being lighthearted. It had to have a scientific basis, but I couldn't imply I cosign these beliefs. I wanted it to be a good-natured, meeting-people-where-they-are piece, the type Taffy Akner does well. Whenever you read her, you don't believe she's signing on to belief systems. She's not shooting fish in a barrel, writing things to make fun. She meets people where they are. There's generosity about that. I thought I could do that, talk about belief formation, how we come to believe what we believe, where we get information, thinking maybe it'll be people talking about the grassy knoll or aliens, whatever. They're playing shuffleboard, drinking mai tais; everyone's having a good time. If that can happen, what does that say about the rest of us?

That is not what happened. The first night was great. The first night, everyone was welcoming. People were so kind. I was excited. I was having great conversations with people. They were being open. By the next morning, things had started to curdle. Someone had looked up *Popular Mechanics* and found the 9/11 conspiracy-debunking issue that they had done several years before that and became irate. One guy approached me the next day and said, you know, if you do anything to smear me, I won't stop until I've exposed you and your paymasters or whatever.

It went from zero to ninety in a space of a couple of hours. Then we started getting disinvited. There were a couple of other journalists on the trip. We started getting asked to leave things or to not attend things. We started getting confrontational stuff from people who had been nice to us. It started to get a little scary, and then it escalated to two people challenging each other to a fight and me being pinned up against a wall between some people. It became a physically frightening, confined space to be in with people who were deeply suspicious, even paranoid, about each other.

I'm assuming you didn't go into this thinking you were going to write in first person.

I thought if anything, I was going to be one of those transparent, touch-point first person to have the reaction shot or the transparent tour guide through the world. I was sad at first when I sat down to write because of everything that had happened. I was sad that I had gotten dragged into the story in a way that the most dramatic event happened around me and how I was perceived. That made me uncomfortable, but that's what happened, so I had to go with it.

Was writing in first person a challenge for you?

It was for that assignment. I've certainly written personal essays when I was younger, and I did an MFA program where I did a fair amount of first-person writing, but as a working journalist, on assignment for *Popular Mechanics*, the last thing you think you're going to do is write any piece so heavily first person. I was not super comfortable with it. But when the events are what they are, you have to be honest about what the situation is.

Were you happy with the first draft that you turned in?

No. Oh, God, no. I think we did seven drafts. I worked with a wonderful guy named Sean Manning, who is now a book editor. Because there were so many moving pieces, we were trying all kinds of things.

I was trying different structures. I was trying different scenes. The main problem I was having is that everything could be a scene because the events started to get so absurd; literally going to the salad bar became the scene. Everything could be a scene. There's a great quote, I believe, from Walker Evans, the famous documentary photographer, and he says a photographer has to be able to see and he has to be able to choose. I was having a lot of trouble with choosing. I could see possibilities everywhere. There were lots of iterations, and lots of drafts trying to get that balance.

Did you have feedback after the story ran?

In the wider world, people respond positively; I was grateful. Folks on the ship, predictably Len and Sherri, prominent characters, wrote a long screed that I was guilty of war crimes, paid by George Soros or something. I haven't looked at it in ages. They were extremely angry. I think they created Twitter accounts trolling me. Other than that I didn't hear from anyone, which is sad. Some people on the trip were lovely. I don't want to give the impression they were all like that.

You were working on your book at the same time you did this. How did you pull that off?

I'd just finished it. Thank goodness. I was nervous, preoccupied with all that was going on. In one way, this was a wonderful break, a different thing than what I'd been working on. If it hadn't been, I don't think I could've done two things at once.

Do you prefer book writing or magazine pieces?

I feel magazine work is my habitat. Everyone has their natural habitat or natural lengths. I'm better and my work is tighter at a shorter length. The process of writing a book changed me especially as a reporter, made me grow beyond what I thought was possible. The idea you're going to create this discrete thing to be packaged, sold, publicly evaluated for months on end is frightening.

I like the rhythms of shorter stories, six months, eight months, in a story then you have this confined space; you have to create within that space. If someone lets me unspool time forever, unspool pages forever, I'll keep going until I drop.

Was your book *Pit Bull* a product of your MFA program?

Not really. I don't even remember the stuff I wrote. I think I wrote mainly personal or cultural criticism. I was one of the few people in that program who didn't have a book idea. I wanted to learn how to do this better; I was groping in the dark. I got my degree in 2009. I never thought I'd write a book until 2012.

I'd give anything to go back, do my MFA again. I was a newspaper reporter who went to do an MFA, then I wrote a memoir, which is what everyone was doing. I'd give anything to take those three years and do a piece of narrative journalism.

You're lucky when you got there you had the reporting background. I was trying to learn all at the same time; it was daunting. It still is. I feel daunted every day by this job.

I was not that great of a reporter. I had four years at a local newspaper. I became better by talking to people like you.

Get the experience working in a newsroom. You knew how to write all kinds of stuff on deadline, how to ask other people for support, how to cultivate sources, those things. That's solid gold. I never worked at a local paper, my greatest professional regret.

A lot of your work is done as a freelancer. What's the market like?

It's frightening. It's hard. The network of people being worked with seems to be shrinking, even as the people who want to do this work is growing thanks, in part, because of Longform and you and Longreads. The number of people who want to do this work is growing, and the number of places to hang it is shrinking. The number of writers being worked with seems to be shrinking, because with fewer pages available, editors are willing to take fewer risks.

On the other hand, I'm encouraged by the interest in long nonfiction narratives in general. What's the explosion of podcasting? People want long stories. They want to be with characters for a long time; sites like the Atavist or newsletters like the Sunday Long Read. These kinds of things make me feel good about the fact that people want these stories out there, and if that's the case, there will always be places to publish.

What's harder for me, not having a staff contract and not having a multidecade reporting career behind me, is that I don't think I'm usually the first person people look at for lots of things. The staff contract people, that's pretty much their wheelhouse.

Everything's changing, and that's always been the case. I'm hopeful that a new story format will arise. I've been told by a lot of people that the book industry is still pretty strong, so that's good to know.

People want stories. Not to go off into a weird tangent, but I think it says so much about the world of artifice and the curated museum of the self that we get through social media and all the things we're concerned about with fake news, that people want these in-depth, true stories about what it means to be alive on this planet. I think that's incredibly encouraging. That's one thing about our wretched species that has not changed over the millennia, and that makes me feel good or comforted.

Mirin Fader

Mirin Fader is a staff writer at the Ringer, where she produces long-form narrative features on sports and athletes, and the author of *Giannis: The Improbable Rise of an NBA MVP*, a biography of Milwaukee Bucks superstar Giannis Antetokounmpo published in 2021 by Hachette Books. In 2019, Folio named Fader in their Top Women in Media "Up and Comer" category. She has also been honored by the Pro Writers Basketball Association, the Associated Press Sports Editor, the U.S. Writers Basketball Association, the Football Writers Association of America, and the Los Angeles Press Club.

In January 2021, Fader's profile of then Green Bay Packers wide receiver Davante Adams looked at how the superstar had changed over the years, especially now that he had become a father. It was the second time that Fader had written about Adams. She profiled him three years earlier when she was at Bleacher Report. She wanted to write about him again after his daughter was born. Ultimately, Fader says it became a story about masculinity and opening up about his feelings and fears of parenthood and how all of that has changed and shaped him as a man as well as a football player.

While the Adams story is full of life, Fader has also written difficult stories tied to the deaths of athletes. In February 2020, she wrote about Gigi Bryant, Kobe's daughter, after the girl died along with several others in the helicopter crash that killed her father. Fader says she wrote that piece because she was annoyed that Gigi had become a footnote in all of the articles about the crash. Everything was focused on Kobe Bryant. Additionally, Fader had been a longtime basketball player and had connections in the girls basketball community that Gigi belonged to, and she knew a lot of people who were mourning that loss.

I spoke with Fader in January 2021, at the height of the COVID pandemic. We talked about her Adams profile and how the pandemic was changing how she reported, as well as other pieces she has written.

Your story on Davante Adams went live on the Ringer on January 14, 2021, just before the divisional playoff games began. What is the focus of the story?

This story is about somebody who's talented at football, but it is so much more about somebody who's evolving in so many different ways off the field. I want to show that the success you see on the field is due to that maturation off the field. He just had a daughter, and he is learning how to love her and is influenced by his mother's love for him. It is a story about masculinity and opening up about those feelings and fears of parenthood and how that's changed and shaped him as a man. I think the confidence and the incredible season that you're seeing from him is due to that evolution off the field.

It was great for an ordinary person to be able to relate to somebody who is an amazing professional athlete.

I got feedback from other men who said similar things, because we think that we should have nothing in common with these people. They make millions of dollars; they're famous; we're not. So many of us live paycheck to paycheck. These themes of love and emotion and humanity is what I think is the beauty of long-form storytelling. You might not be able to relate to Davante in any other way, but you know what it's like to have a daughter and be so overcome with awe and excitement and fear that something could happen to this person, this little human that you love so much. I think it's cool that people were able to see themselves in the story.

How did the piece come about?

Davante was having a great season. I profiled him a couple years back, when I was at Bleacher Report, so I kept in touch a little bit. I thought it would be a good idea to revisit him. I think you want to revisit somebody in a profile when something dramatic has changed in their life. You're not just profiling them again for the sake of it. I think having a daughter, and knowing how close he is with his mom, I was curious how those two relationships went together.

Did you know going in that it was going to center around fatherhood? Or is that something you started to realize the more you talked with him?

I didn't know. I think that's the thing with long-form writing. You have a sense of a couple of things you're curious about. That curiosity is probably one of your biggest tools as a long-form reporter, but you don't know until you sit down and talk with him. I think with him, he's so used to people asking, "What's it like playing with Aaron Rodgers?" I used to joke that our interview was like, I forgot to ask the inevitable Aaron Rodgers question. He was talking so much about his daughter. I think you get your cues from your subject. That's who he wanted to talk about. I asked him, "What is the one thing that keeps you up at night? What is the one thing that's picking at you?" He talked about his daughter. That's the exciting part about this genre. You never know what the story is going to be. But if you're open, it will unfold on its own.

I've done profiles on professional athletes before. I wrote about Kyrie Irving when he was a Cavaliers rookie for *Cleveland Magazine*. I had to write a two-thousand-word profile, but I had fifteen minutes to talk with him. How much time did you have with Adams?

It's so crazy, because that fifteen minutes that you're talking about, I always joke to people: My job is, how can I get to their soul in fifteen minutes? Which is a joke, right? You can't get to somebody's soul in fifteen minutes. I've been on that end of the coin too.

This was different. I had several hours with him, and a couple years ago, I went to his home and I spent the day with him and his wife. I couldn't do that this time because of COVID but definitely had hours and follow-up phone calls and stuff. I think that the industry is in a place where that type of access is rare. I've had other profiles where I had ten minutes with somebody. It's the luck of the draw.

As far as working on this story, I probably wrote it in a week. I was working on another story too, and they were both due before Christmas. It was a time crunch there. Sometimes, you have to pull a story together in two days, sometimes you have six months. That's the part of long-form writing people don't understand. You're not just typing in your room, whimsically taking your sweet time. You have a lot of deadlines, and you're working on several at one time because you know how long it takes to produce one.

How did you talk to Adams for this piece? Was it solely on the phone?

It was on Zoom.

What was that like? I've talked with some other reporters about how they get the details necessary to build a scene. How did you do that?

I was worried at the beginning of the pandemic about how this would affect my work. So much of my work is flying to wherever and noticing little details, like how did his eyelash curl when he talked about this? Was he looking fidgety? Those are things that are important. It's funny that this interview was over Zoom because I've done most of my interviews during the pandemic over the phone. I've found that athletes open up more when they don't have to show their face. I think maybe they're Zoomed out. There's a stiffness to it. I found that the phone call works much better. Adams wanted to do Zoom, I think, because I had spent time with him in a previous profile. There was already that connection.

I think you can use the pandemic as almost an excuse to paint the scene. I have often said in a couple of other story interviews last year, during the height of the pandemic, man, I wish I was here with you right now so I could describe whatever. Can you paint the picture for me as if I was there? It's almost like you can use it as a crutch to get them to visually explain something to you and get those little details that you need.

There's one part in the story where there are some bits of dialogue from a few years ago, when he's in the car after one of his worst games. How do you interview in order to get specific types of information like the fact he got home that night and didn't eat the Thanksgiving turkey and instead got up and went to his room and shut the door?

I always say the first rule of sports writing is you can't be afraid to look stupid. By looking stupid, I mean there's a hesitancy, at least there was for me when I was a bit younger, of feeling like, if I asked this follow-up question, if I asked what he was eating, if I asked the color of the car, is he gonna think I'm weird? You have to drop that because you're going to miss out on a critical detail.

I think you get those details by asking questions such as, I have to ask what kind of car you were in on Thanksgiving. You came home. You said you were miserable. How miserable? Did you cry? Did you shut the door? Can you help me understand how low you felt? That's when he's like, I love Thanksgiving, but I couldn't even eat. I asked, "What's the Thanksgiving meal you typically eat?" It's not being afraid to ask and get that specificity. A lot of times people don't understand why we asked those questions. I've had a lot of athletes say does it matter? Why do you need to know that? They're almost like, she's so weird. I'd rather be called weird than miss out on a critical detail.

Do you ever tell sources that you're going to ask some weird questions and ask them to bear with you because there's a reasoning behind it?

I never say that because I don't want them to feel nervous in any way. Before every interview, I always say I'm going to ask questions, I'm trying to get to know you better, no pressure. I promise this is going to be the least painful thing of your day. I think you want them to feel like they're having a conversation, not an "Interview." If they feel like you're trying to get to know them, they're gonna open up more. I don't even ask about the sport until midway. I think that lets them know that I do care about getting to know them as a person and writing a personal story. It's not that the sport isn't there. It is. The entire second section of the Davante story was all about what makes him so great at football. For me, I'm always like, let's get beyond football. Tell me about your mother.

That is something you don't see often when it comes to profiles on professional athletes: getting away from the field.

I think we're moving towards a much more analytical age. There's nothing wrong with that. I think there's amazing writers that know the game and can understand the nuances, and that's totally cool. But I think there's room for everyone's type of writing. You had Wright Thompson on your podcast. I have grown up wanting to be like him. I think I'll always want to be like him. When you said what you said about relating to Davante, that's how I felt with Wright Thompson's story on Michael Jordan aging. I used to be a basketball player, and leaving basketball was so depressing for me. It was my identity crisis. I related to Wright Thompson's article, even though I should have nothing in common with Michael Jordan and iconic athletes.

I wish there was more of that stuff in sports writing. I wouldn't say it's a lost art, because I can name so many people that are so good at this, but I definitely feel a shift in the beat writer and people like that being a bit more valued.

When you sat down to start writing, did you know immediately how you wanted to start the story?

No. I wish I was better at that. There are some people who write the story from beginning to end in one sitting. I'm like, what? My thoughts are always jumbled. What I know immediately are the images that stand out to me. The one thing I took away from the interview that I wasn't sure if it could be the lead or the ending was the image of him, his daughter was on his lap, and she was falling asleep on him. Originally, that was the ending, but we ended up changing it and moving it up.

In terms of story structure, what does it take to get to the final product?

It comes out of that draft work. I always tell people, as a long-form writer, writing is the least part of what you do. You spend the most time thinking, and thinking doesn't seem like work, but thinking is work. I transcribe everything and look at the material and I always ask myself, what are my best images? Then, what is this story about? It's about Davante, but it's really about masculinity, fatherhood, love, parenting, fear, all those things. Once I know that, I can come up with the structure.

The structure changes a lot too. I can give a lot of credit to my new editor at the Ringer, Matt Dollinger. He smartly pointed out that we needed to play up the Pam and Davante relationship a bit more because it's connected to how Davante is able to be a father. He learned love from his mother. I was lurking there, but I didn't make it explicitly clear until he said that. That helped with the structure, to weave these two relationships together.

It's amazing how big of a role having a good editor can make when you're writing this type of work.

It scares me, the idea of not being edited. I can't think of anything more terrifying. Matt did such a good job with this story. Going from Bleacher Report to the Ringer, I was nervous. I was so close with my editor at Bleacher Report, but I'm so happy with the editing at the Ringer, and I feel sad for a lot of young writers who don't have that close relationship with an editor because I think the editor is the most least valued position in our industry. They're the first to go, and they're the most essential part of how it's all made.

When you're working on a piece, what do you prefer more, the reporting or the writing?

It's equal for me, and I never realized that until I got into my career at Bleacher Report. I get such joy out of the connection that you make reporting with an athlete and their feeling understood or seen. When you get them, there's this connection that happens. It's so amazing. I always call it a reporter's high. It's like runner's high.

Writing is hard. Sometimes, I'm like, wow, this is so bad. I don't think this is English. You're looking at your story and you're like, oh my God, what language is this even in? But I love it. I can't explain it. It brings me such joy. It's the one thing I can do where I feel alive. I know that sounds corny, but I love the feeling of writing even though it's so painful and it can be so frustrating.

Why did you leave Bleacher Report for the Ringer?

We had layoffs, and they dismantled BR Mag, and I was a staff writer for BR Mag, so they let go of everyone except for me. On the one hand, I was fortunate to still have a job there, but on the other hand, my editor was included in those layoffs and literally everyone I worked with, so there wasn't anything there for me anymore. The writing on the wall is so clear that they don't value writing anymore. I tried to stick it out. I stayed for a couple months. I tried to lobby to get my editor rehired but wasn't getting any indication that this would happen.

This is emotional and sad. I love the people that I've worked with. I considered them genuinely my family, my lifelong friends. My agent was like, I think we need to start looking. I probably wouldn't have done that if he had not said that. Change is hard for me. I loved Bleacher Report. It was the best job I ever had. I would have been there forever if that didn't happen.

We started looking and I told him the Ringer was pretty much the top of my list. They're in Los Angeles; I'm in Los Angeles. I interviewed in a couple places, but the Ringer seemed like the best fit. I was so relieved. I was scared to start over, but it's been awesome.

You got your start in newspapers though. Is that correct?

Yes. And thank God I'm not at a newspaper now.

I spent ten years in newspapers. In some ways, so many magazines are going through the same process that newspapers have already been through.

It's the same soundtrack, just different songs. All of these places, they pivot away from writing, and then that doesn't work. I wish everyone would see it's not no writing or all the writing. Writing is one part of what you need to have. You also need to have video and audio. The places that are succeeding have a little bit of everything. It pains me when people think that cutting writing is the answer. It's never been the answer.

For me to spend the first four years of my career at a newspaper, at the *Orange County Register*, that was the best thing ever. I'm glad I got that experience before the demise of local news because that's where you learn to report and write and also to fall in love with the process. The only people that were reading my stories were grandmas of the kids I profiled. You have to love what you do. A lot of people want the perks of being a media person but not actually do the work. When you work for a newspaper, you have to love it. I'm thankful for that experience, but I'm sad for what's happening with newspapers and magazines.

At Bleacher Report, you had two stories that I imagine were incredibly hard to report, especially emotionally. You had a piece on Tyler Skaggs, the California Angels pitcher who died of an accidental overdose, and you wrote about Gianna Bryant, Kobe's daughter, who died along with him and several others in the helicopter crash. What was the reporting like for those pieces?

Those were probably the hardest two stories I've ever done, particularly the Gigi Bryant story. I interviewed thirty people for that story. They were all in the midst of their grief. She had died a week before. The Tyler Skaggs story, they had been grieving already for a year by the time I talked to them, so it's a completely different experience.

I would pick up the phone with Gigi's friends and coaches, and they would start crying. It's hard as a reporter, when you hear somebody crying, and you have to be like, it's okay, I completely understand. Do you want me to call back later? Or, I'm so sorry to barge in on your grief. This is the last thing you'd want to do.

I think it's all about being an empathetic person and an empathetic reporter. It's not, I'm on your side. It's, I hear you, I'm listening to you. I'm trying to understand you. You have to give people the grace that you would want if you were talking about a deeply sensitive thing.

It also comes down to intention. Why, as a reporter, are you trying to write these pieces? With Gigi, I wanted to give her her own space and article because she was always a footnote in Kobe's story. He had a daughter. She loved UConn and the wnba. End of story. I never felt like her story was valued or centered or appreciated.

With Tyler Skaggs, imagine living a whole life, and you have a wife, you have a career that you love, and you end up taking these drugs and dying, and the only thing you're remembered for is that Tyler Skaggs died at an early age or whatever. Humanity, again, was missing. I think your intention as a reporter for these types of deeply traumatic pieces has to be, I want to show the humanity of this person.

What drew you to those two pieces, knowing they would be difficult to report?

The beginning of the Gigi story is just riffing about what it is to love basketball as a young girl. That came straight from my diary because I wrote that after she died. I had grown up in Los Angeles as well, playing basketball, falling in love with basketball. There's so many people I know in the girls basketball community that ended up coaching Gigi and being around Gigi. There was this eerie feeling of understanding this specific community that she was part of.

I was also irritated by the coverage of Gigi. She's so much more than a footnote. I was going to pitch Gigi as a story before she died, and then we decided to not do it because we felt she was too young and didn't want to add that pressure on her career. She's always been lurking in my mind. After she died, I had a dream about her and I don't usually remember my dreams, so that was crazy. I thought, I need to do this.

With the Tyler Skaggs story, that took about nine months to procure the access. I was familiar with the Angels. I had corresponded with him once while I was a young reporter at the *OC Register*. I was in disbelief that this happened. I had interacted with these people. From a local standpoint, I was like, I want to do this story. I was bothered by the TMZ coverage of him dead by overdose, and people were saying such horrific things. I felt sad that that was his legacy, and I wanted to find out who he was as a person.

Latria Graham

Latria Graham is a writer, editor, and cultural critic who has written about the dynamics of race, gender norms, class, and nerd-culture, among other things. She is currently writing about her attempt as a Black writer to preserve her family's legacy and its one-hundred-year-old farm. It will shed a new light on the epidemic of Black land ownership loss and redefine her own identity and sense of rootedness.

Graham almost never became a writer. She went to Dartmouth College to study biomedical engineering, but she realized she didn't love it. She went back to her love of English and theater. After finishing her undergraduate degree, she worked as a library page at the New York Society Library where writers like Tom Wolfe and other major New York City writers would come in and use the library's space for their work.

Graham ultimately completed an MFA at the New School in New York City but found it difficult because she had to fly south to take care of her father, who had been diagnosed with cancer. Her dad died in 2013, and Graham struggled with grief for a long time. Ultimately, she turned to writing.

Graham has written for dozens of publications, everything from *Garden & Gun* to *Southern Living*, from *Outside* to *espnW*. She has also written for the *New York Times, Atlanta Journal-Constitution, Los Angeles Times*, and the *Spartanburg Herald-Journal*.

I spoke with Graham in June 2019.

I'm impressed by the variety of things you write about but also the styles and even the genres of writing that you do. How do you define yourself as a writer, and how have you gotten to where you are now?

It goes back to high school and realizing that I loved language, I loved words. I would read a book a day, from the time that I could read. I kept up with that through middle school, but all of the writers that I was reading and being taught in class and where you would learn more about their biography, for the most part, they were these dead white dudes from the 1800s, and they died in a gutter under sketchy circumstances, like Edgar Allen Poe. I did not see that as a lifestyle or a career path. I did not understand that there was someone whose job was to sit down and report things every day and put it out.

My family, being from this working-class background, watched the news on television. We were not the type of family that got a newspaper delivered to our doorstep every day. I did not grow up reading these great magazine writers, until I went to the Governor's School. My senior year was the first time I'd ever read or can remember reading a living author. So I didn't see it as a career path.

What did you study in college?

I went to Dartmouth to study to be a biomedical engineer because biomedical engineers make money, and writers don't, but I had this almost nervous breakdown. I struggled with math. It was difficult and it was not truly what I wanted to do. I realized I wanted to be an English major and theater minor but was scared of it. I did what we called national and oral traditions, which means I married a lot of slave oral traditions with medieval literature and these other oral histories, and analyzed them and did my pieces on that.

What happened when you changed majors?

I discovered Zora Neale Hurston and some of these other writers that were anthropological. I started discovering living writers. I spent some time with Lucille Clifton when she came up to Dartmouth. I was like, okay, I'm going to do this whole writing thing and graduated in the fall of 2008.

What happened next?

I moved into a New York City apartment because back then that seemed where all the writers went. I move in that day, and the bottom falls out of the economy, and it's the start of the recession. We didn't know that it was a recession. We didn't realize how big it would be. That would not become apparent until December or January, but I had this apartment and I needed a job. I sent out about one hundred applications, and I got this job with the New York Society Library as a library page, working for minimum wage. I would work, and Tom Wolfe would come in there. A lot of actual, major New York writers would come upstairs and use the writing room space to do their work. I got to engage with people that wrote books for a living, that wrote magazine articles. I spent a lot of time doing research, and that's where I got a lot of my archival chops, and eventually ended up going to graduate school for my MFA in creative nonfiction.

Did your writing change in the MFA program?

In my second year, my dad got cancer, and I had to try to figure out a way to stay in school and finish this degree but also start earning money. For the first three or four days of the week, I would be in New York City, and I would go to school, and then I would take the train down to Spartanburg to pick him up and take him to Atlanta for his treatments. Then I would reverse it. My mom had to keep working for the insurance. My brother was already in school. My dad could not take himself. And we needed money.

I started writing these essays. I was in a class with Brooke Obie. She was at *Ebony*, and she knew I was writing about being Black with an eating disorder and struggling with mental health. She was like, we need something like this for the site. Will you write this essay? I wrote that essay, and it was the first published piece that I had out there. I realized I can make money from my brain and stories.

My dad died, unfortunately, in September 2013, and I struggled for a while to figure out who I was going to be. I struggled with grief for a long time. I took some time and was like, what do you want to do? I want to write, and I kept telling my mom that, but I didn't know how to get started. I got started by trying to figure out my dad.

I'm still searching for not the perfect job, but the job that allows me to work remotely and be curious about a bunch of different things. I write so many different things, which is what I'm like. What am I curious about that I don't understand, or what's interesting, but I would like to know more about, and I've gone that direction.

Did you ultimately finish the MFA?

I did finish the MFA by the skin of my teeth and the grace of God. Susan Cheever, bless her. She got the first draft of my thesis, and she was like, completely start over. I had to completely rewrite that, and I have no idea how I did it. At this point, my dad was on a feeding tube, and I was having to feed him all this other stuff. I rewrote my thesis in between tube feedings. I don't remember that time of my life because I was trying to survive it. But I did graduate with that in 2013.

I'm fascinated with journalists who have MFA degrees. I also have an MFA in creative nonfiction. I'm assuming that a lot of the work you did was probably essays in an MFA program.

That's what everyone was writing. The first story that I ever submitted was more of a creative nonfiction long-form piece about this woman who had burned down her house, and they weren't into it. I think maybe the New York MFA at that time was confessional, sex lady, close to the skin, New York stories. I thought it was edgy and interesting, and all that, but maybe I should have gone somewhere that was less like New York because I'm not a New York writer.

I was a newspaper reporter who got an MFA, and then I went back to newspapers. I found that even though I wrote a memoir, it made me a better newspaper reporter. Do you think that writing stuff that is not journalism helped make you a better journalist?

I think so. It allowed me so much more freedom. Coming from my background, I didn't know what I could and could not do in newspaper stories. I had never written for newspapers, yet, and so I was engaging in the senses. They always say, "Show don't tell." It made me think about space in a different way, and voice. The way I think about language, I think about it like music. The rhythm, the cadence of a sentence, the rhythm and cadence of someone's voice, how they sound, what acoustically is happening in a scene.

You're allowed to do that more in creative nonfiction. I come out of that tradition of creative nonfiction, where you're able to access and tap into so many different parts of yourself, that I don't know if you would get [that] at a traditional journalism program. The objective and subjective are rubbing up against one another. That's something that I got to do a little bit more of in the MFA.

You've published several essays. One is titled "Why, As a Black Woman, I Finally Decided to Take to the Streets." It was published in August of 2016. Can you tell me about that piece and how it ultimately came about?

That was born out of frustration. This was right after the shooting that happened in Charlotte. People were finally, we've had Mike Brown, we got Trayvon Martin, people in the South were getting agitated, because, it seemed like this was pre–Alton Sterling, it seemed like this rash of Black people being killed by the police was happening.

The South is hot. I found out through Instagram that there was going to be this rally and this march, and my family, being from the Deep South and fearing repercussions, had never been to a march. That was not something we did. My family was not the type to go and sit at the lunch counter sit-ins and stuff like that. My mom was too young. My dad did not because of being in rural settings and white terrorism that could and would happen to people.

That piece was what happened when I decided to put my body on the line. What is at risk? I started dating my boyfriend, and we wanted to get married and have a family. I felt like I was in some ways marching for not my future but for the future of my family, my hopeful family. I took my boyfriend's camera, and I wanted to see what happened. I went in that line where you're both the person in this march, but you're also observing what's happening. I ended up taking about two thousand pictures. I was not a trained photographer at that point, so I had no idea what I was doing, but I knew I needed to be out there.

My mom went because she was too young during the civil rights movement to go and march. She got out there to see her experience and my experience and be able to talk about it because my family did not talk about white terrorism. We talked about discrimination, but we did not talk about the bigger thing of white supremacy. The piece was trying to unravel my feelings on it.

You had another essay that ran on espnW called "Harry Potter Virtual Running Groups Helped Me Conquer My Depression." Can you tell me about it?

I have a great relationship with espnW, and I was working with editor Jenisha Watts at that time. It may have been around the anniversary of Harry Potter. At that point, I belonged to Hogwarts Running Club. They've changed the name because of some of the Warner Brothers kerfuffle that's happening, and it's called Potterhead Running Clubs. I'm still active in it, and they do medals and all that.

In the African American community and maybe other communities of color, it is hard to talk about mental health, but we're able to talk about exercise. That piece came about because they were getting ready to do a couple pieces on Harry Potter at that point, and I was like, I have this tie to this club, which has raised over $8 million in charitable donations through Charity Miles, which is an app where you run and it gives you X number of dollars or X number of pennies or a quarter or something per mile.

I started running and God bless my best friend, Jill Stevens. I was super suicidal for my birthday. I've struggled with depression, at least since I was about eight or nine years old. We didn't have the word for it until I went to college. I had an eating disorder from age ten or eleven up through probably about twenty-two. And so, you know, she called me for my birthday, and I was like, I don't want to be here anymore. She's like, I need you to make a list of all the things that you want to do to give you a reason to live, and running was on that list. It allows me to get outside of myself. It gives me a challenge. It gives me a bodily challenge that takes me out of my brain.

I was telling them about that. I had gone to the ESPN offices at that point and was talking about my body and the things you're up against. There's nothing like running for a shiny medal and knowing that things will get better.

I was lucky they took that piece. It's not silly but quirky for the type of writing that I do. I still run that same path whenever I'm at home. And Harry Potter came out, it was a story about a ten-year-old boy, trying to find himself. It came out when I was ten years old, so I grew up with Harry Potter in a way that maybe previous or subsequent generations didn't.

When you're spending time with a source, do you talk about your own life as well?

When it's relevant, I definitely do. When we're talking about change or fear or whatever, they want to know exactly why the hell you want into their lives, or why you're asking this specific question. I try to be open about that. I tell them if you want to know something about me, I will tell you about my life.

What do you prefer to write: essays or reported journalistic pieces?

It depends on where I am in my brain space. My mom's been sick for the last ten months. She had a back surgery that did not go well. She had to relearn how to walk. I have not written a single essay during this time because my life feels too close for me to examine it.

I'm doing a lot of pieces on art for magazines. I'm doing a lot more reporting. I'm taking myself out of it right now. I'm also doing some of the shorter pieces. I have a couple of long-form pieces that are taking years to report something. I'm working on a story about a principal in North Carolina, and that's in year two. I realize I'm not in the headspace to write that.

Sometimes when the world is crappy, and things feel urgent, that's generally when the essays come out, when it's like clawing at my throat. I've got essay ideas written down right now, but I don't sit down and say, okay, I'm gonna write this nice, beautiful essay and then go sell it. It usually has to be something that I'm ashamed of or that is rattling around in my body that I can't get rid of.

David Grann

David Grann is an award-winning staff writer at the *New Yorker* and the number-one *New York Times* best-selling author of *The Wager: A Tale of Shipwreck, Mutiny and Murder*. His previous book, *Killers of the Flower Moon: The Osage Murders and the Birth of the FBI,* documented one of the most sinister crimes and racial injustices in American history. The book was a finalist for the National Book Award and has been adapted into a major motion picture. Grann is also the author of *The Lost City of Z, The Devil and Sherlock Holmes,* and *The White Darkness*.

Killers of the Flower Moon is one of the darkest stories that Grann has ever reported. He has said that he has never written about a scenario where good and evil were so obvious and defined. Grann says the job is always a challenge.

"It's something I have to work at," he says. "There are writers who are much more naturally gifted than I am."

One thing Grann brings to his work is a dedication to making sure that every single detail is factually correct, even when he is writing about something that happened a century ago.

"If you want to write narrative history, . . . you want to give the reader a real sense of who these human beings were," he says. "You want to have a sense of what the world was like, how it smelled, what the streets looked like, what the houses looked like, how people dressed. . . . That's a time-consuming process.

"It's those small little things, sometimes seemingly meaningless, but important to get right."

Before joining the *New Yorker* in 2003, Grann was a senior editor at the *New Republic*, and, from 1995 until 1996, the executive editor of the newspaper the *Hill*. He holds master's degrees in international relations from the Fletcher School of Law and Diplomacy as well as in creative writing from Boston University. After graduating from

Connecticut College in 1989, he received a Thomas Watson Fellowship and did research in Mexico, where he began his journalism career.

I spoke with Grann in June 2017, shortly after *Killers of the Flower Moon* came out.

***Killers of the Flower Moon* is about the Osage murders and the birth of the FBI. Can you tell me a little more about the book?**

The book is about the Osage Indians of Oklahoma, who in the 1920s, because of oil deposits under their land, became the wealthiest people per capita in the world. They lived in mansions, and they had white servants. Their wealth belied long-standing stereotypes of Native Americans, and then, during this time period, they began to be mysteriously murdered in one of the FBI and J. Edgar Hoover's first major homicide investigations.

How did you find out about what happened to the Osage tribe?

I had never heard about any of this. I was talking to a historian who mentioned the Osage and how the topic hadn't been written about. I did a little bit of research and was amazed and shocked that this was something I knew nothing about and had not been taught in my books or in history classes.

I made a trip out to the Osage territory, and I visited the Osage Nation Museum. While there I noticed this great panoramic photograph on the wall. It was taken in 1924, and it showed members of the tribe along with white settlers. It seemed innocent, but as I was looking at it, I noticed that a portion of the photograph had been cut out. I asked the museum director what had happened to it, and she said it contained a figure so frightening that she decided to remove it. She then pointed to that missing panel and said the devil was standing right there.

For me, that moment is what the book grew out of, trying to understand who that figure was and the anguishing history he embodied, and out of the fact that the Osage had removed that picture, not to forget, but because they couldn't forget. Yet so many people, including myself, had either forgotten or never had any knowledge of these crimes.

I had also never heard of this at all, and that is surprising given how diabolical it was.

It was deeply sinister. Mollie Burkhart, who I write a lot about, is at the center. Her family becomes the prime target of this conspiracy to target the Osage wealth. To give a little bit of context, the Osage had once controlled much of the Midwest of the country, all the way from Kansas to the edge of the Rockies. Thomas Jefferson had referred to them as a great nation. He promised them in a meeting with the delegation of Osage chiefs in 1803 that he would treat them only as friends, but within a few years, the federal government began to push them off their land.

Within a few decades, the Osage were forced to cede more than 100 million acres of their ancestral land. They were pushed into an area in Kansas, where they were once more under siege in the 1860s. They were forced to sell their land, and an Osage chief stood up and said they should all move to what was then Indian Territory, in what would later become Oklahoma. He said that because the land was rocky and infertile and the white man considered it worthless, they would finally leave the Osage alone.

The migrations had taken a tremendous toll on them, and there were only a few thousand of them left when the Osage migrated to Indian Territory, and then lo and behold, this seemingly forsaken land turned out to be sitting upon this massive oil field. Then the Osage, in these sinister crimes, began to be targeted.

When you made the first trip there, did you go thinking there was a book that could be done?

I didn't know at that time. I thought this is a story that on its face seemed incredibly important. My instinct was that in some form, it needed to be told, but before I went out there, I didn't know what material was available, and I didn't have a sense of the contours of the story. I didn't yet have an emotional connection to the material either, and I think one needs that when they begin a long process. At that point, it was all preliminary, just a research trip. I had not decided for sure that it would be a book.

Even after that trip, I spent many months writing Freedom of Information Act requests to various government institutions, tracking down descendants, and trying to find out what existed in archives, to see if I could tell the story. At that point, I knew I wanted to tell the story, and then the next question was, was there enough material to actually tell it?

So much of this book comes through archival research. What's that process like for you?

I still am, in many ways, a contemporary reporter. I cover a lot of events where you're dealing with living sources. But in recent years, I've done stories that often involve a good deal of history. This project involved more historical research than anything that I had done before.

In some ways, the processes are similar in that you're pursuing every possible lead of information. You spend a lot more time in the archives. In some ways, it can be tedious because you end up looking through lots of old folders, not sure what you will find. Then it can produce unexpected results. For this book, I spent a lot of time in the archives in Ft. Worth, which is a branch of the National Archive[s]. It's a place that looks like something out of *Raiders of the Lost Ark*. It's this massive warehouse, and I would literally spend weeks out there, pulling files, not knowing what I would find. Then suddenly, you open one up, and there would be, for example, secret grand jury testimony.

In many ways, the reporting processes are similar. In this book, even though it was historical, I tracked down the descendants of both the murderers and the victims, both to gather more archival research from them but also to collect oral histories from them.

How were you able to track down these descendants, given it's been a long time?

It was a long process. I did a lot through ancestry.com. I rented a boarding house in Osage County and stayed there to track down descendants who would hopefully lead me to other descendants.

But it was a process. For example, I tracked down Mollie's granddaughter, who was helpful, but it took me a couple years to find her.

Mollie, in many ways, is the emotional connection in the book. When did you learn about her, and when did you realize she could be the character that would hold everything together?

I knew about her early on. I knew that Mollie's family was at the center of the murders, that her family was targeted in this sinister way. Her older sister Anna disappears, and she's found a week later shot in the back of the head. Mollie's mother dies of suspected poisoning. Mollie had a younger sister named Rita who lived nearby, and one night, about three in the morning, Mollie woke up. She heard a loud explosion. She went to the window and looked out in the direction of her sister's house, and she saw this orange ball rising in the sky. Somebody had planted a bomb under her sister's house, killing her sister and her sister's husband and an eighteen-year-old white maid who lived in the house with them.

I knew some of these basic details, but one of the things that struck me was when I would read these little bits of detail about these crimes, Mollie was just a sentence. She had almost no agency. Yet here she was, obviously at the center of the story. Early on, I wanted to get the Osage perspective, and I thought many of the accounts lacked emotion because you didn't have a sense of what this was like for the people who were actually living through it, the people who were the targets.

I did my best with what I could find to record that perspective and get that sense of emotion. To me, Mollie is, in many ways, the heart and soul of the book. And she's the conscience of the book as well.

How much time did you spend reporting on this project?

I would say the project, probably from beginning to end, probably took five years, but the actual intensive work took place over four years. There was a period of about a year where I was just writing to institutions to see what kind of material was available, and then probably another year after that doing intensive reporting. Then I began writing and outlining and doing more reporting to fill in the gaps.

I would visit the Osage Nation territory every year and stay, usually for several weeks, and I spent several weeks at various archives around the country every year.

How did you balance this with also doing work for the *New Yorker*?

Not very well, sadly. I really disappeared from the magazine. I wish I were quicker, and I wish I was a better juggler. Early on, I was able to work at the *New Yorker* when I was waiting for the Freedom of Information Act requests to come in and see what materials I would find. There was a good year where I was productive at the *New Yorker*, but there was about a two-year span where I went down the rabbit hole and was not able to juggle well.

The rabbit hole is a great metaphor for doing research in archives for a nonfiction book. The only way to do it well is to go into the archives and go deeper and deeper.

You have to stay in them. If you want to write narrative history, which is what I aspire to do, you want to give the reader a real sense of who these human beings were. You want to have a sense of what the world was like, how it smelled, what the streets looked like, what the houses looked like, how people dressed, to get fragments of dialogue from letters and court transcripts. That's a time-consuming process, and it involves a slower process than if you're witnessing something.

I would have to interrogate sentences. For instance, you're looking at transcripts and sit down and write something. You knew the investigators went to somebody's house, and you start to write, "The investigator showed up on their stoop and . . . " Suddenly, you have to look at that sentence and say, wait a second, did they have a stoop? Was there a porch? You look for photographs, and maybe you find them and you say, oh, okay, they did have a porch. Or, you don't find them, and you have to then rewrite that sentence and just say they showed up at their door.

It's that forensic meticulousness that is a time-consuming, slow process. When you are witnessing something, you know exactly what the door looked like, or you can call the person up and say, "When you got to the house, were you on the stoop?" It's those small little things, sometimes seemingly meaningless, but important to get right in all aspects, that is time consuming.

Was there anything, as you were reporting, that surprised you?

I would say the thing that surprised me most was the breadth of the conspiracy. The FBI was ultimately able to capture some of the killers, but their working theory was that there was a singular evil figure that had henchmen who perpetrated these crimes.

The more I dug into the archives, the more I interviewed Osage descendants and gathered evidence, the more I realized that this was much less a story about who did it than who didn't do it and that there was a culture of killing around the community. So many members of society within this community were complicit in these crimes, either directly profiting from them, from payoffs, corruption, or from silence. There were many willing executioners, and that is something that shocked me, and still shocks me, and took my breath away.

Did this research give you any insights into who we are as a country today?

There are chapters of our history that we often neglect and ignore. The Osage intimately know this history, but I don't think the rest of us can understand the formation of this country if you don't understand cases like this. This story is a microcosm of so many of the forces that played out over centuries in the clash between white settlers and Native Americans. It gives you insights into the prejudices of the time.

To this day, descendants of both the murderers and the victims live in the same neighborhoods, and their fates are intertwined. In many ways, that's the story of America. You can't understand the country, even today, unless you understand cases like this.

What is your writing process like?

Writing for me is always a challenge. It does not come naturally to me. It's something I have to work at. There are writers who are much more naturally gifted than I am. For me, a big part of the writing process is just sitting my rump down at a desk and devoting the hours and keep going back at it and overcoming doubts, which I suppose a lot of writers do. I don't know if there are many secrets other than working through it.

I do certain things. I'll often read great writers that might inspire me while writing. When I was working on this book, I would often read a lot of western writers. I wanted the style of the book to be fairly simplistic, to have a kind of western style. I read people like Willa Cather, Wallace Stegner, people like that, for inspiration. John Joseph Mathews, who's a great Osage writer, was somebody I returned to over and over again. He wrote during this period, not about the murders, but he's a beautiful, exquisite writer. He describes the environment, what the world looked like, and also has a real understanding of Osage traditions and Osage sensibilities.

Even if I wasn't directly reading these people because they were going to be in the book itself, they sometimes helped me find inspiration in the writing process.

How did you land on the unique structure of the book's narrative?

I never structured a book like this. It's told in three chronicles, largely from the point of view of three separate people: the first person, Mollie Burkhart; the second person, one of the FBI agents who leads the undercover operation trying to crack the case; and the final perspective, in the present, from me. There was a good one-year period when I was doing the research and gathering the material, where I was bewildered about how to structure the book, to the point where I wasn't sure if I could actually do the book because I didn't know how to tell it.

I found it overwhelming because there were so many different murders that spanned so many years. There were so many different FBI investigations. There were private investigators too. At first I didn't find a way to have control of the material. Interestingly enough, I was reading the novel Absalom, Absalom!, a novel I had never read by Faulkner, and I was reading it and noticed that he had three narrators retelling history, each from their point of view. I said to myself that could work for this.

What were some of the challenges?

There wasn't one central figure that could carry you through the whole history because it spans so long. So the structure solved a lot of problems. It also got at what was one of the central themes of the book, which is about the elusiveness of history and that each narrator in the book, or each individual who is trying to make sense of a bewildering world around them, only has partial information. They're all reliable narrators. Mollie's a reliable narrator. Tom White, who's the FBI agent, is a reliable narrator, and I hope I'm a reliable narrator.

There's a wonderful metaphor that the Osage have, in the old days, when they would send people out in a trying time, they would refer to them as the "travelers in the mist." In a way we are all travelers in the mist trying to make sense of this world and trying to make sense of history. That's a challenging, elusive process.

It let me get at that theme, which I think is important to this book; there is a certain unknowability to the story that needs to be reckoned with.

Elon Green

Elon Green is a freelance writer and the author of *Last Call: A True Story of Love, Lust, and Murder in Queer New York*. The book is about several men, presumed to be gay, who were murdered in New York City in the early 1990s. Green focused the book on those men's lives, as well as the investigations into their deaths, all of which was happening as the AIDS epidemic exploded. Green gathered a massive amount of court and police records to put together his book proposal. Interviews with people helped him understand the story he wanted to tell more than anything though.

"These didn't all end up in the book, but I talked to 160 people, many of them multiple times, I'm sure to their utter exhaustion," Green says. "They were very patient with me."

While many writers claim the only way they can do their work is by writing one thousand or two thousand or however many words a day, Green says every single day is different for him when he is working on a freelance story or his book.

"For me, the writing was entirely driven by the reporting," he says. "So if that day, I couldn't get the information I needed, then I probably wasn't going to be doing any writing. . . . The reporting was my way forward."

Green has written for a number of publications, including the *New York Times Magazine*, the *New Yorker*, the *Awl*, *New York*, the *Appeal*, and the *Atlantic*. He has also done a lot of Nieman Storyboard story annotations, interviewing the likes of Gay Talese, Mike Sager, Rachel Kaadzi Ghansah, John Jeremiah Sullivan, Tom Wolfe, and Jeff Sharlet.

"A lot of those annotations were basically my journalism school," Green says. "I didn't go to J-school, and I got fired by my college paper, but the annotations taught me how to report and to write."

I talked with Green about *Last Call* in March 2021.

Can you tell me about your book, *Last Call*?

It's about the stories of men who were picked up in piano bars in New York City in the early nineties. They were presumed to be gay. Their bodies were left outside of the city, sometimes dismembered in garbage bags. The book is about their lives, but it's also about the investigations into the deaths set against the political backdrop and the AIDS epidemic.

I couldn't get over, as I was reading the book, how I had never heard about any of this.

You're not alone. In the entire two or three years of pretty intensive reporting for the book, I only met a single person, not directly connected to the case, who was familiar with the case. I happened to meet him because I was drinking at Marie's Crisis in the village and I was talking to the bartender about the book. The man next to me said, "Oh, I know about this because it changed the way I conducted myself and it changed my dating life." He was the anomaly.

How did you learn about it?

Pretty accidentally. It was just a Google search that led me to an October 1994 edition of the *Advocate*, and three or four pages into a story about antiqueer violence was a few paragraphs about this case, which at the time hadn't been solved.

Do you remember what you were searching for on Google?

I have no idea what the Google search was. I was passively looking for a book idea because I had just come back from San Francisco. I went to see if I could expand an older story about some murders in San Francisco into a book, and I concluded that I couldn't. I wanted to keep researching in the same vein because I was intrigued, if not obsessed, with the issues brought forth by these unsolved cases, meaning the politics and media coverage, and the neglected victims.

What about this actually grabbed your attention and made you start to think that maybe there was a book idea there?

It was really the lives of the men. That's what grabbed me, but what convinced me that it could be a book, as opposed to a feature, was when I had gotten hold of some of the trial transcripts. Of all things, I was reading the testimony of a sanitation worker, and he was recounting for the jury his day, which was mundane, until it wasn't when he discovered some body parts in New Jersey. What made me think it was a book is that the testimony was so granular, and so quietly dramatic, that I could see it. I thought well, that's a scene. The dirty secret of journalism is you don't need scenes in features, but if you don't have scenes, you can't write a book.

You focus a lot on the men who were killed, telling their stories. Why did you want to focus on that?

Because in focusing on them, not only could I tell the stories of their lives, which I think you have to do, if you want to write about true crime or anything that is moral and worth doing. But in writing about their lives, that also allowed me to write about what was happening around them. Not just literally, in the locations and the spaces, but also the constraints they were under, politically, socially. It allowed me to write about the world around them. If I hadn't written about them, and had them at the center, it would have been difficult to do everything else.

One thing that I couldn't stop thinking about as I was reading the book is the sheer volume of reporting that you had to do. How did you gather all of the information that allowed you to tell the story?

First and foremost, those trial transcripts were invaluable. They provided the spine of the story, or at least the story as I originally understood it, and allowed me to write the book proposal. There were also eventually police files that were given to me, binders that were prepared for the murder trial, documents handed over by friends and family that were related to the story.

The most valuable, I think, were primary interviews. These didn't all end up in the book, but I talked to 160 people, many of them multiple times, I'm sure to their utter exhaustion. When I would interview detectives, I would often reinterview them with each successive chapter and oftentimes ask them the same questions. I talked to them a lot during the proposal period, but then when I got to the part of the book that they played a role in, I reinterviewed them. They were very patient with me.

Did you ever have to explain to them why you were asking the same questions?

No. They're detectives. They've asked a lot of questions of people before, often in many different ways. So that I think was one part of the process. They absolutely did not have any confusion about that. Oftentimes, they wondered why I was trying so hard. They felt that my insistence on getting every little detail right was not necessarily warranted, but I plowed ahead.

What was it like when you approached the families of the men who were killed?

Sometimes they outright refused, which I certainly understood. No matter what my intentions were, to them, I was reopening an old wound. I get that because on some level that's exactly what I'm doing. And then some family members were willing to talk to me to varying degrees. I was lucky to have that. I did talk to one relative of the murderer, and it was by far the most contentious conversation I had during the entire book writing period.

You tried to get in touch with the murderer as well, right?

Yes, although I have to say, that was mostly out of due diligence. I don't even know if I would have wanted him to agree to an interview because of how that would have ultimately shaped the book.

Were the trial transcripts the first thing you attempted to get when you started thinking, I want to do something on this?

Once I read a few stories and realized how interesting it was, yeah, that was my first stop. I called the courthouse, and they said, "We don't have the transcripts. The court stenographer has them, and she's retired and living in Utah." I called her, and she charged me thousands and thousands of dollars for a fraction of the trial. Luckily, eventually, I got everything, including an unredacted version of voir dire from the prosecutor.

Once you had done all of this reporting, how did you organize it before you sat down to write?

A lot of the book derives from what was probably a thirty-page timeline of events, as I understood them, that I would keep adding to. It was sequential, but as far as the structure of the book, I owe that almost entirely to Carrie Frye. She is now an extraordinary editor-for-hire, but mine was the first book proposal she worked on. I dumped what must have been fifty or sixty pages of notes on her, and she came back with a book structure.

This was the first book proposal you'd written. What was that like?

It was interesting. A book proposal is not just a sample chapter. You're taking into account the commercial prospects for the book, and so you have to think about it not just through your eyes, but the eyes of the publisher. It's a fascinating exercise.

What was the biggest challenge for you, both in the reporting and the writing?

The biggest reporting and writing challenge was chapter 5, which was about Anthony Marrero, who was a sex worker. He was the third victim, in 1993. That was a tremendous challenge because I had so little biographical detail to work with, and the biographical details are what drove the other chapters about the victims.

I had to figure out a way around it, in some sleight of hand, so I had to shift the emphasis to the milieu of male sex work in New York. That became the story. Also, this was one of the cases where the detectives were extremely helpful in recounting their interactions with the family members. One of the reasons, or the primary reason, I talked to the detectives so often wasn't for their perspective, it was for their recollections of the men and what they learned about them so I could get more information about them. I was essentially pumping them for sources.

How much time did it take you to do all the reporting? And how much time did you spend writing?

That's one in the same. I never stopped reporting. I never understand people who say that they do the reporting for the first half and then they do the writing for the second half. It never worked like that for me. I was reporting up until the last day. From the time I signed the book deal, which was the day I began writing the book, to when I turned it in, it was about eighteen months.

I can't even imagine how you pulled all that reporting off in a year and a half.

It's because I had done an extraordinary amount of reporting for the proposal. I had to interview forty-five people for the proposal because, oftentimes, proposals are based on previously published works. And this one was not.

Did you ever think that you would try to do a magazine piece on this first and then go the book route?

I considered it, and I even had lunch once with Megan Greenwell back when she was at *Esquire*. I told her I was thinking about it. And then I ran this by my friend David Grann, who told me that was stupid and that I should save everything for the proposal.

When you're working on a project like this, what is your typical day like?

There is no typical day. I think that people who manage to write every day congrats to them. I don't know how that works. For me, the writing was entirely driven by the reporting. So if that day, I couldn't get the information I needed, then I probably wasn't going to be doing any writing because I was also writing the book in sequence, so I wasn't skipping around.

The reporting was my way forward. One of the reasons that the reporting never stopped is because when you're writing something, whether it's a book or a story, the more writing you do, the more you see the holes in your story, and you have questions. For example, when I was writing a chapter about a *New York Law Journal* typesetter, Michael Sakara, who was murdered in 1993, I realized, I don't know what he did as a typesetter. So I got a hold of this guy who had consulted on the movie, *The Post*, the Steven Spielberg movie, and he took a couple of hours to walk me through what Michael would have done for a living. You have to allow yourself to take these digressions because it flushes out the character.

Michael was one of the men that I connected with, I think maybe because he was from Ohio, close to where I grew up.

Well, yeah, but I also should say one of the reasons he connects with people is I have the most information on him. He comes off as well-rounded.

You give context to the places that are involved in this too. You don't just say he's from Ohio, but you are able to go into great depth in terms of showing early family life and where he lived. That's all character building.

It was also to satisfy my own curiosity, because my overarching question was, how do these guys end up in New York at any given time, and you have to figure out where they come from. Especially once I started working on the Boston chapter, I became conscious of how little of queer life had actually been documented and how scattered the scholarship was when it existed. I realized I had this opportunity, if not an obligation, to document it any way I could. My understanding is that, until this book came out, there was not a single sentence published about queer life in Youngstown, Ohio. I don't say that to pat myself on the back. I say that to talk about the lack of scholarship that's been done. It's appalling.

What has attracted you to true crime writing?

Nothing. If I have written any true crime, it's by accident. I'm attracted to stories. I'm attracted to people, and that's it.

You have been anthologized in a true crime anthology, and this book, one of the categories it's in on Amazon is true crime. But it's the conflict, right? There are characters, and there are people who've been impacted and had their lives changed.

That's exactly right. So much of the genre is crap. The whole time I was working on this book, to me, I was writing a work of history. The true crime-ness of it was a catalyst and allowed me to write the history and to write about their lives. True crime that is focused on the crime is pretty worthless.

Writing is often considered a solitary endeavor, but you mentioned in the acknowledgments of your book so many amazing writers who

helped you: Paige Williams, Pamela Colloff, Jason Fagone, Eva Holland, David Grann, Sarah Weinman. How did they help you on this project?

David Grann did line edits on the first five chapters or so. He taught me how to space out biographical information and ensure that when I was introducing that information, it was basically tied to the police investigation, and I wasn't dropping it in the chapters indiscriminately. Pam Colloff edited and fact-checked the forensic chapter. Friends like Lyz Lenz and Sarah Weinman read everything multiple times. I wanted people from certain cities to review those chapters to make sure that I didn't come off like a carpetbagger. So, Vince Guerreri, a journalist from Ohio, read the Youngstown chapter. And Duncan Black read the chapter on Philly.

Writing a book is you making yourself aware of how little you actually know, and it's stupid of me to not take advantage of other people's knowledge if they're willing to help you. I wanted as many eyeballs on this as possible.

That's why I do this podcast. I get to talk to people about how they do the awesome stuff that they do, and then I'm learning from them. Did you learn anything that will help you when you write your next book?

Sure. I already took those lessons in the book and the subsequent chapters, but it's also bled into subsequent writing. Once you learn those lessons, they're hard to forget.

Several years ago you did the annotation of Gay Talese's "Frank Sinatra Has a Cold" for Nieman Storyboard. What was that like?

I've had some out-of-body experiences in my career. That certainly was one of them. I spent two days with him at his house. I spent a lot of that time glancing at the tape recorder to make sure that it was functioning because I couldn't believe the stuff he was saying so energetically. It was a wonderful experience.

A lot of those annotations were basically my journalism school. I didn't go to J-school, and I got fired by my college paper, but the annotations taught me how to report and to write. The Talese one was maybe an exception.

What do you mean by "maybe an exception"?

First of all, Talese takes a lot of notes. I don't take any notes. And I certainly am not going to be taking notes on shirt boards. I think that Talese's methods have not aged well. I think he wrote some and reported some extraordinary stuff, but I would not use them as a guide.

I remember that this annotation is where he talks about working with the source to craft the perfect quote.

That's right. He got into some trouble for that. I always run quotes by my sources, and if they misspoke or if they got something wrong, they have the opportunity to correct it, but they don't get to massage a quote.

When you went to college, you didn't study journalism, but did you know you wanted to get into journalism at some point in college?

No, I didn't. I wanted to go into film. I studied film.

What drew you to journalism then?

I ended up at the *New York Observer* in 2002, but I was on the business side. I was writing what they called advertorials at the time, which is now called native advertising. I was writing it for advertisers like bmw and so forth, lots of businesses on the Upper East Side of Manhattan. And then after about a year of doing that, the editor of the paper, Peter Kaplan, his assistant went on vacation and realized that she did not want to be his assistant when she came back, so he offered me the job. I jumped at it because the newsroom of the *Observer* at that time was quite remarkable.

I have to ask because I'm the advisor of a student newspaper here at Fairfield University. How did you get fired from the student newspaper?

Oh, it's not a fun story, and I will not be telling it.

Vanessa Grigoriadis

Vanessa Grigoriadis is a National Magazine Award-winning writer who has made a career of reporting on a wide variety of subjects, ranging from celebrities to youth movements, from pop culture to sexual assaults on college campuses. In 2017, her book *Blurred Lines: Rethinking Sex, Power, and Consent on Campus* covered the awakening of the #MeToo movement at colleges and universities around the country and the ways college women were fighting entrenched sexism and sexual assault while also celebrating their own sexuality.

Grigoriadis has also excelled at reporting and writing celebrity profiles, projects that, while perhaps not as weighty as college campus sexual assault, are still a difficult type of reporting, at least to write the high-quality profiles for which she is known. Grigoriadis won a National Magazine Award in profile writing in 2007 for her story on fashion designer Karl Lagerfeld. The story ran in *New York* magazine. She's also written about everyone from Taylor Swift to Britney Spears to Justin Bieber. She was reporting the *Rolling Stone* profile on Spears right around the time the pop singer was having her breakdown in 2007 and, in many ways, pulled off a modern-day "Frank Sinatra Has a Cold" because she was never given access to Spears and instead spent the vast majority of her time following around the paparazzi who were following Spears everywhere.

Grigoriadis has a reputation as a reporter who isn't profiling celebrities simply because she loves celebrities, and indeed, some celebrities, or at least one in particular (Gwyneth Paltrow), didn't like the way she approached reporting about those who are superfamous. The piece on Paltrow, which had been planned for by *Vanity Fair*, never actually ran.

Grigoriadis has written for the *New York Times Magazine*, *Rolling Stone*, *Vanity Fair*, *New York*, *Gawker*, and many other publications.

Nowadays, Grigoriadis is also involved in podcasting. She cofounded Campside Media, a podcast company devoted to narrative nonfiction storytelling.

I've spoken with Grigoriadis twice. In 2014, we talked about her work profiling celebrities, including Justin Bieber, whom she has written about twice. In 2017, we talked about *Blurred Lines* and the reporting and writing of that book.

You just had your second piece focused on Justin Bieber published. What is the newer story about, and how did it play off the first one that you wrote for *Rolling Stone* in 2011?

First of all, the first one was an all-access piece, and this was a no-access piece. There was a distinct relationship between the two, because I used some of the outtakes from the first, but mostly [I used] my impression and my knowledge of him to color this story.

What drew you to Bieber in the first place?

This time, I would say that my editors wanted a story. That was the impetus. I hadn't thought about Justin Bieber in a while. The first time, however, I was totally enthralled with the man that he was going to become. I was weirdly into Justin Bieber for somebody who was way too old to be into Justin Bieber. I was thrilled when I got the assignment from *Rolling Stone*, which I probably got because I told my editors several times how in love with Justin Bieber I was.

Your new story follows this path of how someone who is incredibly popular can become incredibly disliked. And it's not just Bieber. There are other child superstars that this happens to.

I think the larger point that I was trying to make is if you look at the landscape, there was a time when we thought, "Oh, how tragic to be a child star." It's the beginning of your life, and then you live a long life of infamy and alcohol dependence and misery trying to live up to this image of your youthful self that of course was never you to begin with. When I got this assignment, I thought, oh my God, what am I going to write about Justin Bieber now in six thousand words?

He's not running around L.A. in a wig dating a paparazzo. He's in a private jet. He's not going outside. He's not that easy to get to. I thought, well, what can I say in this story?

The idea that I had was that if you look today at who the biggest pop stars are and the most meaningful cultural figures, there's a huge number of them that were stars when they were young. I thought this could be an interesting thing to point out and turn this a little bit on its head and say even if you don't think of Katy Perry as a child star, she was one who had a record deal by the time she was fifteen. The list is long. It's from Taylor Swift and Katy Perry to Rihanna and Chris Brown and Drake.

What happened with the Gwyneth Paltrow story?

I wrote a piece for *Vanity Fair*. There was a public kerfuffle over it. It was not in any way, shape, or form the piece that was being talked about in the media. Nobody saw the piece because it never was published. It was a reminder that there's always a lot of artifice involved when you are profiling a celebrity. There's a lot of people involved. To me, I'm much more interested in celebrities as cultural artifacts, what they say about us, because they've become so popular. When America responds, there's a reason. I'm interested in looking at those reasons and why some people fall and rise in that hierarchy, dependent on what is going on in the country.

How do you find story ideas that are in front of everybody right now, but aren't being reported?

I don't know if I love pop culture as much as I like to write about pop culture. I think it's hard to find story ideas if you're constantly looking at Twitter or Facebook or blogs. I think that there's a lot of originality that's missing in those venues. While it may be helpful to be like, oh, lots of people are responding to this; maybe I should write about this.

I think that it's about figuring out what you're interested in, what draws you, what do you think is funny, and what you will watch seven episodes of and talk to your friends about and then trying to write something about that. That's always where I start.

You recently wrote a piece headlined "The Revolution against Campus Sexual Assault." What type of research did you have to do before you actually started going out and talking to people for that story?

I didn't do a ton. I did read a bunch of the *New York Times* articles, some of which were specifically on the people I was interviewing. I read a funny story by Katie Baker and Buzzfeed. I think she was at Jezebel before. She's a good reporter covering sexual assault; a bunch of stuff out of the *Columbia Spectator* to see what was going on on campus, the way the student newspaper was covering it.

There was still a large learning curve on that story. There's been so much coverage of sexual assault. The actual release and the administrative stuff around it, it's a little hard to understand what Title IX is. When did it start to cover sexual assault? Why are all these people filing now? What does it mean to open an investigation? When does the investigation stop? What is it that schools are supposed to be providing to students that students are saying they're not? What's at stake here? The other issue is that what schools are supposed to be providing and what activists want the schools to provide can be different things.

The initial reporting you did for that piece resulted in the book *Blurred Lines*. What is the book about?

Emma Sulkowicz is a woman who some people know as "mattress girl." She was a Columbia student who said that she was going to carry a mattress, a real mattress, a fifty-pound, six-foot-long mattress, like the one she had in her dorm room, around Columbia's campus for an entire year, until the university either punished the boy that she said raped her, which they had refused to do, or until she graduated. This was a stunning move by an undergraduate student in 2014.

Her story became a viral sensation. It was the story of September 2014 that people couldn't believe. They were agog or aghast at what she was doing and what the university might have done to her. It brought to light the issue of campus sexual assault.

When I saw all of that happening, and I was perfectly poised to write about it because I had already interviewed her and was planning to do a story about what was going on at Columbia, I thought, okay, this is an interesting book because we have women beginning to talk out across the country. We have policy that is actually changing. We have intense national media glare. I thought we're stepping into a fascinating moment here, and I could spend the next couple of years trying to capture it. So then I quickly wrote a proposal, and my agent said, "Why didn't you have this proposal written before the article came out?" I said, "I didn't know it was a great idea."

Was the proposal you wrote focused primarily on Emma, or was it broader?

It was much broader. The idea for the book was we know that this is becoming an enormous media story. But how is this playing out at campuses across the country, and how are students across the country actually dealing with this problem, metabolizing it? How are guys shifting the way they think about women and sex in response? What is the real rhetoric that's coming from the Emma Sulkowicz, radical feminist wing of those campuses? And how is that changing people's opinions on what should be considered consensual and what should not?

Was this the first book proposal you had written?

This was the first book proposal I'd written. I had ideas for books, and I had certainly written memos. But I had never written a proposal.

What was that like? I like to ask reporters this question, especially with regards to the type of writing and reporting that goes into a proposal.

I didn't find it to be too difficult, but the proposal is also the easiest part, because it's almost like a marketing document, like a business plan. We will do this, and everybody will love it, and it will be so great; the general concept you need to get across to people who might want to buy your book. So it's all potential. I'm going to interview these people, and here's a couple of the people that I interviewed and what they have to say. So here's a taste of it. It still was a substantial proposal. It was a fifty-page proposal, but it wasn't one of those proposals that also includes a forty-page chapter. It didn't include a table of contents that made it clear that I had a game plan.

As I was reading the book, I was constantly struck by how you were able to get students to open up and talk about stuff that we don't talk about as a society. How do you get them to open up like that?

First of all, I'm a reporter. This is what I do for a living. This is how I make my money, by connecting with people during in-person interviews, knowing how to comport myself to get the ultimate best answers that you can get out of somebody in that setting. That's how I put food on my table. I'm known for profiles where people say a lot of interesting stuff and maybe stuff they shouldn't say and they say it to me. But they wouldn't say it to a different reporter, because that other reporter might ask questions in the wrong order or might give them some sense that they're not being heard or might ask boring questions.

I pride myself on that and consider myself a reporter first, a face-to-face, let's break it down in person, together, kind of reporter. I do think that talking with students is working to my strengths. In the practical matter, if there was a swipe card to get into a dorm, I waited for somebody to open the door, and then I went in. I didn't tell any corporate communications department that I was a reporter on campus to interview students.

I just wandered into the campus center and looked around the room and said, "Who looks interesting to me here? Who looks dynamic?" And I think it's pretty easy when you get into a room to see who seems verbal, who's gesticulating wildly with a friend. That's the person I want to talk to because that's going to give me the most dynamic quotes and the least prepackaged one.

How many students did you talk to overall for the book?

I interviewed probably about 120 students in the end, and I think there are probably about twenty students who are developed characters in the book, and most of those people I had more than one conversation with. I did follow-ups with them, even if they only appear in the book once. I definitely followed up to get more detail or see how they were doing.

Did your reporting change in any way for this book versus a magazine piece?

It was totally different in pretty much every way. Long-form, I'm talking about six-thousand-word stories. I have figured out how to do that over the years, and it's not stressful for me. It's stressful landing the subject to make sure I can get everything I need from this person. Can I talk to not only the person but the people around the person? And will I get enough time? How do I coordinate a trip to Kentucky to see this person and get the maximum scenic value out of those trips.

If you travel to Kentucky to do an interview, you want to make sure you can see the person in different locations; you can see that person at home and then going to the person's workplace and maybe see something else. And for a long-form story you need to place the person in different settings and milieus and be able to describe action in those places. That's the nuts and bolts of long-form writing.

But here, how do you write a reported book about such a difficult topic? What is the thesis of this book? The thesis of the book ended up being that there's a new standard of sexual consent for the millennial generation, and what's happening on campus is ultimately going to be replicated throughout the country, which we're starting to see with the Harvey Weinstein situation and all of these women speaking out about sexual harassment in the workplace. They're speaking out about sexual harassment that runs the gamut, from what Harvey Weinstein did, all the way to perverted jokes in an office. The same thing is happening on campus, where sexual assault means a lot of different things that it might not have meant to the Gen X or Boomer generation.

I like how the book is broken up into the three parts: Consensual, Nonconsensual, and The Man. How and when did those section themes come about?

There were so many drafts. I understood at the beginning that I was going to have to tell a number of stories and tell them charily, fully. Actual stories, like this is what happened between these two people at the University of Texas, and here's how it all went down. But when I was halfway through, I realized the macro story, about how American culture is shifting in terms of the way we think about sexual assault, is the story I want to tell.

These other stories that I have with these characters should not be told so fully that they take people away from that initial idea. So I read Peggy Orenstein's book, *Girls and Sex*, and after I read that book, I was like, this is probably a good model for me, where Peggy is present in that book, and she's moving readers towards her own conclusions, and the characters are secondary. I went from thinking about a book that would've been filled with a lot of profiles of different college students, to a book that would be more essay driven and have secondary characters. Once I realized that these characters don't need to recur that much, they can be introduced and then disappear. Once I thought of that, that was when I came up with this three-part structure. The idea was, instead of hitting everybody over the head with all the rape stories at the beginning, let's do the consensual part of sex first on campus. Let's establish what consensual sex on campus looks like and then build up to a crescendo of now here's what sexual assault also looks like.

Eva Holland

Eva Holland is a freelance writer living in Canada's Yukon Territory. She is the author of *Nerve: Adventures in the Science of Fear*. She has reported and written extensively about the outdoors and wilderness, as well as science, sports, and travel.

In *Nerve*, Holland merges science reporting and memoir, tying together her relationship to fear and her efforts to see if she can change and become less afraid. One of her fears was dealing with the unexpected death of her mother, who died of a stroke while Holland was on a backcountry canoe trip in northern British Columbia.

In the book, Holland looks into the science of phobias and trauma, touches on anxiety, and tries to look at what we know about these conditions, why people have them, and whether they can be cured.

Holland has written for *Wired*, *Outside*, Longreads, *Pacific Standard*, SB Nation Longform, and many others. Her stories have been noted in *Best American Essays*, *Best American Sports Writing*, *Best American Science and Nature Writing*, and *Best American Travel Writing*.

I spoke with Holland twice, once in March 2014 about her "Chasing Alexander Supertramp" story as well as work she had done for SB Nation Longform and again in April 2020 about *Nerve* and her freelance writing career.

How did the idea for *Nerve* come about?

A few things happened that led to me writing this book. The first was that my mom died suddenly in July of 2015. She had a stroke. and for complicated reasons, I always feared my mom's death. Obviously nobody wants their parents to die, but it was front of mind for me in a way that I think it's not for a lot of people. My mom had been an orphan and talked a lot about the loss of her parents and how that affected her . . . so when my mom died, I realized that my worst fear had come true. As time passed, I realized I was not as deeply affected as she had been.

Obviously, I was grieving a loss, but I was not undone by it in the same ways that she had been. I realized maybe I had faced my worst fear and survived, and that made me feel powerful, and it made me want to see if I could change my other fears as well.

Then two more things happened. The first was that I had this pretty intense panic attack on an ice-climbing trip a few months after my mom died. That's described in the prologue of the book as an inciting incident: where I refused to come down from this mountain and I put my life at risk and put other people at risk as well. I'd been uncomfortable with heights for a long time, but I hadn't ever done anything like that before. That made me determined to figure out what the hell was going on and why I had done that.

At that point, I thought of it as a personal project, not a professional project. And then two months after that, I had the last in a series of serious car accidents. I rolled my car into a ditch in April 2016, and I had been thinking about the idea of a book about fear that day while I was driving on the highway. That night in the hospital I was like, yeah, okay, you've got to do the book about this now because obviously the universe is sending you some kind of message.

Once you latched onto this idea, you had to write a book proposal. Had you done that before?

That was why I was thinking about the idea of a book about fear as I was driving along the highway that day because my previous proposal I had decided earlier that day to let it sit on the shelf. It hadn't worked out the way I hoped it would. I had put together a proposal about the future of a changing Arctic, the past, present, and future. It was a little bit wonkier and the word that we got back from publishers was a lot of "Eva seems great, but I dunno about Arctic wankery. Can she send us something with broader commercial appeal?" I was driving along the highway that day thinking: What is something that I do?

I always ask myself with stories, and I have the same question with book projects, what do I bring to the table that nobody else does? I was trying to think about what is an area of broad appeal and interest where I have something to say, something different to bring to the table. That's when I started thinking about my experiences with fear, having this fear of heights, and then having acquired a fear of driving after these accidents, and then my relationship to fear around my mom's death. I was like, okay, maybe I have something to say here. My first step after I got out of the hospital and got home was to send a note to my agent with a two-paragraph summary of my idea.

She said go for it.

That summer, 2016, I started actively working on the proposal. I worked on two sample chapters that summer, one of which was the one where I go skydiving and the other one where I try to learn to rock climb as a form of exposure therapy. That became an article in *Esquire*. That summer, I was working on the proposal, and then life happened. There was some back-and-forth with my agent trying to strengthen the proposal, but I was putting it down for months at a time, doing other things, because the thing about a book proposal is the fact that nobody pays you to do it, so it always took the backseat to paying work. Then I got it together in time for early 2018, and it went out to publishers in March and April, and I got the deal. Then I had a pretty quick turnaround. I had one year to turn in the first draft.

How did the book-writing process compare to the magazine work you've done?

I enjoy the process of writing sometimes more than others. Obviously, sometimes I'm in deadline hell like anybody else . . . I liked that it was mine, and I wasn't worried about a kill fee. I liked that sense of ownership, although that also makes it scarier of course because it's on you. I liked digging in deeper into a subject. I liked having what felt like a greater level of creative autonomy. Books are so flexible.

I love magazine stories, and I love magazine story structure, but I guess it's like writing a particular form of poetry where there's rules about what you can do, and the fun is playing within those rules. A book is a free verse. You can do what you want. It was also hard at times. I did get significantly behind schedule on the writing, and I had three months of hell at the end before the deadline. I was cranking words out, and that was hard and scary because I got to a point where I was like, you have to get it done and hope that it's okay.

In _Nerve_ you're a big part, as a character. Do you like writing about yourself?

I do. People that have followed my magazine work know I do this a lot, whether through actual personal writing or immersion reporting, where you use yourself as a tool in the story, but it's not necessarily all that personal.

I came out of creative writing rather than journalism, so first person feels natural to me. I'm conscious of the fact that a lot of people view it as self-indulgent, and so when I put myself in a story, I try to have a reason to be in there and to be clear about what that reason is, rather than doing it for the sake of doing it. I also try to make sure I do at least one traditional third-person journalistic feature per year so that people know that I can and I'm not a one-trick pony or somebody who only writes about myself.

Your mom's death is a big part of this book. I imagine that was emotionally difficult. How did you pull yourself through that writing?

I'm realizing as we're talking that I dragged my feet on this proposal for two years, and I wonder if it wasn't partly because I wasn't ready to write about my mom because by the time I sat down to do it, I felt fairly well equipped to do it. Chapter 1 and chapter 3 detail the events around my mom's death and then the aftermath for me. I will say that some of those sections I wrote a long time ago before I even started thinking about this book. I started writing about my experiences in the ICU before we turned off my mom's life support, if not immediately within a couple of months of her death. I was taking notes immediately. I knew I was going to write about it, and I didn't know what else to do except to start.

I was on a backcountry canoe trip in the wilderness of northern British Columbia when my mom had a stroke. And so I had to be evacuated out to the coast to get to a town in Alaska to be able to fly out to get to the hospital. I have a detail in the book; I say that I rode out to the coast on top of 7,500 pounds of Chinook salmon, and I know that because I asked someone how much salmon was in the boat, and then, I wrote it down in my journal, so that instinct for reporting was there from the beginning.

The most vivid sections about turning off the life support machines at the hospital, I wrote a long time ago. And then I didn't come back to them for years. I didn't feel able to look at them or edit them. And when I did come back to them, it was hard. I didn't do it until I felt able to. I was also writing the bulk of this book in the depths of a Yukon winter in an apartment in the dark. There were some dark nights of wallowing around in the worst moments of my life. The book is not as bleak as I'm probably making it sound. I originally envisioned the book as a funny, Mary Roach style, wacky science of fear. I think there are still some elements of humor in it.

How did you make sure that you got the scientific complexity in the book right?

That was probably my biggest area of imposter syndrome for this book. I felt more capable with the psychology stuff. Handling the neuroscience information was intimidating. I don't have a STEM background at all. I tried to read widely, and I talked to smart people and cross-referenced things and started feeling better with some of the famous case studies that I go over when they started to crop up in six or seven or eight of my sources. I felt I was on pretty solid ground then. Then the biggest thing I did was I hired a fact-checker. My friend Jane fact-checked the science half of the book for me. I didn't attempt to fact-check the memoir, partly to save money because I was paying by the hour and partly because it's difficult to fact-check a memoir, particularly when a lot of it is set in my own head or is scenes between me and my mom, who is dead. I had Jane check the science, and in particular, what I had her look at was my framing of the research, not only if I had misunderstood what I was reading in the journal articles, like misrepresenting the results, but also framing them appropriately in terms of what they mean and what they suggest. We went through my language and eliminated just about any instance of the word "prove." Instead, it was like, "the findings suggest that." I think that's often where science writing can go wrong, not in a total misunderstanding of the findings but in framing them incorrectly in terms of what they mean for the bigger picture.

In 2013, you wrote a piece "Chasing Alexander Supertramp." Why did you want to write that story?

I'd been hearing for a few years about the people I call the McCandless Pilgrims. These kids, they're mostly young, try to hike to the bus that Christopher McCandless died in. It can be a risky trip, depending on conditions. Almost every summer it seemed like I was hearing news reports about people being rescued. At some point last spring, it occurred to me that they'd be an interesting group to write about. I've never been that fascinated by McCandless myself, but I was fascinated by the people that were fascinated by him.

You mention in the story that you've never been fascinated by him, but you understand him because you've also gone out into the wilderness.

I felt like I should be a fan because I can sympathize with the idea of wanting to get away from normal life. I quit my job and became a freelance writer and moved to the Yukon, so I have some things in common with Chris McCandless. But I was never able to fully get behind his philosophy and how far he took it.

You mentioned that you had something in common with McCandless. Do you feel like that gave you some insight into the people that you wanted to write about?

I hope so. I think it was doing the trip that helped me. I went into it thinking these people were nuts, and meeting them and interviewing them and watching some of them get into some pretty serious trouble made them seem more real to me and made me more understanding. Although I still don't think it's a good idea to try to cross that river and visit the bus if you're not prepared. The whole experience of reporting made me more understanding of the phenomenon.

What happened when a group that you followed crossed the Teklanika River?

I wasn't going to go to the bus because I didn't feel safe crossing the river alone because the water was quite high. My plan was to hike down to the river, which is the main obstacle, and look at it and be able to describe it well in my story. It's the crux of the whole problem, this river. I hoped I might run into some hikers along the way, but I had no idea. I did run into a group of five, and I hiked with them for a couple of hours until we got to the river. Then I was going to watch them cross. They had given me permission to photograph them and take video for my story. Two of them went across first and, with some difficulty, made it across okay. Then the next three tried to cross and all three of them were knocked off their feet and swept downstream.

Two of them got out relatively quickly, but one of them was in the water for a long time. I'm not sure, maybe ten minutes. It was pretty hectic. But the problem is the river is fast moving and the water is cold, and the air, once you get out of the river, is really cold. So we were concerned that he would drown and, even if he didn't drown, that he would die of hypothermia.

That scene illustrates another point that journalists face sometimes when they're witnessing something bad happen: Do you keep your distance and be the reporter and watch, or do you jump in and try to help? What went through your mind as you were watching this happen?

I didn't start to think about how it would impact the story again until later. But I was filming this happening, and I made the decision to stop filming when things started getting bad. My editor later said, "Oh, I wish you'd kept filming." I guess I don't have the photojournalist killer instinct. I didn't feel that it would be right. I felt like the situation was spiraling out of control, and I wanted to have my hands free. I abandoned all pretense of objective reporter mode and got involved in trying to get Rick out of the river. And then I thought about it a lot later, how that changed the story because, obviously, I became personally invested in it in a way that I hadn't planned on.

I'm not sure what I could've done differently. I couldn't have stood there and watched. I was the only person on the town side of the river at that point. Everybody else got out on the far side. So if somebody had needed to go for a rescue, it would have been me. I spent a lot of time thinking about how that changes the story and my role. I actually spent most of the hike back by myself after he'd gotten out of the river, more or less safely, thinking about if I ever would have written anything again if he'd died, which was a dark place to be in for a few hours, hiking back alone.

You mentioned in the story wondering whether or not they were going to cross that river no matter what because they knew a reporter was watching.

To me, when we got to the river, it didn't look like something I wanted to wade out into. It was running fast and cold and at least waist deep. They didn't even talk about not crossing, and I wasn't sure if that was because they were shy about expressing doubts among themselves—some of the group was more gung-ho than others—or if me standing there with a camera was affecting their behavior. They didn't even seem to consider turning back. I wondered what role I may have played in that. I thought about saying that they shouldn't go, but, again, I didn't think that was my role. I wasn't a member of the group, and I wanted the photos of them crossing. So I never said, "Hey, guys, maybe you shouldn't do this." Nobody did.

What was it like interviewing Chris McCandless's parents?

It came up out of the blue. I hadn't been sure about approaching the family. I'm pretty shy about approaching people that are grieving or that have lost somebody and pestering them to answer my questions. But the photo editor reached out to them to get permission to use Chris's photos from the bus, and they offered to be interviewed. It was interesting to talk to them. I don't know if they had done interviews about the pilgrim phenomenon before, and I wanted to be careful about how I asked them about it because I didn't want them to feel like I was blaming them in any way for promoting Chris and promoting his journey.

Obviously, it's the continued awareness of *Into the Wild* that sends these kids back there. The parents were keen to point out that they don't try to encourage anybody to go to the bus, and if they get inquiries, they try to tell people, get a guide. Get a pack raft. Do it right. Do it safely. One young woman has died trying to reach the bus. It's a terrible irony that people are trying to make a pilgrimage to this site where this young man died, and they're risking their lives to do it.

Mitchell S. Jackson

Mitchell S. Jackson, a contributing writer for *Esquire* and the acclaimed author of *Survival Math* and *The Residue Years*, won a Pulitzer Prize and a National Magazine Award in 2021 for his story in *Runner's World* about the life and death of Ahmaud Arbery. A noted lecturer and currently the John O. Whiteman Dean's Distinguished Professor in the Department of English at Arizona State University, Jackson's work has appeared, too, in *Harper's*, *Harper's Bazaar*, *VQR*, *Tin House*, Vice, the *Guardian* and the *New York Times*. A formerly incarcerated person and a social justice advocate, the native of Portland, Oregon—even now, even after all he's accomplished—is reluctant to self-identify as a reporter or as a journalist per se. He is, he says, a writer. "When I think of my identity as an artist, it's as a writer first, and then I think of myself probably as a fiction writer, even though I've written much more nonfiction, and journalist or reporter has never been a part of the way that I see myself in the world," he says. "But I know that I am a writer."

He writes with an uncommon combination of lyricism and righteous anger. "I would never want to just report the information. To me, anybody can do that, so it's almost like I gotta filter it through me and the me is the singing," he says. "It's how I say I'm this person at this age from this experience without announcing my biography. And I do it in everything. Like, if that's not there, then I don't wanna publish it."

In this conversation, he talked primarily about two of his most seminal works: the *Runner's World* award winner and his piece in *Esquire* in 2022 about Supreme Court justice Clarence Thomas.

Jackson was interviewed in 2022.

I want to start with one of the more remarkable paragraphs I think I've ever read. In *Runner's World*, you wrote: "Peoples, I invite you to ask yourself, just what is a runner's world? Ask yourself who deserves to run? Who has the right? Ask who's a runner? What's their so-called race? Their gender? Their class? Ask yourself where do they live, where do they run? Where can't they live and run? Ask what are the sanctions for asserting their right to live and run—shit—to exist in the world? Ask why? Ask why? Ask why?" In *Runner's World*, you are writing that sentence and then writing that paragraph. Help us understand the roots of that paragraph.

Well, it's two things. One, it's my response to the convention of a nut graph. And I remember—it probably was the first round of edits—Leah Flickinger, who was the editor on that piece, or one of them, she was like, "I like this, but I want to get at why this matters to our audience." And so I started to ask questions, those same questions, and the whole piece tries to answer them—but I was really just interested in that inquiry. And the other thing that I'm always constantly doing is trying to—what's the word?—I'm trying to implicate the reader in the piece. So, if you are a runner, is this how you feel? Why do you feel that way? I'm always trying to figure out a way to turn the piece back on the reader and have them ask themselves a question.

More broadly, this piece and others, Clarence Thomas and plenty of other stories, you've written, there's something almost sort of—there's a righteous anger.

Yeah.

How did you get to that place?

Because I was a young person who didn't really read—I played sports, and then I sold drugs for a little while, and I wasn't really picking up the *New York Times* and reading what was the latest national news—I didn't think that hard about my circumstances and all the exigencies that went into them. And so it's like discovering that the fix is on and all the ways in which your life and the people that you love have had circumscribed experiences—and then being angry, right? That's the righteous anger. Then what do you do with that information? So for me it's like finding out all the ways that Clarence Thomas has been working against people that look like him and being righteously angry about that, finding out why the McMichaels thought that they had the power to keep this man from moving through the world. I think that's the fuel for it. Whereas another writer who had been reading or paying more attention might have had these feelings twenty or thirty years ago, I've come into them ten, fifteen years ago. The anger is still fresh.

At the risk of asking an obvious question, what happened ten, fifteen years ago to make you curious about why and enabled you to channel it in this way?

Deciding to become a writer, which was probably now twenty-two years ago, when I was in prison. But more to the point is writing my first novel, which was about my childhood and youth—in doing that, I had to research what were those circumstances. And so, once you come across the information, if you're a thinker, then you're going to start investigating. And if you felt these repercussions acutely, like I have, then you're moved to keep going in that direction. Like, everything that I needed to know about how the American dream is bifurcated—to me, it's in my experience in Portland, Oregon. And then I just kind of extrapolate that experience onto other locations and figure out the nuances and how they did it, when the blueprint is pretty much the same everywhere.

Is it fair for me to think that you started to learn how to be a reporter by reporting out your own story?

Well, the strange thing is, I don't even know if I know how to be a reporter.

You just described a process through which you became activated in your own curiosity about, essentially, why is this happening to me, right? You're almost reporting for [a] memoir. Maybe you're not thinking about it in this way, but you're reporting.

Yeah.

You're reporting—whether you're reporting your own story or Ahmaud Arbery's story or Clarence Thomas's story.

I think I just get back to being a writer, because also I came out of fiction, right? So the first book was a novel, even though I interviewed my mother and I talked to some of my childhood friends, and I walked around the neighborhood. So it's really connected to creative nonfiction. And then my second book was an essay collection, so that was a lot more research, and it also included interviews. So I was doing reporting, but to me, it's an identity, right? When I think of my identity as an artist, it's as a writer first, and then I think of myself probably as a fiction writer, even though I've written much more nonfiction, and journalist or reporter has never been a part of the way that I see myself in the world—even though I know that I'm doing this as a profession. And I think I feel a little apprehensive about even claiming that because I was never really trained in that way.

You know Ryan D'Agostino, right? Ryan is a trained journalist, and what he can do with editing, what he can do with the headline, or figuring out the nut graph—because he's trained, he has so much experience—and I tell him, "Man, what it takes you an hour or two to do, it takes me a week." And so, for me to claim journalist, I would have to be able to do what Ryan does, and I can't do that. But I know that I am a writer because I love the language, I love the story, I love all of those things about it. But that journalist thing feels like, once you claim it, you gotta be it, and I don't know if I am it.

From where I sit, one could not write that piece in *Runner's World*, one could not write the Clarence Thomas piece, one could not write a

lot of the things you've written, without being a reporter—whether or not you self-identify as such. So maybe let's strip away the actual words reporter or reporting—and let's just start with the *Runner's World* piece—how did you go about doing that?

What I had was an initial contact. When Leah and Ryan called, they said they talked to his high school coach and he said he's willing to talk. And then I would say, "What's your fondest memory of Maud?" And he would tell me a story, and he would mention some names, and then I would say, "Can you connect me with them?" That's really how the Arbery piece got reported out because I didn't go there. This was all over the phone. So, whenever I would talk to someone and they would mention someone that was important in Ahmaud's life, I would just ask for the contact. And I kept stringing it along. Another person that was really helpful was Larry Hobbs, who was the reporter at the *Brunswick News*. He helped me with a lot of stuff, but one was kind of understanding the landscape. I was looking at Google Maps and I was zooming in on homes and looking at geographic stuff, but it is a different thing, I think, to live there, so he was very helpful. And then he was helpful with getting the information like the autopsy reports and the police reports. Being a professor, I teach what's a primary source and a secondary source—so understanding that is helpful too. But usually I'll just go in, and I'll have an idea of one or two people I want to talk to, and I'm trying to go in with at least a working thesis. Because I think you can do a lot of reporting that doesn't bear out because you didn't have a kind of game plan going in.

So you went in with a working thesis, or did that working thesis develop after a handful of early conversations, or how did that go from the kernel of the idea to the beginning of the congealing of the piece?

I watched a *New York Times* video. It was twelve minutes. It was the last twelve minutes of Ahmaud Arbery's life. And I watched that thing over and over, and it had all the forensics and where he went and everything was in there, and then I started thinking, but what about the rest of his life? And for me, every time I hear about some-one getting killed, I don't know what else is extinguished with them. And so, for me, the thesis became: How can I paint a portrait of this guy that sheds some light on the other part of him? The most important part—like, not the twelve minutes but the other part of him. But I will say, when I saw that twelve minutes, I knew I wanted to do a tick-tock though.

How did you arrive at the structure, both the tick-tock of those twelve minutes, but also, of course, the world through which he is running, the time and space and history through which he's running?

In my essay collection, I would always take a personal moment—say, my aunt getting killed as a sex worker—and I would say, okay, where do I start with this? Okay, let's go back to the history of sex work. Where does that, how far does that, take me? Okay, well, if now I know about the history of sex work, what do I know about serial killing? So when I got to Maud, and I knew that he was from this place that I didn't know much about, and that he was running—I'm, like, okay, I have to discover the history of running as a pastime in America. And then certainly I have to ground this in Georgia. So now I have to do a lot of research on that. I guess, basically, what I'm saying is I'm always looking for the context, and the context just keeps broadening.

Did this apply, too, to the Clarence Thomas piece? What did you take from the *Runner's World* piece into that *Esquire* piece?

I love big chunks of exposition, where I can really just write sen-tences, and also trying to figure out what breaks something out of convention. So, the Gullah, to me, that was the thing that I had going in. I didn't even have a story, and I was, like, I wanna write in Gullah, which is strange because I call myself not a journalist, so then how do I know what the hell the convention is anyway?

Maybe this is your superpower. You're not bound by convention. You just do what you want. You don't call yourself a reporter; you don't call yourself a journalist; you just let it rip.

There's also using different modes, like speaking to the reader, speaking directly, and in this case, I'll speak directly to him—to Clarence Thomas. Those kinds of rhetorical devices that really come outta fiction—I can take that and use it in creative nonfiction. Always figuring out a way to be able to sing. Because mostly what I wanna do is mess with sentences. And I can't do that with quotes. So I gotta have a section where I have some space to do that.

Is that what you look to do the most, even more than, in some sense, the story itself?

Yep. Well, I should say, I think they're now equal. If you would've asked me this ten years ago, I would've said, man, I studied with this guy named Gordon Lish, this old editor from the seventies and eighties, and he used to just talk about sentences. I studied with him for three years, and all we talked about was how to make a good sentence. But you can't care about sentence making over a slain young person's life. And so I wanna respect that and honor that, and I take that very seriously, but I also, in the composing part, I want to be able to sing. So, if I can sing and say these important things about my subject, that's the win-win. But I would never want to just report the information. To me, anybody can do that, so it's almost like I gotta filter it through me and the me is the singing.

One of the differences between these two seminal pieces of yours: In the *Runner's World* piece, you are talking to the reader—"Peoples . . ."—and in the piece about Clarence Thomas, it's him—"My god, dude, what the hell happened to you?"

Yeah.

You're talking to him with that righteous anger. So let me back up to that first section of the Thomas piece because, to me, it is one of the more interesting decisions you make. You're asking the reader to read two different languages.

It was about the earliest decision that I made. I made that decision before I ever sat down. I had gone, Ryan and I had actually gone, to his hometown, and I had already kind of known about the Gullah, but then the first person we interviewed was like a historian of Savannah. And he was talking about how important it was in the community, and then we were, like, "Can you speak it?" And he was like, "No, I can't speak it, and I barely understand it." And so then I went to the cannery where his parents used to work—it's now a museum—and the woman there is a native who speaks Gullah. I had never heard it, and I said, "Can you say something to me?" And I thought it was gonna be like black vernacular—but, man, I could not understand a word she said. But also I came in having read about Clarence and knowing that he's claimed that he didn't really speak English until he was five years old or something. He spoke this language. So that's an important part of his life. Then we met the guy who remembered him and his birth, and he said, "Yeah, I remember when Clarence was born," and then he started telling the story. I was, like, oh, man—I remember turning to Ryan, and I said, "I am going to tell the story of this man's birth in Gullah."

And what did Ryan say?

Ryan was, like, "Yeah . . ."

So he's on board from the get-go.

He's on board from the get-go. So that's when we knew we needed a translator. And we thought about how to do it, like running side by side, but then when I sent the opening—that opening was the very first thing I wrote, and I sent it to Ryan and he sent it to the translator. And when he sent it back, he translated it exactly how it appears in the magazine. It was like me, then him, me, then him. We just left it like that.

There is a certain, like, useful music to the Gullah. I can't recall another situation in which like a story of that sort of scope starts in that way. Ryan was the editor on both these stories?

So—kind of. Ryan and I were supposed to cowrite the Clarence Thomas piece. And the reason we started so late was because we did a lot of the reporting together. We did probably equal reporting, but I went to D.C. by myself. We spent a lot of time talking about the piece and what we were gonna do, but we could not figure out how to write it, how to cowrite. I'm like, my voice is my voice, I don't know how we're gonna do this. What do we do? Divide up sections? And so we waited until basically it was too late. And then Ryan says, "Man, I don't think I can do this. I think you're gonna have to do it." So he became the editor then.

Do you consciously think of what you singularly can bring to a piece like that about Clarence Thomas?

I think, I hope, that I'm always myself in a piece—and by that I mean a forty-seven-year-old man from Portland, Oregon, with two children and a mom who struggled with addiction and a single-parent home and prison and college and the novel behind me. And so I feel in that sense like I'm unique in working in this space. And then if you add on that I'm the Black guy, the one Black guy that anybody knows, that studied with Gordon Lish—so how do I bring not just my biography but also my skill set? You gotta have the information, right? You need to have the pov. But for me it's the sentence, it's the language, so I'm always going into the piece, like, okay, I know I can come by the information if I do enough reporting, but then it's, like, well, how am I gonna sing it? I think if I were just a trained journalist

I don't know if I would have that same value system about language . . . And how do you write about someone that you loathe? How do you be fair? Because I'm, like, there was a point at which Clarence Thomas was just a little kid or a baby and he wanted the same things the rest of us did. And he was not destined—well, maybe he was destined to be this terrible person, but he existed before that. And so a part of that opening is getting us to remember that he's a human.

That's an interesting thought. Do you see it as, like, a half-polemic, or are you trying to avoid that?

Definitely trying to avoid the polemic. Because that's like 99 percent of the stuff that's in the world on him. And so I couldn't write that I hate Clarence and here's all the reasons. To me that's not very interesting. I'm, like, what am I saying beyond Clarence Thomas hates his people? What is beyond that?

And so how did you go about answering that for yourself before you answered it for your readers?

Imagining him as a child. Understanding where he came from. Reading his memoir and reading about the hurt that he experienced with his father leaving, the hurt that he experienced with his grandfather kind of disowning him after he dropped out of the seminary, this kind of chip on his shoulder, and I think he's imagined about, you know, he don't want no help, but then everybody's helping him. I'm trying to imagine him being at those far-right conventions with his wife as a keynote speaker and him in the front row looking at all these people who really want him dead. If you think about Martin Luther King's the ultimate logic of racism is genocide, like, these people don't want you to live, and you're sitting there grinning and skinning with them while your wife is up there giving hate speeches. So, for me, that's a really tragic figure. As smart as he is, as accomplished as he is—you don't have a tribe. And to me that's a real lonely place to be. If civilization or society is people with other people and you don't have no people, that's a lonely, tragic life.

There's a certain—what's the right way to put this?—it's not slang, but there are words you use or ways you use words that other people either don't try or wouldn't try or can't get away—

Absolutely.

And why?

That's what I live for.

"Hella loose gravel"—that kind of phraseology in the Thomas piece.

It's how I say I'm this person at this age from this experience without announcing my biography. And I do it in everything. Like, if that's not there, then I don't wanna publish it. And another thing, the conventional or standard English, we know that it's exclusionary, right? So it's a way for me to assert how much we matter and how much the language has excluded us and how the rules are fixed. It's like an argument inside of just the language that I'm using.

Chris Jones

A journalist who spent the majority of his time writing for *Esquire*, Chris Jones began a second career as a screenwriter, first for the Netflix series *Away*, based on his *Esquire* story of the same name. Jones is also the author of two books: *Out of Orbit*, about three astronauts stuck on the International Space Station, and *The Eye Test: A Case for Human Creativity in the Age of Analytics*.

Jones left *Esquire* in 2016 but had been thinking about screenwriting for some time.

"For me, screenwriting is like using the same muscles to play a different sport," Jones says. "I'm still doing what I'm supposed to be doing. . . . It's just a different form."

Jones is probably best known for his National Magazine Award–winning story "The Things That Carried Him" about a soldier killed in Iraq and his trip back to an Indiana cemetery. Widely considered one of the greatest magazine pieces ever written, it's told in reverse chronology. Jones says it was the hardest piece for him to write, emotionally, in his career.

"That story knocked me flat," he says. "I went into a deep depression afterwards, because of how heavy the material was and how hard those conversations are, but after I was finished, I felt like I was lost. I didn't know what I could write that would ever match it."

Before leaving *Esquire*, Jones went on to write a series of remarkable stories, including a profile of Roger Ebert, after Ebert could no longer speak with his voice, and one about the 2011 night when dangerous exotic animals were turned loose on a farm in Zanesville, Ohio. Jones simply focused on that one night and wrote a series of horrific and frightening scenes that showed readers exactly what local police officers faced. In many ways, it showed how he could easily move into screenwriting.

I spoke with Jones twice, once in 2014 about his profile of Kenneth Feinberg, an attorney who determines how much money the survivors or their families receive after a tragedy, and in 2019, a more general conversation about the differences between writing narrative journalism and screenplays.

You wrote a piece for *Esquire* that was a profile of a man named Kenneth Feinberg. Who is he?

Feinberg is a lawyer by training. His job is to come in after tragedy strikes and decide what it's worth if you lose your husband or your wife or you lose an arm or a leg. Starting with 9/11 and all the way up through the Boston Marathon bombing, he's been the guy who's done this hard math.

Why did you want to write about him?

If I have tics when it comes to writing, one of them would be I'm drawn to stories about life and death. My editor sometimes jokes that unless there's a corpse in my story I'm not happy with it. I don't know why that is. I think it feels more important to me if it's about that kind of thing. I thought Ken presented a lot of interesting philosophical questions that I wrestle with a lot, for reasons I can't articulate. For a story like this you need a person who can carry a story, and I felt like Ken was a guy who could.

In this story, you're able to show Feinberg change fairly dramatically.

I can't remember now who said it, but a great movie has conflict, and it also has change. The main character goes through some transformation. In this case over the years that Ken has done this work, he's gone through a pretty dramatic philosophical change.

What's interesting about Ken is he'll concede that he's more empathetic than he used to be and probably a better listener, but the people around him have seen a dramatic change in him. That helped me follow him through this journey that he's going on. I like stories that have movement. Through time you can watch Ken grow from the first few times he got these phone calls until today, when he's become an expert at tragedy. He knows things about tragedy and our responses to them that most of us don't know.

How much did you know about him going into the story?

I knew about his work. I had heard him on the radio talking about having to put a value on things like traumatic amputations and what someone's arm is worth, and is that worth the same as a leg, and what's a brain injury worth, and if you lost a hand, what's that worth?

Those questions, I thought, were fascinating. What is the value of life and what is the value of the parts of our body that most of us would deem essential to a good life? Most of the stories written about Ken focused on how he decides those numbers. I find that interesting, but I also wanted to look at how doing that math has changed him, how it's affected his own life, whether he views life differently having done this work.

Did you know that he made himself available to meet with all the victims of the tragedies that he oversees the disbursement of funds for?

I didn't know the extent of it. As part of his practice, you can appeal his decisions. If you feel like you haven't gotten a fair shake, you can go to him and explain why you think you deserve more. He first did this during 9/11. Ken took criticism from the victims' families especially, for not giving enough, for undervaluing the lives of the people lost that day. And as part of that process, Ken said, "I will meet with you." To his surprise, more than nine hundred families wanted to meet with him. He does this work for free and spent thirty-three months of his life unpaid, sitting down and enduring these terrible stories of loss. That was probably the thing about Ken that struck me the most.

You show those meetings well. In one, the widow has terminal cancer and needs the money fast, and in another, the other widow has no idea her husband had a girlfriend and a family across town. Were those easy ones to choose?

Yes and no. The first one was pretty obvious because Ken went into those meetings not knowing what to expect. I think after that first meeting, she said she was fine with the settlement but she needed it right away. She said, "I have terminal cancer. I don't have long to live. I want to set this money up in a trust fund before I'm gone." Ken got her the money quickly, and as it turns out, she died within a couple of months. Ken said to me, "I knew after that one that I was in for rough sledding."

I actually wrestled pretty hard about including the firefighter that ended up having the secret family across town. It was super compelling, but ethically part of me was worried that that firefighter's widow still doesn't know that this other secret family exists. If she somehow reads this story and recognizes herself from the description, am I the one who's telling her? I didn't particularly want that responsibility. I didn't want to be that person.

In the end Ken didn't tell the firefighter's widow. He wrote two checks: one for the original family and another one for the secret family. He decided it wasn't his job to tell the widow either. Because she was so distraught over the loss of this man, that if she then found he wasn't who she thought he was, then who knows what she might do? I wrestled with including that anecdote at all. Ultimately I decided it needed to be there. That's one of those ethical dilemmas. I'm still not sure I made the right decision. When you write stories like this, you run into those moments where you're like, well, what's the right thing to do here.

Why did you lead the story with a hypothetical situation?

In a film, they always wrestle with the exposition, with who has to tell the story. I had to have that bit of exposition in there where I explain what Ken does. This is a relatively recent phenomenon, not a job that existed in 1986. As it happens, as I was on the ferry going to see Ken for the first time in Martha's Vineyard, I noticed a man with a black bag over his shoulder, and I was like, what if one of these backpacks explodes?

That's how I set up that situation. As if something terrible had happened on that ferry ride, and if a fund had been set up in response to it, the man I was going to see would be the man who would disperse that money. I hoped that would draw the reader in.

When you get to the dollar amounts for the victims, I had to stop reading when I got to Newtown, even though I only had three more paragraphs to read. Did you expect the reader to be impacted that way by that type of ending?

I'd be lying if I said I didn't want readers to feel something, not just with this story, but with any story I write. I wanted readers to feel something with this story. What I wanted to get across more than anything is the burden that Ken carries with him for having done this work. Toward the end I list the tragedies and how much people got. That paragraph for me, where I list the victims and what they were worth or what they got paid or what their families got paid was my way of trying to bring home that point that ultimately this is almost saintly work that Ken does. The temptation would be to try to soften it for the reader, but I don't think that's right. My job is not to make the reader feel better that these tragedies happened. That paragraph is blunt, a slap in the face. But two hundred and some thousand dollars for each of those twenty children? That's horrible. I didn't want to sugarcoat it.

It's horrific that these tragedies happen. For whatever reason, people decide that money is the solution to the problem. I think it's something we need to think about. It's a pretty American instinct to see something bad happen to people and then write a check, but only for certain things—explosions or shootings or things like that. That's in some ways an interesting reaction. That's what that paragraph is.

I want people to be affected by it. I don't think we should try to make ourselves feel better about those things. I don't believe it had anything to do with God. I don't believe it had anything to do with fate. I believe that it had to do with a guy with a gun that he shouldn't have had, who shot a bunch of kids in the weeks before Christmas.

What's been the hardest story you've written?

Emotionally? The hardest for me emotionally was "The Things That Carried Him," the story of how a soldier gets back from Iraq. I followed one soldier's journey back from Iraq to the cemetery he's buried in just down the road from his mom's house. For eight months, I had that story to work on, and I was driven to write that story as well as I could. When it was gone, I didn't know what to do with myself. That story was the hardest to work on by far.

You also wrote a piece about the immediate moments after President Kennedy was killed, and it ran around the fiftieth anniversary of the assassination.

That story originally started as a screenplay. I pitched it as a movie and wrote a good chunk of a script. I got to that place where I had lots of Hollywood meetings, and people expressing interest, but I needed someone to commit to it before I would commit to it. When people are starting new careers, part of the deal is that often you have to do some speculative work, but I think of myself as a professional writer, so I wanted someone to pay me to write that script. I'd never written a script before, so of course no one wanted to pay me to write one and it died on the vine. I'd done a lot of research on the script, and I didn't want it to disappear.

My editor knew that I had been working on it. As it so happens, *Esquire*'s eightieth anniversary issue was October, and they were looking at this long survey of time and what had happened over these last eighty years and what it meant for the future. I took the research that I had done for the script and instead put it into a magazine story.

How did the reporting differ on this piece versus a piece like the one on Feinberg?

I don't normally do historical pieces. Normally I'm talking to people who are at an event, doing as much firsthand reporting as I can. In this case, there aren't that many people who are still alive from that point. It was fifty years ago. Luckily, on the flip side there is this tremendous archive of material that's available. I was looking at transcripts and old interviews while also trying to talk to people who were on the plane, but there's limited firsthand information. Most of it came from these documents.

Do you have goals in your mind when you sit down to start writing?

There are certain stories where you have an opportunity to make something that people will remember. My goal when I sit down and write one of those is usually "don't screw it up." If you have the reporting, your job as a writer now is to present what is hopefully good reporting in a way that doesn't get in the way. I think the biggest mistake young writers make when they want to write something with feeling is they overwrite. There's no such thing as overreporting. There is such a thing as overwriting.

I think back to the first story I tried to do with emotional weight, back when I was a newspaper reporter. A triathlete died during a triathlon. He was a likable guy and had a ton of friends and family who were upset. I remember my editor taking me aside after my first draft and he said, "You're trying too hard. Just let me feel it. Don't tell me what to feel and don't tell me that this is the point where the strings come in and this is the point where you cry. Let the story do the work."

My fear when I sit down and write something is that I'm gonna mess it up. There have been stories where I have the reporting. I know I've got the goods, and now, I have to make sure I present it in a way that doesn't blunt the impact of the material.

Do you ever sit down and write while you're reporting, or do you wait until you're pretty much done with all the reporting?

One of the things about being on the road, especially as a magazine writer, is you're alone. You're usually somewhere by yourself. Often I would go back to my hotel and write as a means of passing the time. What I've found is that there'll be days where you do reporting and I find I want to write it when it's all fresh in my head. I rarely start writing at the beginning of the story and then write to the end. I'll write middles; I'll write scenes. That's usually what comes out of me at night. I'm trying to think of a good example—like the Zanesville animal shooting story.

I remember coming home after spending a day with Sam Kopchak out on his farm. Then after coming back to the Hampton Inn in Zanesville, I started writing scenes. I wrote the horse scene, what turned out to be the opening scene, that night in my hotel. I didn't know it was the opener. But I knew I wanted to write that scene when it was fresh. I also like writing. I like writing without looking at my notes. I find that interrupts things. I feel pretty confident about what I'm writing about, and I can go back and check my notes and get the quotes right later. In the immediate aftermath of reporting something, you don't have to sit there and check every detail. You can write and then go fix it up.

When the bulk of your reporting is done, are you putting all of the pieces together, like a puzzle?

I can't think of a single instance where I sat down and wrote the first word and then went chunk, chunk, chunk to the end. I don't think

I've ever done that in my life. When I'm done reporting and I'm home, my job is to take this patchwork and try to put it in a good order and fill in the blanks and make sure it has some structure. I'm making a collage.

When do you start thinking about the theme?

Early, often in the pitch. You can't do a magazine story that doesn't have a theme. And then when you're reporting, hopefully you have a moment where you go, oh, that's what the story is.

Did you have an idea of what the theme would be when you pitched your profile of Roger Ebert?

I had this idea that Roger was still expressing as much as he ever expressed, using the written word as opposed to the spoken word, and in some ways, this language was almost more powerful. It was hard to articulate until I got the scene where he was yelling, where he wrote, he typed out about Disney pulling down the videos, and then, he made the font on the screen bigger and bigger and bigger and bigger. I was like, there's my theme. You can do everything that you can in spoken words in written words. It's just a different form.

The Zanesville story was almost entirely scenes, right?

Just scenes. That story doesn't have a theme. The whole goal for that story was to scare the shit out of you. That was my version of a horror movie. There was no higher purpose. That's an exception to the theme rule.

When we're talking about screenwriting, that's probably the story that's the most cinematic. It has no backstory. It doesn't have that second section where you're cast back in time. This is what happened that night. That's what a movie is, right? It's setting scenes and letting the actors do the work. The difference between screenwriting and narrative journalism is in narrative journalism you have the last word. In screenwriting, you're giving an outline, and then, other people fill in the blanks.

You were a writer on the Netflix show Away, which was based on a story you wrote for the magazine. Did you always want to get into screenwriting?

I wouldn't say always. I was happy being a journalist. It was an itch mostly, like I want to try something else.

For me, screenwriting is like using the same muscles to play a different sport. I'm still doing what I'm supposed to be doing. With journalism, I could see what was happening to magazines. It was going to be hard to be a full-time magazine writer. I had to start thinking about what else I was going to do, and screenwriting became a thing.

Are you seeing more people who write narrative journalism or are magazine writers moving towards television and film?

There's a few of us. It's not the easiest transition, just like in journalism, because you need that first crazy person to say yes to you. It's hard to convince them that you can do it. You're in that terrible catch-22 where you need a clip to prove that you can do this. Screenwriting is the same thing, where you need that first person who goes, "I know you've never done this, but I feel like you could." That's a leap that someone has to make, and it's hard to convince someone that you can.

While you and I might say that narrative journalism and screenwriting aren't that different—we're just collecting scenes and putting them in a compelling order—screenwriters and directors don't see it that way. They look at a newspaper story, and they don't see anything that resembles a movie. A few people have made the shift, and it's an obvious time to try to make it because probably, for the first time in history, it's easier to get a TV show made than to land a ten-thousand-word story somewhere.

It is hard to land a big, long-form piece of narrative journalism nowadays. Where will the people who do this well end up telling their stories?

TV and film are natural or books. It's all about telling stories. People have told stories since cave paintings, so I'm not worried we're going to stop telling stories. Just the form might be changing, at least for me. I'd still like to do journalism. I'm sure I will. But I don't mind the idea that maybe one day people will think of me, if they think of me at all, as a screenwriter. I just want to be a guy who tells stories for a living. I'm not fussy about the form.

Have you ever considered yourself a great writer?

This is an absolute stone-cold fact: I was the worst writer at *Esquire*. Charlie Pierce, Tom Chiarella, Tom Junod, compared to them, it's like, what am I doing? I was the worst writer of sentences. I still don't think of myself as a very good writer. I think I'm a good reporter, and I think I understand people.

I've always thought reporting is by far the most important part of writing narrative journalism. If you can't go out and get people to tell you about their lives, then you're not going to write good narrative journalism.

If you are a good reporter and not a good writer, you can make a living as a nonfiction writer. But if you're a good writer and you can't report for shit? We all know writers who try to mask their terrible reporting with their prose, but you can see through it from a thousand miles away.

Tom Junod

Tom Junod is one of the most celebrated magazine writers of his generation. He's won two National Magazine Awards and been a finalist ten times. In 1998, he profiled Fred Rogers for *Esquire*, which inspired the 2018 documentary *Won't You Be My Neighbor* (in which Junod was interviewed) and was adapted to a 2019 feature film *A Beautiful Day in the Neighborhood*, which starred Tom Hanks as Mister Rogers and included Junod as a character in the film. Junod writes in strong voices from a variety of vantage points. His Rogers profile, "Can You Say . . . Hero?", was written in the voice of Mister Rogers. In 1999, Junod's six-thousand-word profile of rapper Lil Bow Wow took the form of a rap.

Junod, two decades later, still profiles in strong narrative voices, including a piece on former NFL offensive tackle Eugene Monroe, who quit to use marijuana, easing the pain that football caused. That piece led with a back-and-forth with Monroe, midworkout, comparing the sensory experience of football to drug use in a flurry of simile. It was Junod's first reported piece for *ESPN the Magazine*. "The stories that interest me are often wrestling matches between writer and subject," Junod says. He also says his stories take shape in the revision process. The Monroe profile went through four major revisions before publication. Junod says he couldn't get it right. "There's a lot in journalism [left] on the cutting room floor," he says. "There's often that moment when you realize you've relinquished the thing that has driven you there. . . . Part of the process for me is trying to be true to that force that is making you sit at the desk every day."

Junod's two National Magazine Awards came for pieces he wrote for *GQ*: "The Abortionist," a profile of John Britton, an abortion doctor, and "The Rapist Says He's Sorry," a profile of a serial rapist who was undergoing therapy.

Junod and I spoke in July 2018 about Rogers and in December 2016 about the Monroe profile and his jump from *Esquire* to ESPN.

Did you watch Mister Rogers as a youngster?

I grew up knowing who he was, but when in the 1970s—when Mister Rogers came to the national consciousness—I was twelve. I was too old for Fred, and he struck me as a mamby-pamby guy, the last guy you'd want to associate yourself with when you're twelve years old.

What was it like when you started spending time with Fred Rogers?

You meet someone every once in a while that has you completely out-flanked. That's what I was with Fred the moment I walked through the door: disoriented. I don't mean that as a chess player, but he was always two or three steps ahead of me. I was walking into, not just a stranger's apartment—Fred, at the time, was a stranger to me—but into a completely new world. And that's what it was.

The voice in "Can You Say. . . . Hero?" is something that makes the story stand out because, in so many ways, you wrote it in the voice of Mister Rogers. How did you pull that off?

I don't think I wrote it in any other way. It was a matter of executing it well or not. I wrote a lot in that voice before I was able to control it, but at the time, I was not concerned as a writer. I was pretty comfortable giving that a shot.

When you spend time with somebody, especially when that person is as extraordinary as Fred, you want to somehow not fail the extraordinary nature of those transactions, of that person. You don't want to do this conventional thing if the person is extraordinary. I put that pressure on myself no matter what I'm writing. You don't want to fail the material, because the material is better than you. I tried to live up to Fred's example, in prose and in the moral push of the story.

What was it like when you saw the documentary?

I was anxious about how I did. It was all new to me. I saw it at the premiere in Pittsburgh. Fred's family, his son and his wife, were there. I was relieved I didn't make an ass of myself.

But the second time, I saw it in Atlanta, with my family and friends, and was moved. I was joltingly moved. I shed tears. Fred was a miraculous person, so singular a human being. The footage of him is so powerful, from the first time you see him to the last. The movie brings him back; you hear Fred again.

The other thing I thought was just how lucky I was to have been assigned that story. Because that story did come as an assignment. It wasn't: Oh, I think it would be great to write about Mister Rogers. That story came out of the editorial process. I was asked if I wanted to do it, I did it, and twenty years later, we're still talking about it. I mean, how often does that happen? It's one of life's turns that you know at the time it's remarkable, but you don't know that you're still going to be talking about it twenty years later.

What part of the movie touched you the most?

The first time I saw it, I was left agape by the footage of Fred and Jeff Erlanger, of Fred and Koko, the gorilla. The second time, the thing that kicked me was when Fred, as Daniel the Striped Tiger, asked, "Am I a mistake?" That killed me. It was the vulnerability of children, of us all. He put his finger on what to me is the unmentionable, unsayable concern, which is not "why am I here?" but "am I here for the wrong reasons?" It reminded me of my own childhood very much. I'm writing a memoir of my childhood right now, and so all this has come to affect me.

Your Rogers profile starts with a lost stuffed animal, Bunny Wunny. How did that come about?

That was one of the first decisions I made. I don't think that came late in the game, because it was also part of my introduction to Fred. I went to his apartment, talked about Old Rabbit; he took my picture; I forgot my pen, and the next day, he had an envelope that said Tom's Pen. That remains unopened on my desk. All of that was part of my introduction to him. It's like writing anything: You start and the door opens or it doesn't. With that particular idea, the door opened.

What impact did this story, spending a significant amount of time with Fred Rogers, have on you?

When I was going to see Fred, I was [also] trying to write a story for *Esquire* about the quarterback Jeff George, a person who had squandered his gifts, not known as easy to get along with, and also who did not cooperate on the story. I was trying to write about this guy and was completely stymied. I couldn't write it because I was coming from such a bad place in regard to what I was trying to do as a writer at that time: trying to take Jeff George down. I was trying to use George as a symbol for everything that was wrong in the NFL. I was in Pittsburgh, and I would spend a day with Fred, and then at night, I would go back to the hotel and try to write that story and get nowhere. It was brutal. It felt like I was writing with a piece of chalk on the street.

I was full of doubt. I'd come to *Esquire* and was having a hard time living up to what I was supposed to be, and then that thing happened with Fred and the prayer, and that night, I went back to the hotel and wrote the Jeff George story. That was the first opening. And you know, the Jeff George story turned out okay. It wasn't a story I was particularly proud of, but I did it. I didn't disgrace myself doing it. But I was opened up by Fred and that prayer when I started writing again.

What Fred taught me is you can be a good, effective, and penetrating writer . . . and you don't have to be an asshole. That was the most important thing. You could revere somebody, yet honor yourself.

You moved to ESPN in 2016 and your first reported piece for the magazine was about Eugene Monroe, a recently retired NFL player. What drew you to him as a story subject?

I'd seen that he had become the first active player to challenge the NFL about its marijuana rules in March 2016, [months] before I made the move to ESPN. I was interested right away because how many players smoke pot in the NFL? For him to become the first and the only player for a time to challenge the NFL on this, that showed a lot about the NFL itself, how the players regard it, and how afraid they are of being who they are.

It didn't seem like anybody was covering that issue, because I thought there was a bigger issue there: What happens to football when players start taking responsibility for their own health decisions? The marijuana issue is part of that much larger issue when it comes to the NFL. Right from the start, I felt I could pick something that might be somewhat entertaining and approachable, about a guy who basically quits football to smoke weed. And then move on to larger issues. That is precisely what I like doing as a journalist: writing about one person or incident as a way to get at something much larger. Eugene turned out to be the perfect guy because he didn't quit just to smoke weed. He was incredibly eloquent and articulate about his reasons for making the choices he did.

I found the opening scene compelling. It pulls you into the story. Why did you choose to lead that way, with you smoking marijuana with Monroe?

I've always been an advocate of not being particularly coy when you're writing stories. I've talked to journalists who have written stories that have said, well, when I was reporting, such and such happened in such and such a way and it was amazing. I ask, "Did you put that in the story?" You hear with more frequency than you think, "Well, no, I didn't." And they say they didn't think it was possible or the right thing to do or that their editors would allow it.

There's a lot in journalism [left] on the cutting room floor. This story was about a guy who gave up everything: his career, which entailed his being paid $8 million a year (with offers from two teams to play again, even after the Ravens cut him), and he gave that up in order to heal himself through smoking pot. I don't want to make it sound like he was just wanting to get high. I don't think that's the case. But he was looking to treat himself through cannabis. I went out to his house, and he offered me that experience, that ritual that he has made the center of his life. He allowed me to enter, so I did, and I wrote about it. It's the center of his life, so I can't see why it shouldn't be at the center of my story.

Did you talk with your editor to see if that was something ESPN would be cool with in the magazine?

It was a pretty interesting experience. This was my first story for ESPN, and I wasn't cautious exactly but definitely not certain either. I ended up writing four separate drafts. With the first draft, I knew I didn't get it. I knew it was not the right way to go. It was stiff, a bit formal. I didn't know what my ESPN voice should be. Should it be different than the *Esquire* voice? Should it be more sporty? What would that even mean?

The second draft was the one where I figured, if I'm going to write this story, I should, at least in parts of it, sound like I'm stoned. So I wrote that, and that was the draft that my editor liked the energy [of], except he thought it was a mess. Structurally, it was. And so I did a third draft, which was more well-crafted structurally but a buttoned-up piece that did not start with me getting stoned with Eugene. I mentioned it in the middle but didn't make it the centerpiece of the story. That was the piece that went to some of the higher-ups at ESPN, and the response was unanimous, which was: What happened to Tom getting stoned? It was restored on the fourth draft by not just my editor but the editor of the magazine and the editor of the whole enterprise group. They were all for it.

I've always found you to have one of the most unique voices in magazine writing. You capture the personality of the person you're writing about. What's your mindset as you're reporting, and do you think about how you are going to nail this particular voice in every piece?

I think that is the challenge of all long-form journalism. You are writing those stories as a testament to the people you're writing about, but you're also challenging those voices over the length of the story with your own. The stories that interest me are often wrestling matches between writer and subject. I'm not the first person to say or notice that, but I'm definitely interested in stories that provide that opportunity. I bring a strong voice and point of view to the stories I'm writing, but I try to respect the voices and the points of view of the people I'm writing about. It's the struggle but also the fun of writing stories.

Is that something that comes through revision, or is it often something you are able to get at on the first draft?

The thing with revision, it's amazing how many times you write first drafts that are not true, at least for me. I'm amazed at how many times I write first drafts that are not true to the original impetus behind the story. They're not even true to all the interesting things that happened during the reporting. The second draft is a way to get those things back.

The last story I wrote for *Esquire* is about a young woman who went missing and has never been found here in my hometown of Marietta, Georgia. I wrote the story for David Granger and completed a first draft, and he read it and told me, you know, this is a pretty good story about a fucked up young woman, but it's not much more than that. He goes, "When you were reporting and writing this story, you were obsessed with it . . . not only were you obsessed with it, you told me that everyone that comes into contact with the story, the people investigating the disappearance, they're obsessed with it.

So . . . why? Because that doesn't come through." I said we were obsessed with it because of the mystery, because her disappearance doesn't make any sense, yet she's gone and people walk through the world, through the empty space she left. He was like, "Why don't you write that?"

There's often that moment when you realize you've relinquished the thing that has driven you there. Why writers do that, I'm not exactly sure. Part of the process for me is trying to be true to that force that is making you sit at the desk every day. That goes back to the question that you asked originally: Why did I write about smoking pot with Eugene? Because that was the moment.

With Monroe, one of the things that I found interesting is the way you're able to flip the addiction. So often, the addiction is perceived as drugs. In the piece, you write that the addiction is actually football.

That perception came after we had gotten high when he was on the phone with his personal trainer. Eugene was telling the trainer over the phone, while working out, why he'd quit, and the trainer was giving him inspirational messages about all the things that he had done and what his stance meant to other players. I was like, wow, this is like an intervention . . . but it's not about drugs. Using cannabis is the thing he's trying to get to, and the thing he is trying to escape is football. It was one of those high insights that stuck, and when I ended up doing the reporting for the piece, I talked to a lot of guys about Eugene who all agreed.

How do you take notes while you're smoking pot with a former professional football player?

My handwriting is never good to begin with, and it went into a kind of Sanskrit after I got high, so the notes were of limited value. I taped it. I don't use tape recorders in every circumstance, but in this particular circumstance, I'm glad I did.

What made you think you should record the conversations for this story?

I couldn't keep up with Eugene. He was such a great talker. One of the great joys of this job is that you either come across great talkers or you ask the questions that make people great talkers. I said to myself, if I'm not capturing this, I'm going to miss out. I don't know if Eugene's insights on football are the best I've ever heard or if the weed had something to do with it, but I've gotta say, Eugene's portrayal of football and what happens on the field is the best I've ever heard.

What's your first step when you set out to start reporting a profile like this?

I'm a big emailer. I write rather long, rather impassioned emails about why I want to talk to my subjects, lay out the areas of my interest and what has compelled me to seek them out. I did it for *GQ* and *Esquire*, I find myself doing it for ESPN and for the book I'm writing, a memoir that requires reporting.

For people who write longer stories, it gives their subjects an idea of what they're getting into as well.

That means a lot. But there's another thing about the Eugene Monroe story that I need to say that goes back to your original question: That story began with me thinking it was an undercovered and underserved story. That did not turn out to be the case. Eugene was in fact profiled the same time I profiled him. Between the time I was contemplating doing it and the time that I did it, it became an extremely well-covered story and Eugene became well versed in talking to journalists. But there's something that happened in the beginning of this story that was a choice that I made, and that was the choice when he wanted to get high. I don't think the relationship that Eugene and I wound up having would have happened if I had said no. I think he would have said okay, and I would have watched him work out. I would not have asked the quintessentially high question, "Hey, what's it like?" That's not a question that you ask if you're not high because it sounds stupid. But that was the question that opened the door in Eugene. The story ended with me talking to Eugene at great length about the addictions that he had to deal with when he was growing up, not his own but his mother's addiction, and her eventual suffering from a heroin overdose. I don't think Eugene would have gone as far with me if I didn't go as far with him.

This was your first reported piece for ESPN. Why did you make the jump, and what are you hoping to do at espn?

I worked with David Granger for twenty-three years, from the time I started working at *GQ* to the time that David got fired at *Esquire*. David was my editor all that time, and we had an extremely close relationship. I was the only writer that David edited throughout his entire tenure as editor-in-chief of *Esquire*. When he got fired, not only did I see the magazine changing in ways I wasn't comfortable with, I wasn't comfortable with the way David had been treated after all the work he'd done there. But that wasn't what drove me; I wanted to start over. David announced his firing on a Friday. I believe the following Tuesday I went up to New York and met with John Skipper and ESPN.

What was it about ESPN that interested you?

I knew so many people there who were doing great work. I read J. R. Moehringer's piece that he did on Alex Rodriguez, which totally respected the thrust of the eccentricities of J.R.'s way of telling a story. I read the twenty-five-thousand-word piece that Wright Thompson wrote about New Orleans in the wake of Katrina, which was a bravura piece of storytelling. I read Eli Saslow's work; I read Seth Wickersham's work. I wanted to be part of that because I could see myself on that particular team. That's what was impressive to me, that ESPN was giving those writers that support.

You mentioned that you're working on a memoir? What is that about?

I'm writing about my dad, finally. I wrote about my dad many times, both at *GQ* and at *Esquire*. At *GQ*, I did a story called "My Father's Fashion Tips," which is about a celebration of the style that my father embodied. Then at *Esquire*, I wrote about his time as a singer during World War II. I'm finally going to use the book to tell the story that I was not able to in magazines. It was always clear growing up that the lives that my mother, my brother and sisters, and I spent with him were not his only life. It's been remarkable uncovering secrets, experiencing one revelation to the next.

Abbott Kahler

Abbott Kahler is a *New York Times* best-selling author of four historical narrative books, most recently, *The Ghosts of Eden Park*, published by Crown in 2019. Those books were published under the name Karen Abbott; she legally changed her name to Abbott Kahler in early 2020.

In March 2021, Kahler published a story simultaneously in *New York* and the Marshall Project about her friend Sara Gruen, the celebrated author of *Water for Elephants*. That story focused on significant issues Gruen faced after her bestseller was published and turned into a major blockbuster film—issues related to her trying to help a man she believed was wrongfully convicted get out of prison. This was the first piece that Kahler wrote under her new name.

Kahler's most recent book, *The Ghosts of Eden Park*, is about the world's most successful bootlegger. His name was George Remus, a man she learned about by watching *Boardwalk Empire*. When she watched the show, she became interested in this side character and wondered if he was based on a real person. He was.

"He was actually one of the inspirations for Jay Gatsby, reportedly," Kahler says.

In 2013, a friend told Kahler that if she Googled "Karen Abbott," her name at the time, it said that she had died in 2010. That's when Kahler started thinking about changing her name.

"I don't know how to explain how weirdly disturbing it was," she says. She ultimately made the name change official just before the pandemic hit in 2020.

Kahler's book *Liar Temptress Soldier Spy* was named one of the best books of the year by *Library Journal*, the *Christian Science Monitor*, and Amazon. *The Ghosts of Eden Park* was an Edgar Award finalist for best fact crime, an Amazon best book of 2019, and a *Smithsonian Magazine* top ten history book of 2019.

I talked with Kahler in April 2021.

You typically write books about people from the 1800s and early 1900s, but recently, you wrote a piece about your friend Sara Gruen. What was that piece about?

Sara is an old and dear friend of mine. We met when we were both aspiring writers, before either of us had published a book, probably around 2003. Once Sara hit the big time with *Water for Elephants*, she had always been a private person, and she never expected that level of fame and exposure, and it was disconcerting for her. It was exciting, of course. She was thrilled to have her book reach such a wide audience and be so beloved, but it was also scary for her in a lot of ways. She started getting weird overtures and people asking for things and people being overly familiar and people doing outright creepy things as well.

Sara got one letter from a prisoner in California. What happened after she received that letter?

Sara is an empathetic person, a generous person. This man who wrote to her actually had a connection to *Water for Elephants*. His grandmother was named Lottie Bell. His daughter was also named Lottie. And Sara had based one of her characters, Lottie the Aerialist, after Charles Murdoch's grandmother. He is the prisoner.

Sara sinks her hooks into something that she's passionate about. She is dogged and relentless and was not going to let it go. At first it seemed like, hey, this is an admirable thing. Nobody expected it to go on for six years. Nobody expected it to eventually take the toll it took on her. But in the beginning, it was like, wow, this is a really generous thing you're trying to do for this man. And then it spiraled out of control.

Obviously, Sara was all right with you writing this piece. When did you realize that you wanted to write about what she had gone through?

The height of her health crisis was when my last book came out. *The Ghosts of Eden Park* was published in August of 2019. I had been worried about Sara in the weeks and months preceding this because she was not communicating as much; she wasn't answering her phone. I was like, well, I'm going to be seeing her soon. I'm going to check on her in person. I happened to have a book event in Nashville and went to stay with Sara, and she was not herself. Our mutual friend Joshilyn Jackson is a great novelist as well, and she had also been there for a book launch and warned me. She said, "She's herself enough to be aware of how badly she is breaking." When I saw her, I was truly terrified that the *Bartonella* and the encephalitis that she was suffering from had permanently injured her brain.

After that immediate crisis had passed, it was probably about in the winter, I said, hey, now that you're on the other side of this and you're able to at least look back on it with some reflection and have some perspective, why don't we tell your story? Would that be cathartic for you? Would that help you in some way? She said it would. She was also still invested in having Charles Murdoch freed from prison, so any publicity that could keep drawing attention to his case was also in her interest.

Interviewing a close friend can be far harder than most people think. What was that like when you spent time talking with Sara for this piece?

I had never done this before. I'd never interviewed a friend, especially about something so personal, not only so personal but so traumatic. It was hard because I knew the points that might upset her, and I had to tread carefully in ways that I would not have tread necessarily had I not known her. She told me to shut the recorder off at times, and I respected that there were things that she spoke to me about off-the-record that I had to respect, and it was making sure that the story was authentically reported. I was trying to be as objective as possible, but how objective can you possibly be, and achieve 100 percent objectivity, when you're interviewing somebody that you've known and loved for nearly two decades?

Have you written in first person before?

Not to that length and not about anything so personal. What I've written in first person before has been my research journeys for my nonfiction books and what interests me in history. I've never written about anything this personal, and it was difficult for me because I'm so used to putting my efforts and energy and imagining myself as somebody else, even somebody who lived hundreds of years ago, and instead, this was quite a different experience.

Beyond interviewing Sara, what other reporting did you do?

I haven't done straight reporting in quite some time. I've been doing history for quite a long time. Before I started writing books, I was a reporter in Philadelphia for six years, and it was a return to those days, trying to find people who didn't want to be found and asking questions that were uncomfortable. I had to talk to one person who is one of the witnesses in Charles Murdoch's case, and she had some mental health issues that were relevant to her testimony, whether her testimony was valid and truthful because she was suffering from delusions and schizoaffective disorder. It was quite a difficult thing to call up her mother and her stepmother and her daughter and talk about the mental health issues and some of the problems that she had been having and how they might have affected her during this whole trial testimony that she had to give that put Charles Murdoch behind bars.

How long did it take for you to report and write this piece?

I started interviewing Sara right before COVID, in February of 2020. Of course, I wanted to go back and see her a couple times, but that wasn't possible. Sara is somebody who was super high risk for contracting COVID. We talked every day. I interviewed her on the phone, and she sent me all of her files. A lot of it was sifting through the work that she had already done and piecing it together in a way that was as concise as I could make it, and as readable as I could make it, something that the average layperson who doesn't know much about the case can follow.

I'm assuming you probably didn't do any traveling at all for the reporting.

I wanted to go see Charles Murdoch. He's still in prison in California. I wanted to go see him and talk to him. That wasn't possible. We exchanged letters and spoke that way. I had to do it all by phone and email.

Did you enjoy doing this type of reporting again?

I did. I wouldn't want to do it full time again. I now have a preference for speaking to dead people. Dead people always do what you want them to do, and they also don't give you that many problems. It was a nice change of pace, and I'm glad I did it. But I'm eager to get back to history.

You mentioned on your website that Sara felt like the interviews were cathartic. I've done interviews with people who've been through something traumatic, and they've told me that going through them actually makes them work through the process itself.

I think that talking about it and having it out there, now she feels like the burden isn't on her alone anymore. Other people are aware of Charles Murdoch's case. They can try to pick up where she left off or at least continue the advocacy.

You've spent your entire writing career using the author's name Karen Abbott, and now you are going by Abbott Kahler. Why did you make the name change?

It's actually a funny story. It was about 2013, and a friend wrote to me and said, did you know if you Google yourself, it says that you died in 2010? I had no idea. This is why you should never Google yourself. I don't know how to explain how weirdly disturbing it was. It creeped me out. And I had also been turning forty at the time and was thinking about changing my name for some family-related stuff. I ended up going to court in New York, and I changed it. My publishers were reluctant for me to have a new name until I became adamant about it. This is another part of the story; I found out that I'm donor conceived, that my father was actually a sperm donor. I found this out right at the beginning of COVID, right when I was writing the story, and it was the last break I needed to make with my past and go on with a new name. My publishers were okay with it at this point, so from now on my books will be published under Abbott Kahler.

All four of your books are historical narratives. The most recent one is *The Ghosts of Eden Park*, which was published in 2019. What do you love about reaching into the past for book ideas?

I guess I should tell the story of how I got into writing about history in the first place. I was coming from a reporter background and was never much interested in history beyond a superficial level. My grandmother told me a story that her mother and her mother's sister had emigrated from Slovenia in 1905. The sister took a trip to Chicago one weekend and was never heard from again. I was always intrigued and haunted by this bit of family lore, and I began looking into what was going on in Chicago in 1905. What forces were converging that led to my great-grandmother's sister disappearing? It turns out that I found something much more interesting. I found an article about Marshall Field Jr., the son of the department store mogul; he got shot in a brothel called the Everleigh Club that was run by these two mysterious southern sisters. It was the most lavish brothel in the world, and you had to pay fifty dollars to get in the door, which, of course, was a huge amount of money in 1900. I forgot all about my missing ancestor and immediately was fascinated by these two sisters. That became *Sin in the Second City*. It wasn't just the sexiness, the lore of this brothel, but the Progressive Era, which was such a fascinating period in American history, and when you think about it, you think of Ida Tarbell and Standard Oil or Upton Sinclair and the FDA, and nobody ever realizes there was this entire nationwide movement to shut down red light districts, and this amazing brothel was at the heart of it. That started my love affair with history, and I took it from there.

The Ghosts of Eden Park, was published in 2019. What's that book about?

It's about the world's most successful bootlegger, George Remus, who in 1920, found a loophole in the Volstead Act, and the loophole was, with a physician's prescription, you could buy, sell, acquire, and distribute alcohol for "medicinal purposes." Of course, he was not distributing alcohol for medicinal purposes. He was such a fantastic character. He spoke of himself in the third person. He was remarkably brilliant. He made anywhere between $20 million and $40 million within the course of a year and a half. That's not adjusted for inflation, that's 1920 money. He was actually one of the inspirations for Jay Gatsby, reportedly. He was this quintessential, roaring twenties character, and I don't think I've ever come across a more interesting person in history.

How did you learn about him?

I learned about him from the show *Boardwalk Empire*. I usually get my ideas from archives and libraries, but I got this one from TV. He is a minor character on *Boardwalk Empire*, and he was used for comic relief. He would come in there and speak of himself in third person. He'd say, "Remus sells good liquor. Remus has the best. You've got to come to Remus." And of course, people like Al Capone were like, "Ain't you Remus?" I was like, is this guy based on a real character? What's the deal here? I looked into him, and of course, he was a real character. I think his life was much more dramatic than anything portrayed on *Boardwalk Empire*, especially the love triangle that develops between George Remus, his glamorous wife, and the prohibition agent who actually put him in jail.

When you're researching these books, you said you like to talk with the dead people. How do you start the reporting and researching whenever you've got a new project?

I was lucky in this case to have found a trial transcript. Let me talk about how exceedingly rare that is, to find a trial transcript from the 1920s. Usually they're lost, or they're discarded. Luckily, this one was preserved. I went up there and I Xeroxed every single page. It was 5,500 pages. It took me about a week of sitting in the Yale University Law Library. It had the most amazing details. One of my favorite details from the trial transcript was that George Remus did not wear underwear. In the 1920s, this was a cause for great alarm. It was the sign of an unsound mind. It actually provided me an opportunity to do something that I don't think is often done in nonfiction, which was to write a who's-done-it. Somebody gets shot on the first page, and then, you don't know who it is until later on when the gun reappears. Any of the characters are crazy enough to shoot each other, and hopefully, it keeps you guessing until you get there.

When you are researching books, are you spending your time in archives? What is a typical day like when you're in the throes of research?

Once I had that 5,500-page trial transcript, it took me four months to go through the entire thing and make an outline. The outline was about eighty-five thousand words, which was almost like the book itself. I'm a big outliner. I think outlines are so key for nonfiction. By the time I finish an outline, I pretty much have a blueprint for the book, including dialogue, including details, including setting the scene.

What are the biggest challenges when you research a book like the ones you write?

You'd rather have too much material than too little, but there was so much material that I was like, how many tangents do I go on? And are they worth going on? If I do go on them, how long should they be? I learned the hard way that you have to know what your tangents are and stick to the prescribed length you want them to be.

When I was researching *Sin in the Second City*, I was looking into early 1900s contraceptive methods, as one does when they're writing a book about prostitution. I ended up going on a tangent and began researching it for about six weeks. It was so fascinating, all the different sheepskins and the douches of this and that. I probably put in a good two paragraphs, and then, by the time the book is published, I think maybe there's a line. I've wasted six weeks of my valuable deadline time, writing something that went nowhere. I'm careful about that now. One of the challenges is knowing if people are going to find this as interesting as I do and is this going to confuse the narrative.

This is a question I ask those who do historical nonfiction research: How do you organize everything as you're collecting it so when you do sit down to write, you're able to find it and do everything that needs done?

If you could see my office right now, you could see how tiny it is. I used to, in the olden days, the analog days, have these filing cabinets where I would have hundreds and hundreds of files all indexed. I'm not a neat freak or anything like that, but when it comes to my research, I'm pretty meticulous. I can't do that anymore. There's too many papers, and I don't have enough space, so I started using Scrivener. It's an invaluable tool if you want to keep all of your information in one space, and it's searchable, and you have different folders. It's like basically an index system filing cabinet on your computer. I found that to be invaluable when I'm creating my outline.

Have you found that doing this type of research and writing has gotten easier now that you've done four book projects?

In *Sin in the Second City*, I had a lot of material, but not nearly as much as I had [for] the Civil War book *Liar Temptress Soldier Spy*. The fact that it was about the Civil War created volumes in and of itself, let alone the details of my characters' lives. You get better every time you do it. You learn to be more efficient with how you plot. I think I'm sure that the same is true of novelists. You get a better feel for what the narrative should look like and the tools you need to create it.

Michael Kruse

Michael Kruse is an award-winning senior staff writer at POLITICO and *POLITICO Magazine*. Kruse focuses on what POLITICO calls "Trumpology." He has written a significant number of stories that dig into Donald Trump's past and how the former president has been portrayed and portrayed himself, and he's done so by talking with hundreds if not thousands of people who have worked with or come into contact with Trump. Kruse also writes profiles of presidential candidates and political notables, doing similar reporting that does not rely on access to the candidates themselves. For his work, Kruse has won the National Press Foundation's Everett McKinley Dirksen Award for Distinguished Reporting of Congress. He was also an honorable mention for the Toner Prize for Excellence in National Political Reporting.

One thing Kruse didn't expect when he started reporting on those who work in Washington, D.C., is that he would spend the vast majority of his time writing about Trump.

"Nobody, even the most well-seasoned Washington journalists, could have predicted how my first couple years at POLITICO would go," he says. "It's fair to say that I went to POLITICO with 0 percent expectation that a large portion of my professional life would be having to become an expert on Donald Trump."

Kruse has also spent a great deal of time writing about towns and counties across the country that were solid Trump bases. Even though those voters frequently lashed out at the media, Kruse said he never felt threatened when he talked with them.

"So many times in Cambria County and in so many places around the country, I find myself in somebody's living room, and these people start bashing the media and don't quite consider me part of 'the media' because I am a person," he says. "When I show up, I am a person. I am a human being. I am the other half of a conversation. I am not the faceless media boogeyman. I am not somebody yelling at them through the television screen."

I spoke with Michael in November 2017 about his work at POLITICO and what it was like to make the change from a daily newspaper to a political magazine and website.

In late 2014, you made the jump from the *Tampa Bay Times*, where you worked as an enterprise reporter, to POLITICO. Why did you make the jump?

A number of reasons. First of all, I thought it would be an interesting challenge, and it has been an interesting challenge. And to be candid, I saw the newspaper industry in general becoming a little bit less certain. That included the *Tampa Bay Times*. For so long, the *Times* was immune to trend lines and industry forces. It certainly didn't suffer from them quite as much because of the relationship with Poynter and the fact that it didn't report to Wall Street, and that's what made it such a great place to be and why I wanted to be there in the first place. But I couldn't quite see with clarity what my world would look like at that newspaper or in regional newspapers in five, ten years, twenty years down the road.

If I was going to leave, I wanted to leave from a position of strength rather than being forced to make some more panicky decision. At that time almost three years ago, I was looking into some options and POLITICO ended up being one of them and seemed like the most attractive opportunity. I had written some profiles of politicians in St. Pete and around Florida, but that definitely was not my specialty. But POLITICO said we like that, we want your fresh eyes. I went up there and started from almost zero in terms of political contacts and even political knowledge but spent the last three years frantically trying to catch up.

You made the jump with your editor Bill Duryea, right?

Yeah. If you make a move like that or any move in some respects, the most important transition, at least professionally, is who are you going to be working with, who's going to be your editor. That is one transition I did not have to make because Bill Duryea, my editor at the *Times* for six or seven years, went with me to POLITICO. It was a huge help especially early on in the first six months to a year, a huge help to transition into Washington and transition into POLITICO with him. It was a transition for him, and it was a transition for me, but we were able to band together and try to make that work and hopefully we have.

When you made the jump, what were some of the goals that you set for yourself? And how is what you're doing now compared to what you thought you might be doing?

In the broadest sense, it's the same job that I've always done, even before I went to St. Pete, back at the *Times Herald Record* in New York state and *Basketball America*. Eyes and ears and pen and pad and work, work, work and be a curious person. I was expecting to be a reporter, just in a different playing field. Obviously as you referenced, nobody, even the most well-seasoned Washington journalists, could have predicted how my first couple years at POLITICO would go.

I remember early on into my time there, I pitched a profile of Bernie Sanders in the sixties and seventies in Vermont because it was an underexplored chapter of his life, of this person who was already at that point starting to become a thorn in Hillary Clinton's side. I pitched this, and I remember hearing back from the experienced editors at POLITICO, through no fault of their own, this was the appropriate response, but the response was, "We should do this fairly quickly because he's going to be not running for long."

I scurried up to Vermont in April or May of 2015 and did that story in a few weeks, and then it ran, and then of course, Bernie Sanders kept running and kept running and kept running. That was an early suggestion, that we all, whether you moved from Florida to politico or whether you have thirty or forty years under your belt in Washington and in politics, we all didn't have any inkling of what was to come. With respect to Donald Trump, I didn't start gearing in on him until the end of 2015 and early '16. I had written a couple things but he was just another candidate.

I feel like you've probably read everything that's ever been written about Donald Trump.

I don't know if that's physically possible because so much has been written about him for so long.

Maybe historically speaking?

Historically speaking, that's what I'm talking about. He's been a public figure for the better part of a half a century. As much as I've tried, I have not read 100 percent of the words generated about Trump, but I would say I'm on a short list of people who've read a huge percentage of not only what has been written or said about him but what he himself has written or at least what somebody hired by him has written with his name on the cover. He is, with the possible exception of Hillary Clinton, he is the most talked about, written about, watched, person in this country for more than a generation. It's fair to say that I went to POLITICO with 0 percent expectation that a large portion of my professional life would be having to become an expert on Donald Trump.

Is there a difference between doing a deep dive into the history of Bernie Sanders versus doing a deep dive into the history of Donald Trump?

Not in terms of mechanics. You are doing your reading and your research, and you're going where you need to go to do that reading and research and to meet with people who knew that person at certain times. One of my approaches, and this was true in Florida but certainly it's been true in Washington, has been to identify chapters of politicians' lives and gear in on them, report those chapters, and then say something larger about that person through that window. It is one way I have at least tried to do distinctive political profiles. One of the biggest differences between working in Florida and Washington for me is competition.

Washington is ultracompetitive. I'd say New York and Washington. There are some exceptions, but there's not a story you're working on where there isn't somebody else working on some version of it. You're looking for ways to do something that feels different and historically minded profiles, that has been one way I have tried to do it. Using history to illuminate a person in the current moment.

Do you like that competition?

Sometimes. It has forced me to report differently, to leave fewer tracks, but that's as simple as not announcing where you are by tweeting or whether that is not leaving email trails that could be forwarded somewhere and making phone calls instead. I don't know if it's a good thing or bad thing for me. It's a thing I have to deal with. In the most materially difficult way for me on occasion, I will hear that somebody else is working on something similar to the one I'm working on, reporting concurrently, and that makes me have to speed it up. Or slow it down considerably and back off. But typically, when I hear from people I'm talking to that somebody else is poking around, I speed up the process and try to beat those other people to publication.

Something I was forced to confront fairly early in my time at POLITICO was the reality that sometimes it's better to be pretty good and first rather than amazingly good and second because if you're going up against a direct competitor, people, once they've read a story, they've read the story. And if another story shows up a week later and it's better, it won't be read as much. Sometimes, that's a calculation that I've been forced to make, along with Bill and along with other editors at POLITICO. And it's a calculation that I would say almost never came up in St. Pete. In St. Pete, it was how do we make this story the best it can possibly be. There was no competition. The competition was with yourself, how good you could make the story.

You wrote a piece that was focused on Johnstown, Pennsylvania. That was a city you visited immediately after the election in 2016. It was a region that voted heavily for Donald Trump. Your story at that point talked about what they wanted to see. Why did you go back?

The idea always in going to Johnstown, Pennsylvania, and Cambria County and that area of the western part of that state and other areas in the Midwest and in the Rust Belt, in the immediate aftermath of the election, the idea was to set up the opportunity to go back at certain times throughout the presidency of Donald Trump, to lay down a marker in November of 2016 that you could then return to and do some comparison and some contrast. I went initially to Johnstown and to Cambria County because a different reporter for POLITICO magazine had gone there in the summer of 2016 and had written this story that, looking back in retrospect, should have been a warning sign for the Clinton campaign.

It detailed the ways in which traditional Democratic voters were abandoning her and her candidacy and were energized by what Trump was saying. In fact, on election day in Cambria County, Trump won by a wide margin and those kinds of places, specifically in Pennsylvania as well as Michigan and Wisconsin, helped make Donald Trump president. So we wanted to go to those places, and this was one of them.

I went there last year in November 2016, the week after the election. I talked to a host of people who had supported Trump on election day. I asked them why, asked them what they were expecting in return for their vote, and wrote a story and then returned almost exactly a year later. So I went the week before November 8th and revisited with most of the people I had spoken to the first time, and what I found was a lot of the things that they said were the most important things in November 2016 were less important or not important at all—repealing and replacing Obamacare, building the wall, fixing the opioid epidemic, and, for them locally, reopening the steel mills that had been closing for fifty years plus and increasing coal jobs. These things were not as important to them. They still support the president as much as if not more than they used to, but the culture wars, to use a broad overused phrase, seem to be animating them more than what we would consider to be particular policy victories or defeats.

When you first went there, given Trump's rhetoric about reporters and the media, was it hard to get people to talk to you as a reporter from Washington, D.C.?

No, and here's the thing about that. So many times in Cambria County and in so many places around the country, I find myself in somebody's living room, and these people start bashing the media and don't quite consider me part of "the media" because I am a person. This has always been my experience, even well before the current moment we're in and the current political media hating moment we're in. My experience has never not been that when I show up somewhere—whether that is in rural Florida as the courts reporter for the Hernando County Bureau of the St. Pete *Times* or as a reporter for POLITICO from Washington—when I show up, I am a person. I am a human being. I am the other half of a conversation. I am not the faceless media boogeyman. I am not somebody yelling at them through the television screen.

For them, the media is the talking heads on whatever cable channel they're watching, people who are talking and not listening, whereas you are the person who's there listening and not talking, right?

Maybe it's as simple as that. When I'm sitting there and I'm listening, I'm not doing anywhere close to most of the talking. With many of the people in western Pennsylvania, both times I've been there for these two stories, I set up a meeting, I show up in their living room or at the appointed restaurant for lunch or whatever, and I ask a couple questions, and I steer the conversation, but basically, I listen to them for an hour, more than an hour, however long they have.

It's rarely not the case, even as they talk about their unwillingness or inability to trust or to like "the media." I think it speaks to the value of presenting yourself as a listener in the largest possible variety of places and across from the largest possible variety of people.

There are some instances in the Johnstown story where you do some talking. There's that one section where you're correcting one of the people that you're interviewing with regards to the golf issue. How do you handle those situations? I think we see how the person you're talking to responds but then when it comes to writing the story, how do you decide how you're going to show that to the reader?

When I have conversations like this in places like Johnstown, I am not there to get into a political argument, obviously. I am not there to be [in a] confrontation in any way. That is counterproductive to my charge. At the same time, I am not going to quote somebody saying something that is not true, and in many cases, I don't use that in a story. It's in my notebook or in my audio file, and it's not something I'm going to use. I think if it shows something that is important for the story and important overall for how to understand where we are as a body politic and as a country, I will step in and steer the conversation in a light nonconfrontational fact-checking kind of way. And that in my experience over the last year creates some revealing exchanges.

Never in any of these sorts of places that helped make Trump president have I gotten into what I call unpleasant exchanges. But I'm trying to establish some fact-based terrain on which to have a valuable revealing conversation that may or may not end up in the final version of the story. What happened in Johnstown and the way I presented it in the story was maybe more explicit than I sometimes do. Perhaps that is one reason it generated the amount of tension it did because those back-and-forths with a few people seemed to show something that either hadn't been shown before in a story or hadn't been shown quite so succinctly or starkly.

The ending of the story has gotten a lot of attention, at least on social media. When did you know that was going to be the ending? Did you know that would be the ending as it happened? Did that come up with talks with editors at POLITICO?

The exchange that is there at the ending I think is another reason this story generated such a tension fueled on Twitter and fueled on Facebook. It comes from a portion of my conversation with this husband and wife, and the wife brings it up; it was not in response to a question first of all. I didn't ask the question about the NFL. She brought it up.

"I want to tell you about this. What's really making me angry is this NFL shit. The kneeling players." That's how she put it. And she says to her husband, "Tell him," meaning me, the reporter sitting in their living room on their easy chair, "Tell him what you say the NFL stands for." And her husband gives her a look like, are we sure we want to go here? I don't have the story in front of me right now, but you can go and read it. He says, "I didn't say that." She says, "No, you did too. You liar." She calls him a liar and then says, "He says the NFL stands for Niggers For Life." And he says, "For life."

Punctuating this crude, racially ignorant, insensitive acronym, I didn't think to myself right then and there that this would be the ending of the piece, partly because sometimes at POLITICO there is a desire to use some of the most grabby stuff higher. There is an understanding, which is the reality, that fewer people read to the end than start reading a story, the metrics, and the way that POLITICO measures these things and analyzes these things is far more sophisticated than I was used to in Florida. There is a compelling reason to not hold back something you think is going to resonate widely.

I wrote that story quickly. I said to Bill, this is what I heard at this house, and I said to him as we discussed the structure, I want to hold that to the end if that flies. Nobody had a problem with that, and as it turned out, I think as a good ending should be, it was a tool to make people read all the way to the end of a 3,500-word piece.

The thing that was surprising to me was that there was language very much like that in the first story out of Johnstown, and it generated next to no buzz. So it was definitely not the first time I had heard that in that area of western Pennsylvania, and it was not the first time it had come up. I didn't ask on either occasion questions that led to these exchanges that then included racist language. But I'm gonna use it because it speaks to this question that is overly binary in my mind; what was it that made some of the Trump supporters support Trump? Was it economic anxiety or was it white supremacy?

If you are more economically anxious, which people certainly are, or most people certainly are in western Pennsylvania because you can't go to the steel mill and work for thirty years and retire comfortably anymore, it doesn't work like that anymore, then maybe you are that much more prone to be looking for somebody to blame, which draws out of you deep-seated bigoted feelings. This is a complicated thing, but I don't want to sanitize it, and if that comes up, especially if it comes up in a way that doesn't strike me as out of character or context, I'm obviously going to use it. This time around it caught fire and was read widely. I can't quote you numbers, but from what I understand, it was one of the more read pieces that I've done in three years at POLITICO.

You talk a lot about the importance of stories. You did that TEDx talk on that subject too. How do you find the stories that you want to tell?

I wish there was a foolproof way. The way I find stories has changed over the course of my time in newspapers and certainly in my time as a generalist. Right now I find stories by reading, more than ever before. I read my paper, looking for articles that hint at in some way a much larger piece. You mentioned that TEDx talk, and I think in that talk I said something like most of the things that run in newspapers are either beginnings or endings.

My job is to find that beginning and stick with it until there is an end or see that ending and report back to the beginning. That's the beginning of or the possibility of a story, beginning, middle, and end conflict resolution, rise and fall story. I read the *Times* looking for those entry points, and I read a lot of other things too. If I'm around the state reporting some story, I pick up newspapers as I go, and I read those newspapers the same way.

I subscribe to a couple dozen magazines. I read those magazines, probably because I like to read and I like to see what else is out there, and I like to learn things, but also I'm scanning. I can't help scanning for stories. Then there is the reality of living a consciously or subconsciously curious life where my wife knows somebody from my step-daughter's school, and that person said something to my wife, and then my wife said something and that was interesting, and I wonder if something is there.

Jeanne Marie Laskas

Jeanne Marie Laskas is the author of eight books and has been published in just about every major magazine in her illustrious career, including the *New Yorker*, *Esquire*, and the *Atlantic*. She is most known for writing about traumatic brain injury in professional football. That work started with her story "Game Brain," which was published by *GQ* in October 2009. The story ultimately became the *New York Times* best-selling book *Concussion*, which was turned into a major motion picture starring Will Smith.

Laskas has been anthologized in *The Best American Sports Writing* five times but says she has zero interest in sports. "I don't even bother with the questions that a sportswriter would ask because I don't even know them," Laskas says. "When I write about a sports figure, I'm writing about a person who happens to play sports."

In many ways, Laskas followed the same model when she profiled Joe Biden in 2013. "I like to write about people that nobody ever heard of, like coal miners and just folks, and the idea for this was, of all the people, wouldn't Joe Biden be just a guy underneath it all," Laskas says. She got one day with Biden, riding around his hometown of Wilmington, Delaware. "The first place we went was to the cemetery," she says. "He wanted to show me this church. He's very enthusiastic. There was this cemetery around it, and then he started talking about who was buried in the cemetery."

This was the cemetery where Biden's first wife and daughter were buried.

"He didn't want to go over to the grave," Laskas says. "It brought me into his mind and his heart in a way that I had not been."

Laskas has been a finalist for the National Magazine Award in feature writing twice and has been anthologized many times. I spoke with Laskas in November 2013. We talked about the Biden profile and "Game Brain."

In July 2013, GQ published your profile on Joe Biden. How did that piece come about?

It was one of those situations where you're chatting with your beloved editor, in this case, Mike Benoist at *GQ*, about who are we interested in. Who is right underneath our noses; who we think we know but we probably don't? Joe Biden popped in. We were both like, yeah, Joe Biden. That's it.

How did you go about getting the access you were given?

That's the whole issue because I like to write about characters. I like to write about people that nobody ever heard of, like coal miners and just folks, and the idea for this was, of all the people, wouldn't Joe Biden be just a guy underneath it all. It seemed like surely we could get to just the guy, but then it did keep coming up that he was the vice president of the United States. That was like, oh yeah, that's right. Okay, this is going to be an obstacle.

I formed a nice relationship with the White House, explaining what my idea was, and they liked the idea, but of course they're used to dealing with the Press Corps, so you get lumped in with the Press Corps for a long time. You need to earn the trust of people.

I spend a lot of time on stories, like a lot of time and research, and in this case, that time was doing a lot of stuff that probably wasn't going to end up being in the story. It was only when I finally got him to agree, that's where the whole story opened up, spending one-on-one time with him at his hometown.

How much time did you spend doing the background work to gain the trust of Joe Biden?

Normally, it would be the trust of the person you're writing about, but in this case, it was a whole team of people who are positioning him in a certain way. It was months, on and off for months. I would drive down to Washington and go to some event he was having at his house, but I'm in the press pool. I'm being roped in with everybody else, just standing there.

It was absorbing. Nothing to write about, though, in those moments. You think, huh, okay. What am I going to write? I had nothing to write about for all that time. It doesn't discourage me if I think that it's all going to end up somewhere. I went to Rome with them to the pope's inauguration. I went to a lot of places, but honestly, Wilmington ended up being the most interesting.

There's the one scene early in the story where you're at the cemetery, and I think that's a striking scene. How did that unfold?

That was interesting because it was right at the beginning of our little trip through memory lane in Wilmington. We were in the motorcade, and I was sitting next to him. This was the closest I'd ever get to him. I don't mean physically. I mean chatty-wise. Up to that point, everything had been a setup interview with fifteen tape recorders going everywhere because the White House is part of it, and everybody's part of it, and everybody's staring at everybody, and it's all very buttoned up.

This is when we're finally meeting in Wilmington, and I had no agenda. I just wanted him to take me where he wanted to go. The first place we went was to the cemetery. He wanted to show me this church. He's very enthusiastic. There was this cemetery around it, and then he started talking about who was buried in the cemetery. It came like that organically out of the moment.

Now, whether he had intended to show me that spot, I don't know, but it certainly was a real quiet moment of, whoa, we're here where his wife was buried. Whoa, we're here where his daughter's buried. He didn't want to go over there. He didn't want to go over to the grave. It brought me into his mind and his heart in a way that I had not been.

The pace of the story, especially in that early part, is almost frantic. I'm assuming you did that on purpose because that's probably what it was like on that day with him.

I'm trying to hammer the reader with the same hammered feeling I got, where you are being taken on a ride. There is no chance to ask, "Why are we going anywhere? What's going on?" It feels like he's yanking you around.

Politicians, it seems to me, are tough to crack and to get the personal story. It's hard to get inside.

Everything needs to be manufactured, especially at the higher levels. It's not a real person. It can't be. It's a mouthpiece for a set of policies. I'm not interested in any of that. The staging of it is the only interesting part but not that interesting. That's always the challenge with any of those. That's why they all read the same, typically.

I was not interested in writing that story. I wanted to write about a character. I wanted to write about, here's what it's like to be vice president. Here's what the job is. I think that was our first idea, but more interesting to me was, what's it feel like to be the vice president?

Were you ever worried that you weren't going to get that?

Mike and I would have a conversation as I would drive home from Washington. Each and every time, it was like, oh boy. Should we pull the plug? I couldn't get close enough. As kind as the White House staff were, and they were wonderful, and I liked them so much, and I formed friendships with them, there was only so much they could allow the vice president to do. I'm not sure why finally they opened up and gave me that Wilmington day. It was only a day. All of that months and months of research was about getting that day in Wilmington.

Have you ever had other stories where you've had months of research that lead to one day that makes the story?

I never know what's going to be interesting. I never go into any of these stories with a set of questions or a set of expectations even. I go with this more throw yourself to the wolves feeling of let's go see what this experience is like. Let's go see what it's like in a coal mine. Let's go see what it's like on an oil rig or any of these places. I go in blind. I go in not knowing.

I always tell people who are starting out, you have to have a high capacity for boredom in this kind of work because a lot of stuff is boring. A lot of stuff is waiting, waiting, waiting, waiting. As you become invisible in front of these people, the longer you're there, the more invisible you become, and then you can start seeing the real action of the world.

Did anything surprise you in the course of reporting the story?

It surprised me how difficult the Press Corps' jobs are. I could never do the job that the White House Press Corps does, where you're going and sitting in a motorcade van for four hours waiting for the person to come out and give a speech, then you're sitting back in the van, typing it on your Blackberry to your editor, and that's your story. I wouldn't know what to write. I wouldn't have a clue. I do think that surprised me a lot, seeing how they work. I admire anything that comes out of that.

There's a line toward the beginning. It's one sentence. "Joe Biden does not pause." That's a great line because it encapsulates him.

That's exactly it. No pause, no chance for you to say, "Wait, what?" Or, "Why are you telling me this?" Because he's already onto the next thing.

There's also that scene where he stops at his old school. What was that like?

I didn't know where we were going. We were touring through the neighborhood, and all of a sudden, it was great because we pulled up into the driveway of this grand school, Archmere Academy. It's a beautiful campus; it looks like a small college. I don't even know where we are. We're just getting out of the car. We started walking, and the Secret Service guys, I thought I knew where they were, but then, more were appearing out of nowhere, swirling. I'm like, where were all these people? It's a whole system going on. He walks into the campus. Nobody knew he was coming.

The students are hanging out for lunch out in the commons area. They look up like, oh, Biden's here. Cool. He's waving, saying "Hey, hey, I used to go to school here. Hi." He was unannounced and completely like a neighbor coming to visit. Then, of course, swarms and swarms of people came around, and he loves it. He loves the attention. He loves what he does.

Did you get any feedback from the vice president after the story ran?

His communications director, she's wonderful. She liked the story and said that pretty much everyone there was happy with the portrayal, even some of his family. Somebody said I really captured him.

How much time did it take you to write the story?

A long time because I'm so slow. I don't remember exactly but several weeks certainly. It's not that long a piece, but I go through so many drafts because I kept thinking that I spent all this time in Rome with the pope and Biden and all of the pomp and circumstances of that and the complications and on Air Force II and all this material. You have all that and you think, well, you've got to use that.

I was overwhelmed with all that material, and I thought, what am

I going to do with all that, because all I want to write about is Wilmington. I had many drafts with a lot of that stuff. It all happened before chronologically. It happened before I got to Wilmington, so the whole first half of the story was all this Rome stuff and all this fancy stuff. It was irrelevant. That's hard to cut. It was like, this thing needs to start in Wilmington.

It seems like such a small idea to go that small, but of course, it's the right idea for that story, for that thing I was trying to capture. It's that tight shot of a real guy dealing with himself as a kid. That's so much more interesting than all the fancy pomp and circumstance of anything. I know it, but I couldn't convince myself of it, so I had to go through many drafts of it.

It's the perfect beginning because you get the franticness and you get where he came from. I think him trying to get into his old house is telling but also funny at the same time.

Isn't that hilarious, that he's trying to get into his house, peeking in a window in his old house, and people aren't even home? He's like, yeah, this is my house. We're peeking in the freaking dining room window looking at the hutch. I'm like, I can't believe this is happening, with the Secret Service guys all out there. By that point, you're so used to it. You're not even sure that that's weird. Not weird, but that it's unusual. You have to keep stepping back and saying, wait a second, this is the vice president of the United States. This is unusual.

You've been anthologized in _The Best American Sports Writing_ multiple times. What draws you to sports?

Nothing draws me to sports. Zero. I have no interest in sports. I keep ending up in sports anthologies. The reason I write about sports is because it started in _Esquire_ when I was there, and Andy Ward was my editor at _Esquire_ at that time, and the idea was since I don't know about sports, since I'm not much of a football fan particularly, isn't it interesting to send someone to write a profile when she has no baggage? I bring no baggage to a football story.

For example, the first sports thing I think I ever did was writing about this big football player named Korey Stringer, who has since died. Andy's idea was, go write about what it feels like to be a lineman and get bashed in every single Sunday. That's your job to get bashed in by these big, humongous people. Just go write about that experience.

I go to the Minnesota Vikings training camp. I know nothing. I don't know the coach's name. I don't know the history of the team. I don't know if this is a good team, a bad team. I knew nothing, so I don't even bother with the questions that a sportswriter would ask because I don't even know them. Instead, that gets me right front and center with the guy, the character, the person. That's the model. When I write about a sports figure, I'm writing about a person who happens to play sports.

I think that's why the sports pieces that you write are so good. It's not necessarily a sports story. Glenn Stout wrote about this in terms of the stories he looks for in *The Best American Sports Writing*. They aren't necessarily sports stories, but they're related to sports in some way.

I totally credit him for pulling out these kinds of stories in those anthologies. I don't mean mine; I mean all of them. I love what he does. He gets it. Those are the kinds of sports writers I would read too. I think he does a fabulous job.

You wrote *Game Brain* in 2009, long before concussions in football were being talked about. What got you onto that story?

I'm going to try and squash this, because again, this one in particular is not the kind of story I do. If you think about that story, it ended up being almost an investigative piece.

Now, flash forward, Andy Ward is now at *GQ*, and he's my editor. I don't want to tell you the whole boring backstory, but let's say I'm writing about this concussion debate that was going on at the time. It wasn't a debate, though, when I was writing about it. It was more like a crisis. Alan Schwarz at the *New York Times* had done fantastic reporting, and there's this guy, Chris Nowinski, who was the PR guy for concussion-related injury who you hear his name a lot in conjunction with the Boston Group, who's doing a lot of research.

I was going to do an update. That's all my intention was back then because I thought the story was already reported. The way I wanted to do the update was I wanted to see a brain. They have all these brains in Boston in these dishes that they had cut and sliced and found this disease in. They didn't have the brain I wanted. I wanted to do this guy Justin Strzelczyk's brain because his backstory I thought was fascinating. I'm like, where's the brain? They kept saying, well, we don't have that one. I'm like, well, where is it? They're like, well, it's in West Virginia. I'm like, why is there a brain in West Virginia?

At that point, there was no press at all having anything to do with this original group who first cracked this case. It was so off the pages I couldn't find anything about it. I will say publicly, Chris Nowinski tried to steer me away from it. It was all then just trying to find this brain.

I found this doctor in West Virginia who knows where the brain is of this dead football player who tells me about this guy, Bennet Omalu, who had discovered basically this disease in football players. He had been squashed by the NFL, which was bad enough, but then squashed by the media; I don't think on purpose, but he was forgotten about.

It was a systematic thing that was happening. It bothered me that the guy who found the disease never got recognized. I went and I found him. That's what I ended up writing about in 2009. I got interested in this scientist's private discovery of this disease. He didn't understand football. He doesn't know what football is. He's got Mike Webster's brain on a dish, and he's trying to figure out how Mike Webster died, and he ends up taking the brain home to his apartment to slice it and dice it and do all they do with brains to find what the secret of this injury was.

My story was basically unraveling the narrative of this guy and this brain slowly step-by-step, unraveling it, untangling. That's mostly what I did in that piece, and it got a lot of attention back in 2009. The congressional hearings happened shortly after that. Lots happened because of the NFL's denial of Bennet Omalu, of his work, and the repeated attempts to silence him. That to me was and still is the story for all these NFL players; the fact that they've been duped, these old guys in particular.

Was it difficult to get Bennet Omalu to talk with you?

I think there was a little team, him and Julian Bales, who was the scientist in West Virginia, and his attorney. They all knew Mike Webster, and so they were all part of that original discovery. I think when they heard that I was interested in unraveling it and telling it and I'm genuinely trying to figure out what the hell happened, and why is the *New York Times* leaving this guy out, why is everybody leaving this guy out, I remember Julian Bales said, "You know what? Stop asking me questions. Just come to this diner in West Virginia and we'll talk." I showed up in this diner, and that's when he explained his version of the whole thing to me. He told Bennet to talk to me, and Bennet did.

Rachel Monroe

Rachel Monroe is a freelance writer and the author of *Savage Appetites: Four True Stories of Women, Crime, and Obsession*. Monroe has published pieces in the *New Yorker*, the *Atlantic*, the *New York Times Magazine*, *New York*, *Outside*, *Wired*, and others. *Savage Appetites* (Scribner, 2019), named a *New York Times* Editor's Choice and a book of the year by *Esquire*, Jezebel, and the *Chicago Tribune*, focuses on four women and the true crime stories they were attached to in varying ways. For instance, one woman played a key role in helping develop forensic science in the 1940s and '50s; another helped get someone wrongfully convicted of a crime released from prison.

Monroe followed the stories of all four women for years, not necessarily with the intention of writing a book but simply because she was interested in them. "At one point, it clicked that not only did they share that each of them had been fascinated by a crime that didn't happen to them but that they approached it from a different perspective," Monroe says. "My brain is wired such that I get serial obsessions, one after another," she says. "I'll get fascinated with something for months, then leave it behind. I always used to feel guilty about that, but that's a great way to be wired for being a freelance writer."

Monroe studied undergraduate fiction under David Foster Wallace at Pomona College in California. She was awarded a Fulbright and studied women and literacy in Morocco. She ultimately ended up in Marfa, Texas, an arts haven of 1,800, seventy miles from the Mexican border in the western part of the state. There, Monroe is also a volunteer firefighter and occasional radio host. Monroe was a finalist for a Livingston Award for Young Journalists in 2016, the same year *New York Magazine* named her one of fifty-six women journalists to read.

I spoke with Monroe about *Savage Appetites* and freelancing in August 2019.

Can you tell me about *Savage Appetites*?

The book originated with a feeling I didn't quite understand, which was that even though I was a journalist, sometimes writing about crime, and knew a lot from a factual perspective, these certain crime stories would still get in my head and seem to provoke a reaction that no other stories did. I would get obsessed. I would stay up late, reading Wikipedia, reading message boards. I didn't quite understand the hold that they had over me. Then I started noticing that other people, particularly women, would talk about crime stories in the same way.

I started working on this book around when this true crime boom started. You would hear people talk about binging stories; appetites in the title is not an accident. People often talk about these stories and their response to these stories in terms of appetite, being hungry for them, craving them, binge eating them. It was curious to me that even though most violent crimes are committed by men, most victims of murder are also men, homicide detectives, prosecuting attorneys . . . all these roles in the crime ecosystem are primarily held by men, but the people consuming the stories are disproportionately women. That was curious to me both about myself, about my friends, and also about the world in general.

Did you know going into the book that it was primarily women who were interested in true crime stories?

It was something I had an anecdotal sense of. Growing up, I always enjoyed these kinds of stories in a dark way. I had certain friends, always female, I knew I could talk about serial killers with. My mother was the same way. I sometimes say that our love language is creepy stories. We send each other emails of terrible things all the time. Then a number of years ago, this study came out that was, as far as I know, the only quantitative analysis of this, and the study found, unsurprisingly, that readers of true crime books were disproportionately female. They had come up with an explanation for why: that women like to read about serial killers because maybe it was a way to help them avoid being killed by a serial killer. To me, that was such a ridiculous explanation for why these stories are so compelling. That was part of the motivation for the book too: coming up with a better answer.

You focused the book on four true crime cases that involved four women in varying ways.

I had been circling around this idea of writing a book along these lines for a long time. I went back and found a half-written draft of a book proposal that I had written about eight years ago, covering similar themes. What was tricky was finding the shape around it. I was interested in crime, and on this metalevel, how these stories are told and why they have such a hold over people, but didn't quite know how to get into that. I had the theme but not the structure. It took a long time for me to figure out a shape that would allow me to explore those ideas. All four women that I write about in this book, I have been following their stories, not necessarily with the intention of writing a book, but following them because I was interested in them for a number of years. At one point, it clicked that not only did they share that each of them had been fascinated by a crime that didn't happen to them but that they approached it from a different perspective.

One of the women who was alive in the 1940s and '50s saw herself as a detective, occupied that role, and became key in the development of forensic science. And then you have somebody like Lorri Davis, who got one of the West Memphis Three off death row, who occupied the role of the defender, the lawyer, which is a different way of relating to a crime story. Another woman acted more like a victim, and another woman identified more with the killer. Once I realized that there were these different facets, that each of them would allow me to explore a different angle on the same topic, that was the first time that I could see it as a book.

How did you settle on the four women that end up in the book? I imagine there's more than four women and four cases that you've been interested in.

I'm always squirreling away things that catch my interest. I don't know if I'm going to ever do anything with them, but they fascinate me. All of these women had been that for me. I had written about a number of them tangentially for other projects. One of the first pieces of writing that I ever wrote and was paid for was about Francis Glessner Lee, the heiress I write about in the detective chapter, who built these amazing, creepy dollhouses that were used to train the police in forensic techniques. It was the first story that I ever pitched mostly because I was living in Baltimore at the time, and I knew these dollhouse murder scenes existed and obviously wanted to see them. They were not open to the public, so I figured, if I write about this for the local weekly, the *Baltimore City Paper*, they'll have to let me go see them, so I wrote a pitch.

You write about your own life as a true crime aficionado. Had you written about yourself much in the past?

I have tended to avoid it. Sometimes in my reporting, I'll have an "I." I like to deploy an "I" to acknowledge that the story is being written by a person with a perspective. But it's not usually like a memoir. I don't talk about myself, my past, or anything like that. It did seem important in a book like this, which focuses on some extreme cases. The four women I write about did transform their lives and take some extraordinary actions, and I didn't want the reader to look at them and say: well, that has nothing to do with me. Those ladies are extreme, obsessed, weird. I'm not like that. My personal interest in these stories is nothing like that. I figured that by being in the book myself, I could serve as a bridge. If the reader thought these women that I'm writing about are taking actions too extreme to understand, I'm halfway there. If you identify with me, maybe we can see the parts of us that are reflected in or refracted through these more dramatic stories.

Of the four women you write about, do you have a favorite?

I don't know if I'm allowed to pick a favorite. They are all special to me in different ways. That's what you're supposed to say. I'll say that Lorri Davis, the woman who saw a documentary about the West Memphis Three—these three teenage boys who were arrested during the Satanic Panic Era for murders that they did not commit—and fell in love with this man essentially through this documentary then started writing him these passionate letters and helped him get out of prison after almost two decades . . . she is a lovely human being. It was interesting to report this book because, in the first section, my subject is dead. The second section, my subject didn't particularly want to talk. The fourth section, my subject was in prison. So Lorri, who is the third section, was the only one that I got to do extended interviews with. She's the one that I ended up feeling personally closest to.

How long did it take you to get the first draft of the manuscript done?

I wrote the first draft in about fifteen months. I was drawing from previous research that I had done and everything in there is pretty much new, that I wrote entirely for the book, but was playing around with some characters in research.

Were you doing freelance work while you were working on this book? And if so, how did you balance it all?

I promised myself that I wouldn't. I did less than I usually do, but every now and then, there were some pieces that I hadn't quite finished by the time I was working on the book and others that came up. It's hard for me to stay focused on one thing. I think that's a problem I have, when I'm working on a piece and feeling like I'm hitting a wall with it. It's easy to get distracted by a new shiny idea and convince myself, oh, if I wrote that, I wouldn't have any problems at all. I still haven't learned that lesson.

Writing a book is funny. As you know, there are low periods and periods of great activity, and it's somewhat out of your control. I tried to smoosh it all together and make it work as best I could.

How did it feel when you sent that first manuscript to your editor?

You know that moment when you jump off the cliff into the water, and there's that period when you're falling that lasts way longer than it should? It's like that, a plummeting sense. But also, I tried to allow myself the space to feel proud of myself. I don't know if you have this problem, but it's hard for me, that phase of creation, the basking phase. I'm trying to encourage my friends to do this more, to sit back and be like, wow, I'm proud of myself. That was hard, and I did that. I've been trying to take the time to . . . before I jump to the anxiety of how's it all going to work out and all the flaws.

You do a lot of freelance work for big national magazines, but you live about as far south as one can live in West Texas. Is it challenging to be a national freelancer in a place as remote as where you live?

In some ways, it's an advantage. In some ways, it's definitely a disadvantage. I live in Marfa, Texas, about seventy miles from the Mexican border and two hundred miles from the nearest airport in El Paso. That two-hundred-mile drive to the airport is one of the big disadvantages. To editors who live primarily in New York, it makes me exotic, which is a testament to how concentrated the media industry is. There's an advantage in that certain things come across my radar before they trickle over to New York. I see certain phenomena quicker than I would if I lived on the East Coast.

I think about a story I wrote for the *New Yorker* a few years ago about essential oils and the multilevel marketing companies that were selling essential oils. I tried to sell that story forever because, from where I was living in rural Texas, this stuff is everywhere. I would try to bring that news to my editors in New York, and they would have no idea what I was talking about. It took a little while before I think that phenomenon started to make its way to New York or to these coastal cities, and then all of a sudden, people were interested.

When did you know that you wanted to be a writer?

Probably from an early age. It was one of the only things that I was ever good at. For a long time, I wanted to be a fiction writer. That was what I imagined my path to be for a long time. I didn't start writing nonfiction until after I got a master's in writing fiction.

What drew you to nonfiction then?

For a long time, I didn't feel like I had permission to write nonfiction. I don't know where I imagined that permission would come, from some imaginary authority outside of me, but I guess I felt like I didn't know enough or that my perspective wasn't valuable or that I didn't have enough to say. Reading fiction was, for me at least, a way to hide. Over time, I grew a little bit more confident, saying what I observed, what I noticed about the world, and I loved it.

I love asking people questions. I love being nosy. My brain is wired such that I get serial obsessions, one after another. I'll get fascinated with something for months, then leave it behind. I always used to feel guilty about that, but that's a great way to be wired for being a freelance writer.

You've got one book down. Is there another one in the works that you can talk about? Are you working on freelance stuff right now?

I'm working on a lot of freelance stuff. I guess it's maybe like once you get a tattoo, when you have a baby, or something—painful while you're doing it, weirdly want to be back in that space as soon as it's over. Writing a book is that way. I'm craving another one and I have a few tentative ideas but nothing I've sat down and confirmed with myself that I want to do.

Ben Montgomery

Ben Montgomery is a *New York Times* best-selling author and a former reporter for the *Tampa Bay Times* and Axios. He was also the founder of the now-defunct but once-beloved and now nonexistent narrative journalism blog Gangrey, where journalists from around the world gathered to discuss great stories. The site became the namesake for my podcast, which has resulted in these conversations.

Montgomery's first book was *Grandma Gatewood's Walk: The Inspiring Story of the Woman Who Saved the Appalachian Trail*. The book landed on the *New York Times* bestseller list and won the 2014 Outdoor Book Award. It was about Emma Gatewood, a sixty-seven-year-old great-grandma who, in 1955, told her family she was going on a walk and then disappeared.

"The next anyone heard of her, she had hiked from Mount Oglethorpe in Georgia to roughly Roanoke, Virginia, along the Appalachian Trail," Montgomery says. "At that time, only five men had completed what's referred to as a through hike, which is a walk in one season of the whole 2,050-mile trail, which ends in Maine on top of Mount Katahdin."

Gatewood became the first woman to solo hike the Appalachian Trail, and the first person of any gender to do it twice and then three times.

Montgomery almost never became a journalist. His plan as a young man had been to become a farmer. The Oklahoma native went to Arkansas Tech University and took a journalism class as an elective. The first assignment, he says, was to write a two-thousand-word article on the subject of his choice. He wrote about pot on campus. A couple of classes later, the professor read the story's lede to the entire class.

"This is how we should be doing it," Montgomery remembers the professor saying.

In 2005, Montgomery started Gangrey.com. He had been working at the *Tampa Tribune* and collecting stories he thought were good. He would paste them into a notebook and carry it around. Blogs started to become popular, and so, with the help of a friend, he launched Gangrey—which, by the way, is still his Twitter handle.

How did you first hear about Emma Gatewood?

She's a distant family member. I remember growing up hearing stories from my mother about Emma Gatewood, who's known even to family members as Grandma Gatewood, which became her trail name. My mom would share these stories that her own mother passed down, and I was always captivated by the eccentric woman who chased away a black bear with her umbrella and who had all these crazy experiences walking late in life. I did a story a couple years ago about an unsolved Florida lynching that got a lot of attention and wound up in the hands of an agent in New York, who wrote me and asked if I had any book ideas. It turns out she liked the idea about doing a biography of Grandma Gatewood, so we were off to the races.

Had you always thought you might write about her at some point?

No. Honestly, it was always this familiar curiosity, and again I was born in seventy-eight, and she died in seventy-three. That side of the family stayed in Ohio, my side of the family moved to Oklahoma, so I never knew a whole lot about her besides these anecdotes that my mother would share as I was growing up. I always assumed that she had been written about a lot.

Once you decided to look at Emma Gatewood as a book subject, where did you start reporting?

I didn't know what it took to do a book. I didn't know what it took to do a book proposal. I didn't know anything about the process before any of this. I was completely oblivious to what this kind of work entails, so basically the pitch was a couple of sentences, no more than two or three sentences to the agent. When she said, "I like this, let's put together a proposal," then you start reporting. First off, it's who's alive that knew her.

That led quickly to her youngest daughter, Lucy Seeds, who originally lived in Jacksonville, Florida, and I had a couple phone conversations with her. I went up to visit her, and fortunately, she's been the keeper of her mother's flame. She had preserved tons of correspondence. She had preserved her mother's diaries that she kept on her hike on the trail. She kept photographs and scrapbooks and all the information you could need. She was willing to share all of that, whatever I wanted, so I had that.

Four of Grandma Gatewood's eleven children were still alive at the time; one has since died unfortunately. I was able to interview all four of them. I did hours of interviewing with them, and then I went in search of anything on the public record having to do with Emma Gatewood. I was primarily tracking down small newspaper articles and papers alongside the trail. Thank God for small town librarians.

Everyone that she had met along the trail, she would make note of their name in her diary, and then, often, she would send them all postcards when she got to the end of the trail. I had a list of about thirty names of people that she met or stayed with on that first hike. I was able to track down probably ten of them who were still living, which I thought was cool. That was pretty much the reporting in a nutshell.

Did you do all of that just for the proposal?

I did probably 5 percent of the reporting to begin with to get the proposal out there, and when the book sold, I launched into deeper, wider reporting. I had about a year to do the book, the reporting and the writing. I couldn't quit my day job, and I couldn't through hike the trail, but I wanted to see places that were important to the story with my own eyes. It involved me going to Harper's Ferry, West Virginia. My wife and I climbed Mount Katahdin, retracing Emma Gatewood's steps. In Mount Oglethorpe in Georgia, I wanted to see the start of the trail. I did a lot of reading about the trail, a lot of reading about 1955, which was a fascinating year in U.S. history, because I wanted to set it firmly in that time.

How did you balance your day job with researching and writing the book?

It was a real challenge. I'm lucky that people at the *Times* were supportive, so if I needed to race off to take a trip, it was typically okay. I had to read eight books about walking. One of the books opens with the history of walking. For six million years, we've relied on bipedal locomotion as our primary means of locomotion, and it's been only the last 100 to 150 years since we have chosen to sit and ride rather than walk. The *Atlantic* published a Thoreau essay called "Walking," so I pitched a newspaper story that allowed me to do reporting for the book and reading for the book while also feeling like I was accomplishing something for my day job. I told my boss I was going to walk to work for a week. No car. I was going to walk everywhere I needed to go for a week in the middle of summer in Florida. He was totally down with it.

One of those days you walked from Tampa to St. Pete and then back in the same day, right?

Yeah, we had a meeting in St. Pete. I can sometimes work in Tampa where my home is. That walk was roughly five miles, so I was doing ten miles to and from work. One morning we had to have a staff meeting in St. Petersburg, and I wanted to show up for that. So I walked there and back. It was a good walk, maybe forty-six miles, I think was what we tallied it at. It was kind of stupid, but it was fun.

Did doing that give you any insight into Emma?

I think so. I'd never taken a long walk like that before. I'd never walked more than twenty miles before. I was trying to get into her head. I was thinking about her a lot. I'm not a sixty-seven-year-old woman, so there's limits to how deep into her psyche I can get. I feel like I connected with her on that long trip.

Toward the end of the book, you climbed the final summit to retrace Emma's final footsteps. What were you hoping to get out of that experience, and did you get it?

We hired a guide. I gave him the sections of Emma's diary that dealt with that little stretch. We wanted to get as close as possible to the ascent she would have taken in 1955. I'm sure you probably know the AT changes dramatically every year. It's rerouted for erosion and other things. I wanted to see what she saw as closely as possible, so we decided to do this hike on the exact day that she finished, September 25th or 26th, 1955. I wanted to stalk her. The whole book felt like trying to chase her ghost, to get as firmly inside of her head as possible, so I could write with authority what her experience was like.

That was an important moment for her, making that final ascent at the end of a long trip. She got this rush of attention. In fact when she got to Katahdin Stream Campground at the bottom of the mountain, she left an AP reporter and a reporter from *Sports Illustrated*, and she wanted to hike this last stretch on her own. They stayed at the bottom waiting for her to return.

What was Katahdin like?

Katahdin is this amazing place. It's true wilderness, even with trails and even if it's in Baxter State Park, it's real wilderness. Thoreau climbed Katahdin and basically went crazy a little bit, calling it this uninhabitable place, this place that man had no purpose being a part of. You start this climb, and hundreds of people do it, maybe thousands of people do it every year now, but it does have this feeling of desperation and this feeling of like, I shouldn't be here. The wind doesn't want me here; the rocks don't want me here. I wanted to get as close to that experience physically as I possibly could. Did I get there? Again, I felt some connection to her. If we walk in the footprints of others, even if they did it sixty years before we did, I think we are still trying to interpret the same path, and I think I achieved that.

Did you learn anything about writing or reporting that you didn't know before you started this book project?

What scared me is I have a tendency to check out of books that are loose or take a while to explore an idea or get from Point A to Point B. I don't like superfluous books. I like books that are tightly written, that are compact. I wanted this to be a solid, brisk magazine story or newspaper article, to almost have the feel of a newspaper article with that speed and that respect for the reader's time. I kept an eye towards that, but at the same time, I felt like a book gave me that link. Seventy-thousand words gives you opportunities that you don't have in a smaller medium.

Your _Tampa Bay Times_ series For Their Own Good received a significant amount of attention. It looked at the history of abuse at Florida's oldest reform school. How did that series come about?

In October of 2008, these five old men who had found each other online, all were former wards of the state of Florida at a place called the Florida School for Boys, which later became known as the Dozier School for Boys. They held a small ceremony/press conference on the campus of Florida's oldest reform school, and one by one, told stories that were incredible. They detailed their abuse. They talked about the beatings they took in a small, dank cinderblock building they referred to as "The White House." The beatings were administered by a one-armed man named Troy Tidwell. Fortunately, a reporter from the Tallahassee Bureau of the Associated Press was at that little event and wrote an AP story that ran in the metro section of the *Tampa Bay Times*.

That's my first brush against that story. When I read it, I walked immediately over to the desk of my editor at the time, Kelley Benham, and the way she tells it is my eyes were wide and I was like, this is crazy if true. We set off shortly after that in pursuit of the question: Is this true what these men are saying?

When did you know you wanted to be a newspaper reporter?

I was going to be a farmer. My grandpa has a cattle farm in Slick, Oklahoma, and I had every intention of going back and helping him run that farm. Then I got married to my high school sweetheart my freshman year of college, and she was basically like no, I want to go to New York. This forced the door open to other possibilities.

I took a journalism class as an extra credit. The feature writing class sounded cool. I'd never been a big newspaper reader before that. I'd never written anything that I was proud of. The first assignment was two thousand words on a subject of your choice, and so I wrote about pot on the campus of Arkansas Tech University, and I turned the story in. A couple of classes later, the professor read that in front of the class. He read the lede on the story, his name was Tommy Mumert, and he was like "This is how we should be doing it." It was such an uplifting moment.

Your third book is *The Man Who Walked Backward*. His name is Plennie Wingo. Who was this guy?

Plennie Lawrence Wingo owned a café in Abilene, Texas, in the 1930s, and when the bottom fell out of the stock market and things started to go south on the front end of the Great Depression, he lost his café to the bank and couldn't pay the bills, so he found himself out of work. He went to work making waffles at a greasy spoon in Abilene. He was making like twelve, seventeen cents an hour, something like that. His take-home pay was pitiful, and he decided that he wasn't going to do this anymore, and he seized on a crazy idea to try to walk around the world backward. He trained for about six months and then set off in early 1931 out of Fort Worth, Texas, wearing sunglasses that had rear view mirrors affixed to the sides of them so he could see behind him, and he set off on a quest to become the first human to ever walk backward around the world.

He walked eight thousand miles backward, which solidified his place in the Guinness Book of World Records as a backward walking champion. You can look at the record today, and he's still got it. Imagine that, nobody has ever tried to walk backward more than eight thousand miles.

How did you come across his story?

I was researching crazy pedestrian stunts for *Grandma Gatewood's Walk*. I found myself reading a lot about walkers, and I kept going down these rabbit holes: first person to walk from Chicago to New York and first person to walk across the country, and there's a guy, it seems like in the 1880s, who walked one thousand miles, but he walked only one mile per hour, and it was on a bet, like his buddy had offered seven Cornish game hens if he could do this or something like that, and that's pretty incredible. We normally walk three or four miles per hour, and he's walking one mile per hour every single hour for more than two weeks, which is unbelievable.

I stumbled across the name Plennie Wingo, and at the time he had a Wikipedia entry that said something like "Plennie L. Wingo is the backward walking champion of the world. He walked 8,000 kilometers backward in 1931," and that was about it. A couple of lines. No real detail on his life. I did a little bit of searching and couldn't turn up anything, and so he existed as a question mark in my head for a long time. I couldn't get him out of my mind for some reason. That, the novelty of what he did and the time in which he did it, which I knew a little bit about, made it so that I couldn't forget him. I finished *Grandma Gatewood's Walk*, and I did a book called *The Leper Spy*, about a woman who was a hero spy for the U.S. during World War II, and my agent naturally started asking what the next idea was, and I thought, let me see if I can learn something about Plennie Wingo. That started the long journey of trying to understand his life and who he was, and also that fascinating era, the early 1930s, when I think we were at our worst.

Grandma Gatewood's Walk took place in the 1950s and before. *The Leper Spy* was a World War II book. And now Plennie Wingo during the Great Depression. How do you do the reporting for projects like this?

I have an active subscription to newspapers.com, which gets better and better as a digitized internet searchable archive of old newspapers. Reporting started like this: you're after two things, one the reporting of his story in particular, two, the context. I've got to learn about that period of time, as well as about his specific journey. I started reading. I bought every book that was on the bestseller list in 1931 and '32. I watched every film I could get my hands on from that era.

The reading of archival newspaper material is another big deal because a lot of times, little important incidents get overlooked by history and get forgotten, and they certainly don't make the history books, and so I look for those little cultural nuggets that help the reader understand where we come from that can serve as the context for a story like this. I almost think about it like I'm gonna report the era as hard as I report the human.

This is a simple arc for Plennie Wingo. But I want to create a character out of the time almost, and then in reporting his trip, I followed his footsteps. I didn't follow his entire route across the United States, but I followed big chunks of it, things that I thought would be important for the book, and then I flew to Hamburg, Germany, and took trains, cars, and buses from Hamburg to Istanbul, following his exact route, stayed in Berlin and Dresden and Hamburg but also like small towns, like Yablanitsa, Bulgaria, where I slept on top of a mountain in the Balkans and tried to communicate with the elders in the community to see if anybody remembered this white Texan who walked through Bulgaria in 1931. It turns out it was pretty fun reporting this book. It gave me a chance to see that part of Europe and learn about this period of time I've always been fascinated by.

When I start doing any type of archival research, I find myself losing track of time and often going down a series of rabbit holes and looking at all sorts of stuff. Does that happen to you too?

It's exactly how I operate. Something will pop into my mind that might be interesting to tell a story about. I wonder if I can create a search string that will introduce me to stories I've never heard about that deal with whatever subject it is I'm thinking of.

How do you keep on task when you're doing that type of stuff?

I can't tell you how much time I spent thinking about Plennie Wingo and why a guy would try to walk backward around the world in 1931, because it was two years, maybe longer than that, between the time I first stumbled across his name and the time I actually started to put together a book proposal. If something interests me, it's hard for me to let it go. Stuff that I'm thinking about right now that I spend five minutes or ten minutes or twenty minutes searching around on, learning about might be the next book. I live my life in those rabbit holes, and it often is a giant distraction and whatever but it's fun.

I think some of the best journalists are those who can't sleep at night because they're thinking about a million different things. It's a blessing and a curse, I guess.

Correct me if I'm wrong, but you were still working at the *Tampa Bay Times* when you started researching this book. Is that correct?

That's correct. I left the *Times* in October of 2017, and the manuscript was due to Little, Brown on December 12 of that same year, so it was my first experience not having to punch a clock and write a book in extra time. I started writing the manuscript in early October and finished on deadline, and it was fantastic. It's so much better this way. Doing *Grandma Gatewood's Walk* and *The Leper Spy*, I'd work all day, and then, I'd come home at night and put the kids in bed and go write for five or six hours, and it's like burning the midnight oil, and it's exhausting, and I would come home and find that I'd lost any creative energy, and so I'd have to try to tap that creative energy. It became a big burden, and I felt like I was going crazy. This break was timely and perfect, and, for the first time, I had a fun time writing a book.

What was it like to go from a daily newspaper reporter to someone who is now a book author?

It was a little scary at first, but I'm lucky that *Grandma Gatewood's Walk* was a successful book, and so financially, I can afford to do this finally. It's been pretty rewarding so far. Because I was interested in doing this, I took a job teaching at the University of Montana, where I've been the T. Anthony Pollner Professorship. It's an endowed professorship, and they bring in a new working journalist every semester to teach one class that he or she designs and to advise the student newspaper. It's been dreamy. I hope I can make this work for a long time because this is quite the life.

You're advising the student newspaper. I did it for eight years in Ohio, and I'm back to advising the student newspaper here at Fairfield University. I did not realize how much I missed it the two years that I wasn't doing it. What's that like for you, and what are those student journalists doing?

I am teaching a class called investigative storytelling, and so I've encouraged my fourteen students to pursue one story that had some impact. I've been essentially teaching them how to do investigative storytelling that people will read when it comes right down to it, and then, the student paper is called the *Montana Kaimin,* and it's made up of a paid staff. It's totally independent, so they do their own thing; they come up with their own stories. They write their own stories. They edit their own stories. I'm there to provide encouragement and feedback and maybe save them from themselves every once in a while, but they did some cool stuff, and I can't stop the idea generation. I have little curiosities like I did as a newspaper reporter, and now, I have a gaggle of students who can go chase down the answers for me. I have to bring it to their pitch meeting, and they've actually turned a couple of my ideas into stories that I think are great. I get tickled by it.

Vann R. Newkirk II

Vann R. Newkirk is a journalist for the *Atlantic* whose work tells the story of America through the lens of race, class, geography, finding lines through politics and health care and justice. One of his most well-known pieces is groundbreaking work on Black farmers in the Mississippi Delta having their land stolen, decade after decade, century after century, and he combines a rigorous re-creation of the paper trail with a series of unforgettable characters.

It's truly generation-defining work. He grew up in North Carolina and attended college at Morehouse. After finishing his undergraduate, he got a master's Degree in public health from the University of North Carolina at Chapel Hill. His podcast, *Floodlines*, takes listeners on a journey into the New Orleans left behind fifteen years after Katrina, finding a new way to tell a story we all thought we knew. That ultimately is his calling card, whether he's writing a story or building an audio one. He is forever showing new Americas, building brick by brick, narrative by narrative, the nation where we would all like to one day call home.

Newkirk was interviewed in 2022.

How do you go from a studying public health to a writing career, and, as a follow-up, did your doctor father want to kill you?

I can take the follow-up first. Hell yeah. I mean, you gotta understand, the public health thing was, that was the first rebellion. I was supposed to be a doctor. I was the first one on either side not born on the farm or in a shotgun house, right? So like it was supposed to be, you get good grades, you go out, and, if not a lawyer, you'd be a doctor. And so I didn't wanna do that. I got as far as like applying to med school, taking the MCAT and applying to med school and realized, you know, I was only doing it because it was what I was supposed to do.

So along the way, I'd taken public health classes with a guy, Bill Jenkins. He was one of the first Black folks in the CDC. And he helped like dismantle the Tuskegee study. So I was like, yeah, I like working with him. He really was a big influence in my life. And I said, "Okay, well, maybe if I don't wanna do medicine, I can try out what Dr. Jenkins does." And there's also a chance to go back home. I went to Carolina for public health school, met the woman who's now my wife there, and I was supposed to go out.

The idea was to get a PhD. So with a master's you have to go and work in the real world. You get a master's, you work for three or four years, you come back and get a PhD. That's how it usually works. So I have a master's candidacy to work for a think tank. The idea was to go back in three or four or five years, get a PhD. But while I was there, a whole lot of different things were, were happening. And I'd been freelancing, just because it was an easy way to make money for somebody who could put subjects and verbs together.

Did you like doing it?

In college, I didn't really care much for it. It really was like they needed a blurb. I was going to concerts for people now are big. I remember one show is Big K.R.I.T., it's like his first show in Atlanta. And there were legit, you know, twenty-five people in the crowd.

But in grad school, I started blogging more with a couple of friends. I wasn't bad at writing. And then I actually did enjoy that.

How did this become a career instead of a hobby?

I realized I really enjoyed it. I liked interviewing people especially. And so it got to the point where like I was freelancing twenty hours a week, working forty, fifty hours a week in a real job. And my wife, who was my girlfriend, she had a good job. And she was like, "You, you should be working one job, and you should take the chance to try it."

Describe the phone call with your father.

(Laughs) Uh, so, um, it was . . . I didn't really tell him.

What was the overlap between public health and journalism?

My first actual full-time journalism [job] was public health. I was writing things that were kind of public health adjacent because Kaiser didn't want me to write about my day job. So the thing that was the most adjacent, too, was: How are people living? How are they getting the groceries? How are they getting their food? When I went to go work for Daily Kos, we were on the earlier side of covering Flint. And that was mostly because people from the CDC and from public health world were like, "You should, you know, really be looking at this thing happening in Flint."

How did you get so good at finding public documents?

I think about public health school. A lot of our work was problem solving, and it was like historical problems on it. So why does this health center have worse outcomes [than] the one down the street, right? If you could look and find an incident like a race riot in the past in that neighborhood, things click. If you're looking at foreclosures, you can tell a place that's gonna be on the downswing in terms of health. A lot of it is pulling strings. So I did already have the basic skills. I knew how to call a county registrar.

What do you think you missed out on by not going to a traditional journalism school, and what do you think you actually gained?

Number one, I didn't know what the hell "тк" meant for a long time. I mean, that's like the basic mechanics of just how to interact with an editor, how to take edits, how to turn around quickly. I default to sports metaphors a lot. A good journalist is like a Tim Duncan, right? He has practiced from every single angle, every single entry pass and knows exactly what he's gonna do and how the ball is going in, right? And you gotta be at that level in order to be able to turn around copy fast. I didn't have that at first. And so a lot of it really was like, I was going home even while I was working. And I was going and taking apart stories, reading, and going to the library. Remember the library? Finding old magazines, finding stories, bringing home as many as possible and, like, actually diagramming. Here's the lead.... Here's how it reconnects to the kicker.

What stories or writers became north stars for you?

So the thing I always wanted to do was *The Case for Reparations*. People remember, obviously, the title, it's *The Case for Reparations*. But the amount of reporting he does . . . He makes the case in a way that nobody has ever done it before, which is, he's establishing a chain of responsibility, right? And I thought that was a useful thing to do, whether I'm making a big case for reparations or whether I'm showing that New Orleans is at fault for lead poisoning.

I thought that was a really good and useful. The other, I don't know if you've read *The Making of the Atomic Bomb* by Richard Rhodes. It's a history of the Manhattan Project. You learn about how to split a fucking atom [*laughs*]. You learn about how the early pogroms in Eastern Europe sent the Jews to universities in Germany, then the Holocaust moved them out to New York. And you see how that becomes a brain trust for [the] Manhattan Project. Every single piece of the story gets told and woven together this really amazing way. I think it's just awesome.

Those were the standards though. The first pieces that I really tried

to read to understand how this works: *The Warmth of Other Suns.*
And also *Hiroshima* by John Hersey.

With your education you could do a lot of jobs. Why this one?

What I tell people today is, if I have a question about the world, I
get paid money to go ask people about it. You can't beat it. You can't
beat it.

Tell me how the Mississippi Delta land theft story came to be.

So as I said before, my mother was born in a shotgun house in
Greenville, Mississippi. My father was born on a hog farm in Eliz-
abethtown, North Carolina. So I grew up with the stories of Black
farmers on my father's side. My mother's side was mostly sharecrop-
pers, not a whole lot of people who owned much, but I grew up on
both sides, like one side that has been dispossessed forever, and had
these stories of working in a white man's land. In my dad's side, I had
so many stories of people who were like the last nub of the family to
hold on to family land. So even as a kid, I saw, okay, that field that's
across them behind Uncle Lonnie's field used to be your aunt Thelia's
field, but they fell behind on the taxes, and now, it's the sheriff's field.

Those stories were at my life's core. I grew up slopping hogs, and
I used to have to go and run around behind this really mean gander
that I hated.

My mother was the first to go to school. My dad was the first to
leave town and not come back. So I had all these questions about
how they came to be. And the story of dispossession of Black farmers
kept popping up. I kept hearing these stories just matter-of-factly,
you know, "Oh, USDA came and took that."

I think, especially in lots of Black spaces, you have barber shops,
churches, you hear this idea of like the capital P plan, right? And it's
kind of like the Jeremiah Wright thing. If you were to say that in

2007, people would look at you like you were crazy, like you were a conspiracy theorist. The more I looked into it, the more I thought about it, the more I saw that there was something there. This was not an intuition. They were real. There's a real paper trail.

So I carried the idea to do something about that with me for years and was between stories and finally told my editor at the *Atlantic*, "Why don't I just look at Black farming for a bit." To their credit, they let me do it.

How did your family react when you sent them the story?

My dad gloated a little bit. He was like, "Yeah, you become your old man." My mother's side, it really resonated with them. There's a couple of posters behind me, a stack behind one, but the poster behind this one is at the cover. And it's a Black farmer from Mississippi on the cover. And they're like, we never thought that would happen. My grandmother was just . . . she cried. I've seen that woman cry a handful of times [in] my life. It was interesting because after I did it, so many other family stories, just started being unlocked. I was just talking to people. It was things that I think they never thought other people would think important.

So my grandfather—my mother's father, he is from [the] Greenwood area. And I just remember having a conversation with him about the story. And he was telling me about how, I got people, going way back, who are holy men out in the fields, because a lot of them didn't have true brick-and-mortar churches. A lot of people did a ministry in the fields. We had people he knew as a kid who did that. You know, he was one of the first black people in the county to ride a damn school bus.

The past isn't dead.

Yeah, yeah. And just always thinking about him going to Vietnam, what that meant and why he chose to go. He said, "You understand that that was the way out." My grandfather has a body shop in Fayetteville, North Carolina. Fort Bragg. He was in the Eighty-Second Airborne. That's a big story. So there's all these stories. I mean, my grandmother is one of, she's one of seventeen. He's one of eighteen. And, you know, my phone was full of people [*laughs*].

What's your process between the end of reporting and the beginning of writing?

I outline a lot. A lot of my outlines end up being longer than a story. A lot of the first round, especially if I'm doing something, like the Black farmer story, where I needed to find people who were the face of the thing, a lot of the first round is like casting almost: going through, looking at the facts of people's lives, looking at people who carry parts of the story. So I'm looking through people stories. Trying to find out who has both the facts and the voice to carry it.

Then what?

I get this from James Fallows and from my editor, Cullen Murphy. There are a lot of different ways the story can end up. A lot of fancy stuff you can do. You can start in the middle; you can start in the end. But the first thing I always do is: Where am I starting, where am I ending, and how do I get from here to here? That's the second step for me in the outline. And then how I actually start to writing is from there. Which of these things is the most readable or the best anecdote that I can get literary with? So for the Black farmer story, that one obviously started in the middle. More toward the end than anything.

You do a lot of podcast work, and I'm curious if there are things that form of storytelling can do that a written piece cannot?

I think it's easy to overlook the obvious things. On a podcast, you can hear people's voices. For me as a southerner, somebody who's interested in language, that's important to me. I think back when there was a whole lot of debate and controversy over how white writers should write how Black southerners—especially those really close to sharecropping and slavery—spoke. And to me, one way that you can get around that debate is if you had recordings. And I really dearly wish we had more recordings of Black people.

I'm doing a show now, and a lot of what we're doing now is focused on D.C. I wanna be able to hear D.C. I wanna be able to hear what it's like. And that's probably hardest in writing, to capture sound as a sense.

I think you can get a more natural sense of emotion, especially if you're trying to do work to connect unfamiliar readers or listeners to a place or to a people. I think you have a couple gifts in audio that you don't have in print. You would have to lean on analogy so much if you're writing a new setting for people who've never been there. Like, if I'm trying to explain to you what it's like to go work in a hog processing plant. You've never been inside a plant, generally. What do I start [with]?

I can say the ceilings are yay high. You can see the carcasses held down by the chains. But if I walk you in there, even with just a recorder, and you hear these chains swing, and you hear the rippers going through the insides, and you hear people shouting, I think it gives you just more of a three-dimensional space. Then you add on to that the emotion, which is the most important part of audio. If I'm talking to a politician for print, I can't really get that. You can lie to me. But I'm doing it for tape, every time somebody swallows or takes a breath before they answer or you can hear 'em tear up or something . . .

Silence matters.

Silence. You get so much more context for emotional cues. In audio, for a story like this, that's gold because the basics of the history are known. We know Hurricane Katrina happened. We've got lots of good history books about what happened with the uprisings after King's assassination. We know roughly what happened. Well, we don't know, what we don't have is what it's like to be a fourteen-year-old and being in the middle of that crowd.

Let's end on craft. Anything else you do between reporting and writing?

I am never done reporting, and that's my problem. Usually I just get to a point, and my editors are like, "Hey, uh . . .

I'm gonna need a draft.

'. . . a story?" . . . Yeah.

Bradford Pearson

Bradford Pearson is a freelance writer, author of *The Eagles of Heart Mountain: A True Story of Football, Incarceration, and Resistances in World War II America*. Pearson has been an editor at *Southwest: The Magazine* and *D Magazine*. *The Eagles of Heart Mountain* is about the best high school football team in Wyoming's history, a team of incarcerated Japanese American teenagers during World War II. Pearson used the story of the Eagles to tell the story of Japanese American life during World War II. He stumbled upon it researching an article for *Cowboys and Indians* magazine in 2013. He traveled to Yellowstone National Park. While there, the person who helped him set up the trip asked if he wanted to visit a museum near Heart Mountain. He learned there was a concentration camp there. He saw a display telling a small part of the story of the high school football team. "That line about the football team ate at me," Pearson says.

He went on to other journalism jobs but couldn't stop thinking about what he saw. He started researching. He learned about the camp's weekly newspaper, found an archive with the issues. "So it had a thorough newspaper. These had thorough game accounts," Pearson says. "I started digging for who the best players were. . . . It snowballed. This was something bigger than what I envisioned."

Pearson has also written for the *New York Times*, *Esquire*, *Time*, and *Salon*, a piece for *Philadelphia Magazine* about being kidnapped as a college student. He ultimately visited one of the kidnappers.

I've talked with Pearson twice, in 2015, about his piece on being kidnapped, and in 2021, about the book.

The Eagles of Heart Mountain is your first book. What's it about?

The best high school football team in the history Wyoming; a group of incarcerated Japanese Americans during World War II. I tried to use the story to tell the story of Japanese American life during the war. I started it in Los Angeles and Mountain View, California. I followed the players to camps in California then Wyoming. The end of the book looks at their lives after the war. It was an opportunity to expand the main narrative and talk about 1940s America, the war, a country losing its moral way.

How did you land upon this story?

In spring 2013, I had a freelance assignment from this magazine, *Cowboys and Indians*. They asked if I wanted to go to Yellowstone for a week to write about Yellowstone. I was twenty-nine, had gotten fired from another journalism job, had nothing to do. I was like, okay.

I went out and worked on the story about Yellowstone. Heart Mountain is at the eastern entrance of the park. One day I was there, and someone that helped coordinate the trip asked if I wanted to go to this small museum where Heart Mountain camp used to be.

I grew up in New York, was taught the broad strokes of Japanese American incarceration in school. I thought, I'll go learn more. I was dumbfounded by how little I knew about this chapter on World War II history. There's a small phrasing on one of the museum's displays I won't say exactly because it gives away the book's ending. It talks about this concentration camp's high school football team; it was interesting. They were very good. That stuck in my head. That was in June 2013; the story came out months later. I mentioned the museum and a sidebar about Yellowstone then didn't think about it.

What brought you back to it?

That line about the football team ate at me. Eventually I got other jobs but couldn't get that sentence out of my head. I started researching the camp and found it had a weekly newspaper. I realized it had a sports section. The Heart Mountain camp had about eleven thousand people. When it was open, it was the third largest city in Wyoming, an unbelievable statistic. So it had a thorough newspaper. These had thorough game accounts. I started digging for who the best players were and their families.

Where did you find the newspapers?

There's an online repository, a nonprofit called Densho in Seattle, with copies. They're dedicated to teaching and remembrance of Japanese American incarceration. They were helpful. There was a man, Bacon Sakatani, an amateur historian who was at Heart Mountain as a kid. He has a digital version of every one of the papers. He sent me a CD with the newspapers. I was able to go through them at my own pace. I would go through each, and in one Word document type out every story about the team or athletics or that mentioned anybody on the team. I created a searchable document that allowed me to have time and place for every player while they were in camp and see how the team changed over the years, what these players were doing outside the team, and the other parts of the camp the newspaper deemed newsworthy.

When did you start thinking this was going to be a book?

There's a lot of people who have this career and think their goal is to write a book. I never saw that for me, but once I started seeing this was a bigger story, beyond a football team, I knew it was a book. There was too much history I needed about why these people were sent to Wyoming and not only who these players were but who their parents were and what they experienced and what all these players experienced.

These guys grew up in Hollywood or Mountain View or Seattle. I needed to write what their lives were like as American teenagers in December 1941. I needed to expand this idea bigger than anything I've done or thought that I'm capable of. I called my agent. I had two possible book ideas. I told him this idea. He said, you need to do this.

Had you done research in historical archives for nonfiction before this?

Not to this scale or in terms of taking multiple trips to different archives, being in different cities, states, booking things, digging through boxes. I've always enjoyed looking for that needle in the haystack idea that ties things together.

There are a couple things in this book I found through a combination of interviews and digging; stuff you spend six months trying to find and ends up being one sentence. I was in the National Archives; I was in archives in Wyoming, UCLA. There are digitized archives at UC Berkeley, Washington State; a few other colleges and universities were helpful. What helped me fill out a lot of their lives is over the course of the seventies, eighties, and nineties, a few of them did oral histories for different organizations and colleges. I was able to use their oral histories to fill out their stories, then fill out some of the time in camp, get a sense of who these guys were, listen to them, and see video of them, even in their seventies. I couldn't pull that from a box score.

There was a set of photos that helped you put together what life was like.

There were two photographers at Heart Mountain. There's some famous photos Ansel Adams took; Dorothea Lange came through. But there were lots of other folks incarcerated. After a while, when the War Relocation Authority allowed folks who were incarcerated cameras, you started to get a sense of who they were, what their lives were like. They weren't staged photos, weren't taken by the War Relocation Authority. There are lots of photos at the National Archives, the Library of Congress, but they're formal. There were a few sets of photos taken by incarcerees I was able to use. Whenever I needed additional color, wherever I needed to get a sense of what a high school dance was like, or working the sugar beet fields, being able to pull up different photos helped fill in a lot of gaps.

Were you able to interview any of the players, and if so, what was that like?

One player, Keiichi Ikeda, who [lives] in Los Angeles. It's interesting, none of these folks I wrote about saw what they achieved on this team as worthy of news or a book. They saw themselves as teenagers playing football. What they did was cool, pretty brave; it inspired a lot of people that had nothing to inspire them for four years. There were times there were eleven thousand people at the camp, and five thousand of them would come watch a game. It was one of the first times in my life I felt I was talking with someone and trying to explain to them what they did, why it was bigger than what they imagined.

You did so much research for this book, archival, but also talking with people. How did you start thinking about how the story would be framed?

I did a lot of research before the proposal, but as soon as I got the book deal, in March of 2018, I read for months: good books, oral histories, watched oral history videos. I read bad books because I didn't want to repeat their mistakes. I read Michelle Malkin, who wrote a book called *In Defense of Internment.* I was like, let me see what this shit is about.

You see ways people have told this story, good or bad. You see where your story fits in, not my story, the story of the Eagles and their families, where you want to line your story up. I saw a way to reach a new audience, tell this story. There's folks who have written memoirs from camp, there are academic books; there aren't many narrative stories. I knew that. That's what I wanted to do. As a white guy, I could tell this story and have it reach an audience that hadn't heard it before. If I could hook this story on football and World War II, I could convince somebody to pull it off the shelf who might not have reached for a story that was, on the cover, a story about Japanese American incarceration. That's an unfortunate reality.

When you were writing, how did you handle the endnotes without losing writing momentum?

I was bad at the beginning. I was angry with myself for not being better with it. Eventually, it becomes second nature. I wrote this sentence, or wrote this paragraph, threw in a comment on the side what the source material is, whether that's a book and a page number, a document, a photo, or a page in an interview with a time note. There's times you write one sentence, there's times you write five hundred words, look back, and say, okay, before you go eat lunch or go to the bathroom—here's a note.

As I was doing endnotes, I saw as the book went along, there were more and more endnotes I'd left [out]. That was when I got better at it. I remember something Sarah Weinman said on Twitter: basically it sucks when you're doing it, but you're going to pat yourself on the back because you were smart about it at the beginning. If I ever write another book, I'll be much smarter about it at the beginning. There's times when you're writing, you're like I know where that came from. You're not that smart. You're not going to be able to remember that six months or eight months later when you're pulling your hair out.

Did you change any writing processes for this much bigger piece of writing?

The book process is harder because you're writing for six straight months or whatever. Sometimes at the end of the day you just want to get one thousand words down and it's garbage, but you know you did it. I tend to be a quick writer after I've done my reporting. That was not the case with the book; that was frustrating. I felt I was beating my head against the wall. How do I translate a four-thousand- or a five-thousand-word story into a ninety-thousand-word story?

Eventually, you realize your tone and style is going to be different, because you can't keep that pace up. There's ways you can write scenes and chapters that closely reflect your actual style; maybe some people can keep that up. The first three chapters were due about a year before the whole book, to make sure I wasn't screwing up. After writing those, I didn't write for six months because I got back into research. When I jumped back into it, to jumpstart my process I wrote a chapter I wanted to, but I knew it acts as a standalone. I wrote it out of order so I could write something I knew would be fun to write, writing that helped me get back into the flow.

How much book work did you have to do when you and your wife and young kids were cooped up in your house because of the pandemic, and how did you get it done?

The first draft was due December 15, 2019. I got my edits back by the end of January. I was going through those. By Monday, March 16, our daycare was closed; everything was shutting down in Philadelphia.

I got my first wave of edits back. It was hard. My wife, an attorney, makes most of our money, so managing her career, two children, and the pressure that comes with writing your first book was crazy difficult. The thing about COVID I've found actually a bit calming is the knowledge everybody is going through something. Some people have kids; that's hard. Some people are alone; that's hard. Some people are seventy; they have to deal with a sick spouse. That was my mantra whenever something was bad. Unless you're super rich, you're going through something right now.

My wife and I split up the days. One of us worked in the morning, one, the afternoon; we both worked at night. I was lucky I wasn't sitting there having to write the draft. I know there's lots of folks doing that. It's been nine months and the book world hasn't stopped; there's people having to write entire books with their kids under their desks or on a computer or whatever their situation. I was lucky I got most of this done right before everything shut down.

That said, when I had to do my endnotes, that was hard. That's not necessarily writing; it's somewhat mindless in terms of having information at your disposal, as long as you've kept good notes, but it's still double-checking. My notes were due around [the] beginning of June. That was the first time that we broke down, and my wife took the kids to her parents' house in Maryland. I was able to do the endnotes, I worked sixteen- to seventeen-hour days and did it in three days straight because I knew they were going to come back.

Are you freelancing again now [that] the book is complete?

Right now, it's a weird time because there's so much promotional stuff that goes on, doing interviews, keeping track with your publicist and marketing people at Atria, Simon and Schuster. I've been freelancing, but I'm not doing journalism. I have a side gig for a content marketing department doing slideshows and information about life insurance policies. It pays well.

I was going to say, it no doubt pays better than freelance journalism at this point.

It does. That was some of the work that I did while writing the book, mostly because it helped me put my mind at ease. It's nice to have your brain work in a completely different way and know that you're getting paid well. I probably won't do as much of that come spring, when I realize I have to get back into the job market. But I never begrudge anyone that works in our field who has to find another way to pay their bills because our field, less and less, is paying bills. I know some people either look down on it or think there's something unethical about it. From my perspective, I've never done anything in that part of my life that has come close to interacting with the work I do in journalism. I've never considered it to be a dilemma for myself. I know it helps pay my kids' daycare bills and helps put money away for them for college and our retirement. If it keeps me being able to have money while I work on freelance stuff, or another book idea, I don't know anyone [who] can begrudge it.

Do you have any tips for college students who might be looking to do freelance journalism and possibly write a book?

You get to tell other people's stories for a living; there's a certain level of respect and dignity you have to have for sources. Use everything at your disposal. When I wrote *Eagles*, I had a bunch of stuff I couldn't put in the book. It just so happened I had a couple ideas: a *New York Times* editor reached out to me. They were doing a special section about the end of World War II, and they were like, do you have any story ideas? That's how I got my first two *Times* bylines, thinking about a story I want to tell in a slightly different way.

In 2015, you wrote a piece for *Philadelphia Magazine* about a time you were kidnapped. What happened?

In March 2006, I walked off campus, was robbed, and thrown in the back of a car, kidnapped. The story goes from there. In the story there's a lot about that first night, but it also talks about what happened in the years after, emotionally, mentally, moving on with life. It scoots back to me reaching out to two of the men that kidnapped me.

I went to a prison in northeast Pennsylvania, met with them over a couple of days, trying to find out about their lives before the kidnapping and what life was like for nine years in a penitentiary.

When you were in college, were you studying journalism?

I studied international relations. Sophomore year I was on the rowing team and got injured. I wasn't going to be able to keep up, come back, and thought, newspapers sound fun. I started covering sports for the school newspaper and eventually picked up an English minor with a concentration in writing.

I'm curious how long after this happened did you start thinking this was something you might write about?

Twelve hours. I got home from the police station late the next night. I talked to my parents, my roommates. The next day everything started spreading on campus. I had an assignment due for literary journalism. It was supposed to be a reported feature. I talked to the professor and said, "Hey, I think I should write about this night instead." The next day I wrote down everything I remembered. I eventually pieced something together.

When did you decide to try and get this published?

Two years ago. At that point, it was a five-thousand-word essay, which to people other than me isn't that interesting. You don't learn anything about me. You don't learn about the guys. It's this somewhat strange night, terrible, but nobody else could learn anything. I started thinking about ways to make it better. I wanted to try to talk to the kidnappers.

What was it like psychologically to write this knowing it was going to be published?

I thought I was past it. I had no idea how I would react the first time I saw them. That made it difficult to write or at least going into the prison the first day. When you know you're going to be writing about yourself, you wonder how much of what's going through your head is you as a victim of a crime reacting or you as someone who's eventually going to write this story creating the script in your mind. I wanted to be levelheaded, go in, and be the strong person I thought I was.

Andrea Pitzer

Andrea Pitzer is a journalist most interested in unearthing lost history. She's authored three books, the most recent of which is *Icebound: Shipwrecked at the Edge of the World*. The book narrates three Arctic voyages from the late 1500s taken by the Dutchman William Barents. *Icebound* ultimately tells the story of the final trip, when Barents and his men were stranded on Nova Zembla in 1596.

All three of Pitzer's books have been focused on the past. Her first book, *The Secret History of Vladimir Nabokov*, looks at the author's life and works and uses information from declassified intelligence files and recovered military history to show how Nabokov hid his own disturbing history in his fiction. Pitzer's second book was *One Long Night: A Global History of Concentration Camps*.

Her work on *Icebound* included three trips to the Arctic. Dutch historians, she says, have spent forty years looking at Barents. There are also some people who have examined the relics from the trips. But rarely do those people overlap.

"Not that many people who handled the relics and looked in the archives have also gone to where [William] Barents's cabin was in the High Arctic," Pitzer says. "What is the thing that I can do that nobody else can do? I want to have a story that not everybody can tell. I want to give people something that's interesting."

In 2009, Pitzer founded Nieman Storyboard, a website dedicated to narrative nonfiction and part of the Nieman Foundation for Journalism at Harvard.

Pitzer left Nieman Storyboard in 2012, when she was working on her first book, but the website has continued to thrive.

I talked with Pitzer in January 2021.

Can you tell me about your book _Icebound_?

It is the story of a Dutch navigator named William Barents and his three voyages to the Arctic at the end of the sixteenth century. Each one gets a little more complicated, and the last one, they end up stuck for the winter in the High Arctic. At a basic level, it's a pretty amazing survival story.

All three of your books are historical nonfiction narratives, but this tells a story from more than four centuries ago. How did you learn about it, and what made you want to write a book about it?

There's three answers to that. I'll try to do each of them briefly. The way I first heard about this story was when I was writing my first book, which was called _The Secret History of Vladimir Nabokov_. In that book, there's a mystery kingdom in one of the Nabokov novels. It's obviously invented. It's called Zembla. A big part of my book was figuring out what Zembla was. The most obvious first answer is that there were these islands north of Russia, called Novaya Zemlya. I went into the history of these islands, and that's where four-hundred-and-some years ago, these guys were stranded. In surveying the entire history of these pretty remote islands, I came across this story. It's one paragraph in my first book, but I always thought I might come back around to it.

The other two answers, which are also relevant, is my second book was the history of concentration camps or detention of civilians. There were concentration camps on six continents during the twentieth century. That was a pretty harrowing book to write, so my second answer for why this book is, there were no concentration camps. I wanted to do something that would let my brain move into a different space and still try to reconcile myself to that second book.

The third reason is I'm interested when I'm doing narrative nonfiction in how we tell stories and what stories we decide to tell. I like to pick things that are difficult to do, and it seems to me that to reconstruct a narrative account from more than four hundred years ago, without overinterpreting, without assigning feelings and emotions that we don't know these guys had, without having a free hand, trying to stick to the history. I wanted the challenge of trying to tell that story because I thought there was still enough there to make it powerful.

The main character in the book is William Barents. He's the explorer who goes on three missions into the Arctic. How did you gather information about him?

We actually don't know a lot about his early life. We know that he was a sailor. We know that he became a respected navigator. He did the first comprehensive mapping of the Mediterranean Sea. He was married, and he had several children. Then he was part of these three Arctic missions. That's what he became legendary for. In terms of diving into the characters of the book, there wasn't a ton of material. I almost had to make their interactions with the place, have the place be an additional character, and then feed off of that.

Characterization was unusual with this book because I characterize them often as a group, which you don't see in narrative nonfiction. You're peeling off these individuals. Certainly, Barents is the heart of this. He's the guy that was on all three of these voyages. We see certain characteristics, certain stubbornness, a certain belief that he's right about the navigation chart and where people should be going and what's the best route to take. We do get pieces of his personality there. But a lot of times what's happening in the book is happening to a whole group of people at once, which I liked as a challenge.

It was important to me to go to the Arctic multiple times, in order to be able to characterize that place and understand what it would be like to be stuck there for the winter for almost a year.

A lot of the reporting is archival work. On your website, it says that you feel most at home in libraries. What is it about libraries and archives that give you that feeling?

It's incredible to go in and see documents, handle items, or get close to the items if they're not handleable, and see what's available. At the Rijksmuseum in Amsterdam, which I went to twice for this book, there was a collection of artifacts from their cabin that had been rescued centuries later and are now in the holdings of the museum. On my first trip there, I saw a bunch of them in the glass cabinets. But last year, I wanted to go back. I made an appointment with the curator who was in charge of those, and it turned out there were a whole bunch of other relics in the depot that they had in storage. He took me there and got them out. We had them on a table in front of us. I could gently, sometimes with gloves and sometimes without, depending on what we were handling, actually touch and see these things that are sometimes even described in the journal. That was an amazing way to connect. I see that as archival material too. Instead of a piece of paper, it's an object.

I felt the same way about the pieces of paper. The Library of Congress—I live just outside D.C.—it's convenient for me to go there, and they had an early folio of the man who went on to have the voyages with Barents and also wrote about it, a record of his that came out within a year or two of when they actually made the voyages. You go to the Library of Congress, get your researcher card, and you don't have to be anybody particularly special. You have to be legit, but you don't have to be famous or have a PhD, and you get this researcher card, and you can go in, and I was able to handle, again, under supervision, this book from 1600 that is an account of the voyages. Looking at that and seeing the original artwork from that, it connects you to that time. Both are so critical in this book. It gives you little details that otherwise you wouldn't have.

When you are looking at that material, how do you take notes? I know some archives I've been in say no cameras and no pens.

I could write a long feature on crazy archive adventures. I was talking about this book from 1600, and by the way, that was written in old Dutch and I couldn't read old Dutch, but I could use a phone camera with no flash, and so I took hundreds of pictures of everything close up. There was a pencil because they didn't want a pen anywhere near these books, and I could write some things down, but mostly it was photo documentation. I have found that in recent years, most archives, if you aren't causing them trouble, are pretty flexible about using nonflash cameras, which is a godsend. I can't tell you how many archives I've come home [from] with two thousand photos and I have to go and sort them, but I'm so lucky to have that.

At one point in *Icebound*, you describe a detailed layout of a ship. How did you do that?

I was super lucky. On my second Arctic expedition, two people who were crew on it were Dutch. And they introduced me to some guys they knew who were building a replica of William Barents's ship. I got in touch with them. I went inside the ship. It didn't have its mast yet, but it was floating in the water. I could actually go stand in that space.

Where did the trips into the Arctic come into play?

I went three times. It's important to me to go to these places if I can. Dutch historians have spent forty years looking at William Barents. They're going to know that material and know Dutch history in a way I can't, so I'm happy to synthesize with my nonfiction stuff. I'm happy to play reporter and bring together a bunch of different ideas and hopefully say something new about them. The thing I can add that maybe those historians don't have a chance to do is to tie that together with being in that physical place. Not that many people who handled the relics and looked in the archives have also gone to where [William] Barents's cabin was in the High Arctic, so I feel like that's—what's the phrase?—value added. What is the thing that I can do that nobody else can do? I want to have a story that not everybody can tell.

A couple other people told me about the Arctic Circle Residency. I applied for that. By this point, I had the book contract. With that, we sailed on a tall ship up around Svalbard. I got to learn how to hold the sails and belay them. It's not exactly the same kind of ship that Barents had. It was actually a bigger ship, and the sails were arranged differently. But I spent as much time as I could at the top of the mast, staying up there for an hour or two. I loved it. It was wonderful. To imagine the first guy that had a recorded history of seeing that same shoreline, that was a wonderful thing.

While I was in Svalbard, they had re-created Barents's hut. I could go and take pictures. It's like the physical version of the archives. They made a version of this cabin, and so getting to know how many paces is it across—how cool was it? What does it feel like to be inside it? I got all this other sensory detail.

How did you make it to the actual ruins?

I'd always wanted to go to the ruins of the cabin, but that's a lot tougher, because it's the Russian Arctic. It's not too far from some military installations, and Russia is pretty serious about all that stuff. I lucked out. A friend of mine recommended me to somebody at this exploration company, and we had an expedition to go to the ruins of Barents's cabin. It was phenomenal to go there and stand on that little spit of land where their cabin was. It gave me so much insight. When I came home, I shut myself up in a little tiny room we have upstairs, and I was furiously trying to capture that feeling of being out on that desolate strip of land.

Once you've got all this information from archives, and you've got the three trips that you took up to the Arctic, how do you organize everything so you can write a book?

I had written some of it before I left, and that was helpful because I already knew where I had gaps and holes and what needed to be filled in. What I hear again and again from reporters and people who write books is to have a timeline to start with. If you're not telling it chronologically, that timeline is still going to help you keep it straight. If you're breaking up or doing some unusual structure, you'll at least have a second parallel thing that you can be looking at. This was told pretty much in straight chronological structure, so it's a little simpler. Then it's, where are the chapter breaks going to be?

It's daunting to write a book. You just have to do it, but how do you even start? For me, it's what's my timeline? What's going in the first chapter, what's going in the second chapter. And then from there, to say, what are the subthemes that I'm working on that I want to come back and touch again? It's almost like making recipes for each chapter, which elements need to be present. Then I break it down into, what is this section about? I tend to write in sections. You can have an 800- to maybe 1,800-word section, and be like, that's what I'm writing today. I'm going to make this good. I'm going to make a nice draft of this today. That's a newspaper article. I can do that.

I'd love to talk about your work on Nieman Storyboard, which you helped launch in 2009. How did the whole site come about?

My husband was a Nieman fellow, and we had two children. We still have them. They were little then; my daughter was not even a year old. My son was two. I had been home with him a lot. We had jointly tried to figure out what journalism fellowship he could apply for that would have spousal benefits that might help me transition back to the workforce. We had no idea that once we got to the Nieman Foundation, that, not only as we expected, there was childcare, so I could start thinking about other things, but there was their Narrative Digest at that time, and the big narrative conference that the foundation hosted. The conference was short-lived. It went on that year, but then, with the economic crash, there was a lot of budget cutting that happened, and the conference ceased to exist in that form.

I had been doing some work with the Narrative Digest and enjoyed it. I felt like there was this need to think in a bigger way about story. There was always this weekly focus on a narrative that was well done in a newspaper, occasionally a photo essay would be included. I was thinking, why limit it there? Why not documentary, film and books, graphic novels, any true story that tried to be accountable, not loosely accountable to the truth, but trying to adhere to it, expanding it beyond what people think of just newspaper journalism? That's not to belittle newspaper journalism at all. I think the heart of narrative journalism in America has been these newspaper reporters. Unfortunately, with the demise of a lot of newspapers, a lot of that energy has gone to other places. I thought it would be great to look at something that was beyond print, and say, what about this whole idea of anything that's a true story.

They were receptive to it. We launched it in 2009, and I stayed until 2012, when I was finishing my first book and managing the small children and Nieman Storyboard. Trying to finish the book was too much. I love what they've gone on to do since Jacqui Banaszynski is there now. She's a star, and interestingly, I think I introduced her or moderated her panel at the last Nieman Narrative Conference. It's this wonderful loop, that this stellar person from a few years ahead of me, who's done this wonderful work, ended up taking over this project and is doing such a great job with it today.

Since you left as editor of Nieman Storyboard, in your eyes, how has narrative journalism and the industry that supports it changed?

I think it's tough. Every newspaper used to have at least a weekly slot, if not a daily slot, to have a long piece. It's gone. When I was there, dealing with some of the other Nieman staff, there were what I would call in my head "Gimme Stories." That's not putting those stories down at all, but there were formulaic stories that could come out that were important, something that links you to the community. But you also want to see people taking chances with stories, and sometimes those features were important to the community but not necessarily tackling new ways of thinking about story.

I feel like when the papers had all those slots, that was a training ground. That's a place where a good reporter can start and tell a story. Now, you have to scramble to be able to do that on your own. You don't have the benefit of these experienced editors a lot of times. I think it's a lot more wild west to do this type of writing. On the other hand, if you have a voice and you work hard at it, you will find someplace on the internet. You can get your work out there, but it's a lot more of a scramble, and I think the public is in some ways less served.

Do you ever hear from young reporters who want to do narrative journalism, and if so, what do you tell them?

Eva Holland is a wonderful narrative journalist up in Canada. She wrote a great book called *Nerve*. At one point, she volunteered on Twitter to help rising journalists that wanted help, whether it's a pitch letter or working on a story or whatever. So many people responded to her that there was no way she could have done it all, so I wrote to her, and I said, "If you want to give me your overflow, I'll take ten people."

I try to put boundaries around it sometimes. I don't have number one bestsellers. I don't have an infinite amount of money to back me up to give time for other things, but I want to help, and so in fits and spurts, I'll do bunches of people, where I try to help them. For better or worse in this business, if you hustle and you have good ideas, there's no reason you can't have four books. There's no reason that, three to five years from now, somebody couldn't be outselling me.

The problem is the system makes it hard. I was astounded at how some of these young people responded to rejection. First of all, it's almost never about you. I always assumed that it's part good if I got rejected. I'm already partway through this. As soon as you start taking it personally, it will eat you up. My first book was rejected by twelve publishers before we got a bite on it. That's the nature of the beast.

I remember when Gay Talese was talking about pitching some story, and he couldn't get anybody to take it for the longest time. I was like, Gay Talese? You can like Gay Talese or not, but he has a track record. When I read that, I passed it along to a lot of people to say, you have to keep going. If there's a passion project that you have, and you get stuck and cannot get anybody to take it, you set it aside but do not give up on it. There's a reason it's speaking to you. It may come to you that there's another way to approach it. More than once, I have found that ideas I thought couldn't move forward, I came back to later and did something even better. Perseverance is the biggest thing.

Eli Saslow

Eli Saslow is a Pulitzer Prize–winning reporter for the *New York Times* and previously worked for the *Washington Post*. He is known for his ability to embed himself with a person or a family for an extended amount of time and come away with a compelling story that shows how real people are impacted by larger issues such as school shootings, racial inequality, the economy, gun ownership, and more.

As the coronavirus pandemic started coming into focus in March 2020, Saslow realized he wasn't going to be able to do that type of reporting, at least for a while. The result was the as-told-to, first-person oral history series Voices from the Pandemic.

As the country's death toll neared five hundred thousand, Saslow had reported nearly thirty oral histories, the stories of doctors and nurses and coroners, retail workers and restaurant owners, educators, older adults who found themselves isolated and alone, and younger adults who couldn't shake the virus. All appeared on the front page of the *Washington Post*. "It was a form of storytelling that could work for this moment," Saslow says. "These conversations with people were restorative for me. I'm so grateful that I was able to do it."

Saslow's series on food stamps in a postrecession America won the Pulitzer Prize for Explanatory Reporting in 2014. Going into that series Saslow wanted to find a way to dig down and focus on those most impacted by food stamps. This is where Saslow stands out as a reporter, finding ways to convince people to let him into their lives, even when they are going through difficult times. The key, Saslow says, is to be an empathetic person. "The truth is, when you can convince somebody that you care and that what they're dealing with is important and that it matters . . . then that's actually empowering for people."

In addition to the Pulitzer, Saslow has also authored two books: *Ten*

Letters: The Stories Americans Tell Their Presidents, and *Rising Out of Hatred: The Awakening of a White Nationalist.*

I spoke with Saslow twice, in December 2016 about his food stamp series, and again in February 2021 for Nieman Storyboard about Voices from the Pandemic.

How did the Voices from the Pandemic series come about?

I've always been interested in oral histories. I admired this book about Chernobyl called *Voices from Chernobyl* that came out several years ago. Early in the pandemic, it became clear that that was going to be a pretty massive ethical and logistical challenge because in order to do that embedded work, I would be getting on a plane and putting the people I was writing about at some measure of risk.

It began with thinking about, what's a way that I can continue to tell intimate, personal, urgent narrative stories? My editor, David Finkel, and I decided let's try oral histories without necessarily knowing how many there would be or if it would be a thing I would do for a few weeks or for, as it turned out to be, almost a year.

How do you find the people that you end up having as subjects in this series?

It's similar to how I search for stories normally. I thought about what's the current pressure point in the pandemic, what would I want to explore and hear about. One week, I'm seeing in the news a bunch of fights about masks breaking out in retail stores, and then, I realized that the people policing masking in the country are these essential workers, retail clerks who make ten or twelve bucks an hour. That's a character I want to know. Then I'd search through news clips and see who was working when a mask blowup happened, and I'd cold call. I'll have maybe a half dozen initial conversations so once I decide who I'm writing about I'm more prepared for those conversations. I would say it's typically, in this series, I'd be on the phone with somebody for a total of five to ten hours and turn that into a 1,500-word piece.

Do you interview differently compared to how you interview for a more traditional narrative?

I've learned a lot about interviewing on this series because I don't have my other reporting tools. I don't have my eyes. I don't have my sense of place. I'm reliant on conversation. Because of the format of the stories, it's important for me to capture a sense of voice and to bring out what it is that makes their voice unique and makes it feel authentic. That led me to be much less direct in interviewing and to be more patient.

I need clay, and conversations are clay. If somebody wants to keep talking, we keep talking. That gives me more to work with. I learned to take less control, to be more comfortable with letting things wander.

Do you do any other reporting on these pieces, or are they simply long conversations with the subject?

For one story about this guy Burnell, who owned a grocery store in the Lower Ninth Ward, I asked him to FaceTime and put me up on the register so I could get a feel for the store. I would also talk to people around that main character so that I could come back to our next conversation with more information, to refresh the person's memory.

Do you miss the other type of interviewing and reporting that you've done?

Definitely. I've loved this, and I've learned a lot from it, and I'll bring some of these lessons back to my narrative reporting. Meeting people over the phone is great, but it only approximates what reporting is like in person, and for me, the heart of this job is getting to go to places when I feel like something important is happening in people's lives. I'm eager to do that again.

How do you take these extensive transcripts and turn them into a 1,500-word story? How is this different from your more traditionally reported narratives?

What's different is the word choice and sentence level. I have much less control. I print out the transcripts of these conversations, and I start with the highlighter, and I highlight things that stick out to me. Then I start thinking about what's the engine of the story.

One character, Francine Bailey, worked at a nursing home and caught this virus there and then brought it home, and despite her best attempts to isolate, she gave it to her mom, and then her mom died. That was a story about guilt and about the cruel fact that this virus doesn't come from nowhere, it comes from somebody, and in this case, she was sure it had come from her. Then I ask myself, not only am I being accurate but also am I being fair, am I telling the story in a way that is authentic and fair to this person's experience while still giving myself permission to make the journalistic choices that we always make about what are the things that are important to include and what are the things that I can leave out?

So every sentence in these pieces are essentially direct quotes, something that was said at one point during the interviews?

Exactly, but piecemeal. I can't change the clay. The transcripts are the transcripts, with mild editing for clarity; I have to stick with that. I can't put words into somebody's mouth. But what I can do is to storify it.

You're a sculptor right? The subjects give you the clay, and now, you've got to sculpt it.

That's exactly right. That's part of the fun of it. It's easy when you're writing a story to obsess overwriting one sentence seventeen different ways, obsessing over the structure and the pacing and questions like "are we beginning and landing at the right places?" But when it comes down to the sentence-to-sentence level? There's nothing we can do. It was the way they said it. There was some freedom in letting go of that.

Did the subjects get to see the pieces before they were published?

No, we decided that would be giving up too much journalistic control. I need to have the power to decide what parts we're going to quote and what parts are not going to be quoted.

What has it been like for you, mentally and emotionally, to spend so much time talking to people who have experienced the worst of the pandemic?

It can be draining. I spent a lot of the year talking to people who were in the middle of being affected by trauma or who were having a hard time and suffering. I can sometimes hang up the phone and feel wiped out. But these are their stories, and then, I hang up the phone from those conversations and I come back to my fortunate, lucky, little pandemic life, where I have three kids who are happy and healthy and a strong marriage and nobody's sick and we have our house in a safe neighborhood. For the people that I'm hanging up on, they go back to the traumas that don't end when I stop talking to them. The real courage in any act of journalism is always on their end. Although sometimes these stories can take something out of me, they give me so much more. If I hadn't been doing work that felt meaningful to me during this year, I would have felt down about that.

In 2014, you won the Pulitzer Prize in Explanatory Reporting for your food stamp series. A lot of people thought you would win for feature writing for your Newtown story that year. Were you surprised at what ultimately ended up winning?

Mostly I feel grateful to win for anything. Like any prize, there's a huge element of luck and happenstance involved in any of that stuff. If there were two things I wrote over the course of the year that were talked about for something like that, then that's great. That's the best

I can do. If one of them won, that was going to be great too, no matter which one it was. Mostly I'm glad that anybody's paying attention to and recognizing the work.

The Pulitzer winner looked at food stamp usage in a postrecession United States. One of the things that is remarkable about the entire series is that you take something as complex as food assistance in this country and boil it down to six poignant stories. How did the idea for the series come about, and how did you figure out how to tell those stories?

My concern about writing about food stamps was that it's this huge, complicated thing. I'm not an expert in economics, and I can be a little intimidated by these big meaty topics. I wanted to get over that, and one of the lessons in the series for me was that you can write interesting, compelling narratives about anything. If you can break them into manageable ideas, and if you can find compelling characters, good narrative stories can still be done.

I had been paying attention to this continuing rise in the food stamp program and was surprised that as the economy was getting better, in this one place, things were still bad and getting worse. I didn't approach it thinking it would be a series. For me, it started out with that I had one or two ideas that felt to me a little bit new about the food stamp program.

The first was how food stamps had become an economy unto themselves. In a lot of towns, the first of the month was not just a day people were waiting for, but one grocery stores and bankers and everybody was waiting for, because 30 or 40 percent of the town depended on this influx of money.

I'd also heard about recruiters whose job is to go around and promote the program. That felt new to me, and I didn't know much about it. That helped to explain the rise in food stamp spending.

I started on those two pieces. The challenge then was to find people and places that would make those ideas not boring, that would make them feel essential and immediate and would make them stories about people's lives and not about trends in a program.

The first story is about the Rhode Island town where one-third of all the residents receive food stamps or assistance from the federal government. How did you identify that town and start there?

Reporting before you get to the place and do in-person, on-the-ground reporting is an underrated part of reporting for narrative stories because it takes a lot of time. It also can save you so much time to know that you're definitely going to the right place. If you rush into something, you might find out that you're not in the right place. In that instance I spent a day or two breaking down the data. That eliminated a lot of places. I knew that I wanted to go to a place that was still receiving food stamps on the first of the month.

Eventually, I realized that Woonsocket was reflective of this trend. I started calling around Woonsocket asking, "Where were the grocery stores that were experiencing this boom in big, reflective ways?" I talked to probably five little grocery store merchants and then finally picked the grocery store and the place to write about and then set off to go to Rhode Island to do it. It's a huge luxury to have the time to report through the process that way. I think that it is some of the most important reporting.

I imagine that a lot of the people you write about, especially those who are struggling in life, might not want the world to know that they're struggling in life. How do you convince them to let you hang out with them for a while?

You don't want to be doing too much convincing. If you have to work super hard to sell somebody on letting you write about them, with these kinds of stories, if it starts out from a place of hesitancy or uncertainty, there's a pretty good chance that people become more uncertain and that it falls apart as you go. You want to make sure that you're not coercing or working too hard to convince people to be written about. It's not good for them, and it's not good for the story.

The truth is, when you can convince somebody that you care and that what they're dealing with is important and that it matters, that it matters not just to them but it matters to a bigger thing that's happening in the country, then that's actually empowering for people. I'm surprised by how willing people are to open up their lives when they think that it's in good hands. Then the challenge becomes developing the trust to go into all the corners of their lives and make sure that I get it right so that when people read it, they're not reading about some stereotype, but they're reading about a person, that the story is fair and honest.

If, as the writer, you don't care at all, or you're indifferent toward the issues of the people that you're writing about, then nobody who's reading is going to care either. I'm not talking about caring in an advocacy type way but in the human way.

The family that you write about in the first story is the Ortiz family. How did you find them?

I didn't find them until I was in Woonsocket. I started spending a bunch of time at this grocery store, and I also started going to a lot of the social service agencies in town where I knew that people, as they were coming up on the end of the month, would go and wait in line at food kitchens. I talked with maybe half dozen or a dozen potential families. I found Rebecka waiting in line at a food kitchen. The fact that she and her husband both worked in grocery stores, and have little kids, felt right pretty quickly.

I knew that a grocery store is not quite human enough to carry a whole narrative. The grocery store owner, Miguel Pichardo, was a good guy. I enjoyed spending time with him and writing about his store. But to do justice to the human effects, I knew I needed another character on the other side who would be going grocery shopping on the first of the month. That's what brought me to Rebecka. After doing some serious explaining of what I wanted to do and why I wanted to do it, they were courageous and open and willing to let me spend a lot of time at their house.

The first day it's always a little bit awkward, and you're explaining why you want to be there and why you want to see them. But usually by three or four days in, people have come to trust you and feel comfortable in your presence, and that's when you feel like you're actually seeing real things happen. I walked with her husband, Jourie, to work late at night and watched him do his work shift. We went grocery shopping with her while her kids were having a meltdown. You get deeper into people's lives as the days go on.

Pulitzer prizing-winning journalist Jim Sheeler [note: *Sheeler was one of Matt's best friends, and he passed away unexpectedly in September 2021; Matt was devastated.*] talks about finding the gray areas and not always presenting people as perfect angels. I was reminded of that when I read the section where you were listing all the people the Ortiz family owed money to, cell phones, electricity, and then one of them was a tattoo parlor.

I received emails from people who said they shouldn't be spending money on tattoos. But life is more complicated than that. If you only write about poor people as victims, or if you only write about characters in stories as victims, first of all, it's not correct. You're not doing justice to them. You're taking all the power away from them, and that's not fair. The best thing to do is not to be reductive and not to simplify. Life is messy sometimes. Any savvy reader can recognize when a story is cleaner than it should be, especially with something like food stamps.

If there was a success in that series, it was that readers understood that these problems are not simple. If these problems were simple, and if people on food stamps were only victims, then they would be solved by now. The big problems in the country are not that simple. If we're writing about them in ways that are reducing them to simple cliché, then we're not doing justice to the problems in the first place, so why bother writing about them?

Was there one story in the series that was more difficult to report and write from an emotional standpoint?

They all had different challenges. One of the stories was set in Texas and was about how this one county—the poorest county in the country with the highest percentage of people on food stamps—is also the most obese, which surprises a lot of people. But people who are on food stamps tend to buy the cheapest foods, things that are the worst for you. As a result, they suffer all kinds of obesity issues, heart disease and diabetes, at disproportionate levels. That was a difficult story because I was looking for characters to write about, and I knew I was going to be putting them in a difficult situation.

It's a lot to ask of somebody to not only write about their poverty and food shortages but also to write about their nine-year-old kids who are starting on insulin. It was difficult to find characters for that story. I also was more careful than in any of the other stories about trying to be sensitive about how I was writing about the issue and portraying them.

Other times can be challenging because, emotionally, you're a reporter, an observer and not an advocate. Being on a bus in Tennessee and spending sixteen-hour days with families who are waiting for their one meal a day and then going back to the hotel and having a quesadilla at the hotel bar, it feels lousy. Even though our job is not to go in and feed people, if they were starving, I would help. Our job is to write about it in a way that people can feel what it's like to be hungry and waiting for the one meal so that hopefully people who are paying attention to the problem can help fix it.

That part still always feels a little bit unclean. The nice part about any of these longer stories is that there are parts of the reporting experience with all of them that stick with me long after the story has run. In some ways that changes you as a reporter.

Leah Sottile

Leah Sottile is a freelance journalist whose work has been featured in the *Washington Post*, the *New York Times Magazine, Playboy, Rolling Stone, California Sunday Magazine*, the *Atlantic*, and more. She worked with Longreads and Oregon Public Broadcasting to write and produce *Bundyville*, a four-part written series and a seven-episode podcast. The written series and the first season of the podcast are about the Cliven Bundy family and its supporters, who had armed standoffs with federal agents on land near the Bundy ranch in Nevada and later at the Malheur National Wildlife Refuge in Oregon.

Sottile's work on this series started when she reported and wrote a breaking news story in early 2016 about the Bundy brothers taking over the wildlife refuge in Oregon. The *Washington Post* called and asked her to cover the court arraignment.

"It was the beginning of a long journey for me in covering this story, and then, I realized it was extremely complicated," Sottile says. "But every single puzzle piece about the whole Bundy story was so interesting that I couldn't look away."

The project started as a print series for Longform. After Sottile had written the first two parts, the idea of a podcast was broached. She reached out to Oregon Public Broadcasting for help in producing the show, and they were on board immediately. "I found the process fascinating," she says. "I was learning on the fly here. . . . I ultimately went back, and I rewrote the first story. I went through probably eight or nine drafts, honing and figuring out what I wanted to do with it."

The *Bundyville* podcast was a hit. It was a National Magazine Award in Podcasting finalist in 2019. Now Sottile is the reporter, writer, and host of *Two Minutes Past Nine*, a BBC Radio 4 podcast about the legacy of the Oklahoma City bombing and how it gets into the heart of America's far-right today.

I spoke with Sottile in May 2018 about *Bundyville*, both the print series and the podcast.

How did *Bundyville*, as a podcast and a written series, come about?

This whole thing started with me writing a single breaking news story back in early 2016 when the Bundy brothers took over the Malheur National Wildlife Refuge in Oregon. Occasionally, I freelance for the *Washington Post*. They called me and asked if I could be in court to cover the arraignment, and I said of course.

It was the beginning of a long journey for me in covering this story, and then, I realized it was extremely complicated, but every single puzzle piece about the whole Bundy story was so interesting that I couldn't look away. For a while after I covered the Oregon trial, I was pitching around this idea of the Nevada trial, which happened in late 2017. My initial interest in it was that about half of a large family was going to be on trial for what happened in Nevada, and I was compelled by that idea of this family being on trial, this father and almost all of his sons.

It started as a story that was supposed to be about the trial in Nevada, and once I started reporting there, and when that resulted in a mistrial, it seemed clear to me that there was a lot more to say than just one long-form piece. That's how it expanded into something a lot bigger.

When in this process did Longreads come into play, as well as the idea of also doing a podcast?

I do a lot of reporting on the front end, and then once I have a good sense of a pitch, I will pitch that to various editors, either that I've worked with or that I want to work with, and try and sell the story to them and then complete the reporting once they've accepted the pitch. Then I ultimately write the story.

I pitched this to quite a few places, and a lot of what the feedback I was getting was that the Bundys were over, there was no interest in talking about them anymore. But I'd worked with Longreads before, and I approached them and told them passionately why this was an important story, maybe in such a way that I didn't to those other editors. My editor there, Mike, immediately was like, yes, we have to do this.

They got involved right before I started covering the trial in Nevada, so that would be October of 2017. When I came back from my first trip to Nevada, I called my editor and said, oh my gosh, this is so crazy. I think we could write a series. He said, you know, we've also been interested in this idea of doing a podcast. I don't know if that's something you're interested in or if you know anybody who can help you with that. What do you think? I immediately knew there were some radio producers here in town that I would like to work with, and Longreads gave me the rope to figure out a way to make it work, and it did.

There's a thoughtful point that comes across in the story, as well as the podcast, on how the Bundy family is, in so many ways, a precursor to what would happen in the 2016 election.

The Oregon trial ended about ten days before the election, and that ended with the jury acquitting them of their charges here. Then Trump was elected, and I felt like I had experienced two punches in the face at the same time. I felt like they had to have been connected. It took me a little bit to figure that out, that once I started reading more about "Trump's America," I started to think this sounds like the folks that I've been writing about for a while. I definitely knew there was something there. There's a lot that's been written about the Bundys, and I seemed to feel like there was a hole that wasn't being filled in, and I couldn't quite figure out what that was as far as the Bundys were concerned. It was this idea that people fell victim to the illusion that they are cowboys, and that makes it okay for them to instruct people to point guns at government agents trying to do their jobs or take over a federal building.

That was a lot of what I was running into with editors that were saying no to the story, was they were hypnotized by this idea that this was a cowboy story or a story about maybe American masculinity, whereas I was realizing as I was pitching, and the more I pitched the more I honed my pitch, that it was about more of a comment on this storm gathering in the wide open spaces in America.

Once you knew you were going to do this as a big story and then later as a series and a podcast, what were some of the first things you did reporting-wise to start reaching out to some of these people?

One of the first things that I did was during the course of the Oregon trial, I was looking at the people who were on trial, and of course there were the Bundys, but there were these other people who acted in minor roles at the refuge occupation, and I became interested in why a kid who was a computer nerd from Ohio would drive halfway across the country to come to this frozen-over bird refuge in the middle of January to join what seemed like a cowboy protest. The first person I wrote about was a guy named David Fry who was ultimately acquitted of charges there. He was also the last person to leave the refuge in Oregon. In the course of that story, I talked to a lot of people, supporters of the Bundys, detractors of the Bundys. I was trying to weigh both sides of the fight that I saw playing out in the courtroom and outside the courtroom.

Early on, I became interested in the vitriol that the two sides felt towards each other. I started talking to people in the courtroom. I was there a lot in court, even when I wasn't getting paid to be there or anything. I would keep going because I wanted them to know my face and be recognized that this was someone who we see writing about this and she's someone who's interested in it.

I've asked Michael Kruse, who writes for POLITICO, what it's like as a reporter to talk with Trump supporters. The media has been vilified in a lot of those communities. Did you have concerns going in as a journalist and talking to some of those who have demonized journalism?

A little. I think that as a freelancer, I have the benefit of always telling people, you know, part of the reason I'm a freelancer is because I want to not be swept up in what the media means to people and try and do things my own way and spend a lot of time working on things and having conversations. Obviously, over the course of the last couple of years, with Bundy stories, but also with other stories I've written, I've definitely been called fake news.

I had an entertaining conversation with someone who called me fake news to my face once at a similar protest as the Bundy's. I said, do you feel like you had to call me fake news? You don't have to say that because the president says that. We had this interesting conversation, and he ultimately was like, I'm sorry I called you fake news.

There have been people who didn't want to talk to me, who wanted to film me as I was asking questions, or that kind of thing, but I get it. I get why people in rural areas don't necessarily trust the media or feel like their stories are being told, but I also worked in a small city for a while in the media. I don't feel like this was new or shocking to me that people didn't trust the media. I feel like I could always go into these stories saying, hey, I get it. The stories of rural America probably aren't being told in the way that you feel is fair. I'm willing to listen to those criticisms.

Is this the first time you've done audio work?

For journalism, yes. I used to host two late-night heavy metal programs on a community radio station, so I have had headphones on and spoken into a microphone before. It was the first time that I had done a straight audio, radio story.

How did you get into journalism?

I started as a music writer. I worked at an alt-weekly in Spokane, Washington, on and off for ten years or so. I was their music editor, but I was also handling investigations at the same time. I went to school for journalism, but my passion has always been music and jumping in vans and following bands around on tour. That's how I got started. It's always funny to me when people realize I have more to my personality besides just reporting.

Did you have to change the way you reported knowing this would be something that people would read as well as listen to?

No, not really. It was great that my editor at Longreads gave me this freedom to say, do you know anybody that you could make a podcast with? During the Oregon trial, Oregon Public Broadcasting here in Portland put together an interesting podcast called *This Land Is Our Land*, which was a tick-tock of the trial as it was playing out. They would have me on as a guest. When Mike asked me if I knew anybody I could make a podcast with, I immediately thought of OPB, and I immediately thought of one of their producers there, Ryan Haas, because I knew that he knew this story as well as I did. I also felt comfortable saying to him, listen, if we're going to do a podcast, I want to come off as authentically me because I think that my approach to reporting is different than a lot of people. It openly became a first-person reporter podcast for that reason.

Did you use any other podcasts as guides for how you might want to do this project?

Definitely. I'm an avid consumer of podcasts. I love the medium. I think when it's successful, it's as exciting to me as long-form. I listen to *Dirty John*. Obviously that was one that my editor at Longreads said they liked. They felt like that could go hand in hand with what I wanted to do. I loved *In the Dark*. I enjoyed *Heaven's Gate*. I felt like it was a similar subject matter in some ways.

There's so many podcasts. I listen to *Reply All* whenever they have news stories. I wanted to be acclimated to what sounds good. I think on the mic, I was able to feel comfortable, like I had been listening and learning all along.

I talked with Christopher Goffard when *Dirty John* came out. With *Dirty John*, there weren't a lot of differences between the printed story and the podcast in terms of structure. With *Bundyville*, they're incredibly different types of pieces. Can you talk about the writing process that you went through?

I found the process fascinating. I was learning on the fly here. I had the first two stories written before I approached OPB about trying to collaborate with them on it. Then I ultimately went back, and I rewrote the first story. I went through probably eight or nine drafts, honing and figuring out what I wanted to do with it.

I know some people are obsessive outliners and have an organized process, but I have an artsy personality, so sometimes I like for it to flow organically. That gets me in trouble sometimes. I probably did more rewriting than I ended up needing to. I think we were also trying to figure out, was I going to get an interview with the Bundys? I'd been trying hard to talk to them, but ultimately, I couldn't talk to them for a long time because they were in jail. Their attorneys were either not passing along my requests for interviews or they straight up didn't want to do it.

I started working on the pieces and then put them on hold. We started writing the podcast. The podcast had to hit on things a little differently, whereas all of the first story that I wrote is unpacking all of the drama around what has happened with the Bundys. Whereas, in radio, you have to hit those things hard. I knew I didn't want to spend a ton of time rehashing what had happened, so we could only allot one episode maximum to hitting on the Bunkerville standoff and the Malheur occupation and the two court trials.

The beauty of the two is they achieve getting the story out there to two completely different audiences. If you're a long-from nerd, you will enjoy the prose of the pieces and you will enjoy the writing as much as I enjoyed writing them. For people who don't have that attention span, the podcast, I've noticed, is getting into the ears and minds of people who would not normally consume long-form stories.

In the written series, the narrative engine is, are you going to get to talk to the Bundy family, so they finally show up in part four when you're doing the interview at the ranch. But in the podcast, those interviews show up much earlier. Why make that decision?

There are podcasts that live on their cliffhangers. I think when we were writing the podcast, we didn't know if we had enough cliffhangers to keep people hanging, but I think we also thought people pretty early would be like, why the heck aren't the Bundys' voices in here? They're talking about all these things that they probably believe or they are maybe upset about. It did feel like we needed to get them in there sooner, whereas with the written pieces, there was so much I could tap into as far as what was out there, like getting into the genealogy and things that wouldn't translate as well to audio. It felt like there was enough there based off of archival videos and old interviews and things like that that allowed the Bundys to come later in the written story.

Had you ever worked on a project this large, for this long a time?

I've definitely worked on projects this large, but I don't know if I have for this long. I think of other stories that have certainly taken six, seven months of interviewing and reporting. Last year I did a story for Longreads about a police shooting in Portland. That was an intensive process, with interviews, and talking to police, talking to victims, but also with lots of reading and court documents.

To see this as the end of a two-year culmination of reporting, that was new. And to present it in two completely different mediums felt at times like I was trying to achieve some journalism feat of strength.

Did you do other freelance work while you were working on this?

I did to a certain point. I wrote a lot for the *Washington Post*. I did some breaking stuff for them. I write for *Outside*. I worked on some stories for *California Sunday*. I am programmed to work a lot. I like to always have lots of things happening. There was a point with *Bundyville* where I couldn't work on anything else. In fact, I almost drove myself to insanity. I cleared my plate as quickly as I could. Part of that was thanks to Longreads. As I wrote the pieces, I would get paid for them, so in a way, it was able to sustain me so I didn't have to take on other work.

How long have you known that you wanted to do this type of journalism?

When I was in high school in the nineties, I was an avid reader of Northwest alt-weeklies. The *Rocket* in Portland, and in Seattle, the *Stranger*. I liked what they did, as far as deep, ambitious, crazy reporting. But I think when I was in college, and I first stumbled on Tom Wolfe and Joan Didion and Susan Orlean, I remember it was like a seismic shift had happened in my life. I was like, I have to figure out a way to do this.

Ambition has never been something I've been lacking. It's more about skills, taking all the time to build up the skills I needed, and the know-how to try and pitch the places that I wanted to write for. I graduated high school in 1999. I started working as a journalist in 2003.

What did you learn in your first job that helps you today?

I started as a city council reporter in Cheney, Washington, which is a tiny farm town. I worked for this little weekly paper there, and I worked there briefly before I moved on to alt-weekly. I discovered early on that, working in a rural community, people wanted to be listened to. I needed to make time for them. As far as music writing was concerned, I learned that I could write beautiful sentences and still make it journalism.

I remember arguing a lot with people at the alt-weekly, people that I worked with. People would say, "Are you a reporter, or are you a writer?" I took a weird offense to that because, I thought, why can't you be both? I don't need to fabricate any details, but I can describe them in the most beautiful way that I can. I feel like that's what Susan Orlean does or Pamela Colloff. They work hard to make sure that they select the right words to describe things appropriately, for people to understand or feel viscerally in that moment. That was the big takeaway, was that you can still write well while also breaking news.

You're a freelance writer, so you're constantly looking for stories to pitch. What types of things—ideas, topics, people—get you excited and pull you in and make you want to write about them?

I've always been obsessed with subcultures. I think that speaks to the music writing that I did and the types of bands that I would write about. In a way, the Bundy story is the ultimate subculture story. It's a whole arm of America right now. I think also, just the American dream; what that means for any number of people, whoever they are. Whether that's a metal band in Spokane, Washington, or a rancher in rural Nevada or protestors in urban Portland. All these ideas that make up America, in their minds, that's something I've always been interested in. The Bundy story felt like the culmination of all of my interests in one place.

I also think as a freelancer, I have the benefit, sometimes, of coming in after the media has left and try to figure out how they all got the story wrong or how we need to develop things that were overlooked. I feel like I learned that from that Michael Kruse story back in the day, where he wrote about the lady who died in her car. I remember him talking about how he jumped up in the dumpster. I feel like that's what I do. I go through everybody's garbage and try to find a good story.

The story is a Florida woman disappeared, but never left home. It's about Kathryn Norris. It's an amazing story.

Anytime people ask me about things that I like, I often send them stories like that and say, print this out and annotate it. Try and figure out how he got this information.

Wright Thompson

Wright Thompson is a senior writer at ESPN and is the author of two books, including the *New York Times* best-selling *Pappyland: A Story of Family, Fine Bourbon, and the Things That Last.* His book *The Cost of These Dreams: Sports Stories and Other Serious Business* is a collection of stories he's written at ESPN over the years. Thompson, who has been included in *Best American Sports Writing* eleven times, was the guest editor of the book in 2015. He was awarded the Dan Jenkins Medal of Excellence in Sports Writing for his 2016 story on Tiger Woods.

Two of the stories included in *The Cost of These Dreams* are pieces I've talked with Thompson about: his 2013 profiles on Michael Jordan and Dan Gable, a legendary wrestling coach.

Thompson was part of a group of student reporters at the University of Missouri's School of Journalism in the late 1990s and early 2000s who have gone on to produce some of the best narrative journalism over the last two decades, including Seth Wickersham, Justin Heckert, Robert Sanchez, and Tony Rehagen. Wickersham works with Thompson at ESPN.

Thompson started his career as an intern and later full-time sportswriter at the *Times-Picayune* in New Orleans before moving on to the *Kansas City Star*. He made the move to ESPN in 2006. He was a National Magazine Award finalist in feature writing in 2014 and 2021 and is now doing television work with his show *True South*, a series focused on southern food and culture.

I've spoken with Thompson twice. In October 2013, we talked about his Jordan and Gable stories. We spoke again In November 2020, when we talked about *Pappyland*, a narrative nonfiction story about bourbon in Kentucky that includes first-person travelogue meditation on ideas of family, inheritance, and home.

You told me when we first started exchanging emails that your Dan Gable profile was a story I should read. What was it about the story that you like?

There was nothing I'd change about it, which is exceedingly rare. I felt like it was a new story about a person who's been written about a lot, which to me is the bar for profiles exceeding or failing on a fundamental level, and I thought that it was structured in such a way that it had none of the stench of journalism on it. I thought that it was like a short story about someone who was real, and I liked that and the way it flowed through time.

Gable seems like somebody who would be intensely personal and not the type of person who opens up his life to a reporter. How did you get him to open up?

I think the main thing is not being shy. I asked a lot of personal questions when I was around, and when you do enough of these stories where you're around and you figure out how to be around in such a way that allows you to do your job, you learn that being a fly on the wall is a myth. You have to figure out the dynamic of the group.

In this case, it was Gable and all of his kids and his wife and all of his grandkids and a bunch of former wrestlers, so it's a silly thing, but the first thing I did, thirty minutes in the door, was make sure I knew everybody's name, and I think there were eighteen people there. It became a party trick, where they would be like, all right, name everybody, and I would go through it, and I blended in pretty quickly.

How long did it take you as a reporter to get to the point where you had no qualms about asking anything?

I have never been terribly shy. I think it starts with the first email. You start off, and you want to send the first email in such a way that gets you to be able to write the story you want to write. I don't ever want to have to defend something I know is wrong, and so I'm blunt in the first emails to people about what it is I want to do and why, and I think that if they've said yes to that, they understand what's going on. I say over and over and over to people, I'm not your friend. I feel comfortable going in, and I'm here to ask questions you might not want to answer.

What drew you to Gable in the first place?

I'd just done that Jordan story, and I got an email about the Jordan story from the head of the Dan Gable Museum, and I don't remember the exact timing, but two or three days after the Jordan story ran, the IOC announced they were cutting wrestling, so Gable was reintroduced into my head at about the same time, and my first thought when I heard about the IOC is Dan Gable must be having an aneurysm. I felt I needed to go see Dan Gable, and that was the extent of the idea.

Do you do a lot of work by email, at least in setting stories up?

I like to write a letter to people saying this is what I want to do. With Gable, it was much simpler. It was, I want to come talk to you about your life and about how the ioc decision fits into the arc of it, and I think it's a testament to how much he was willing to bring attention to this issue, that with few questions, he was willing to say yeah come on. He was open.

At the end of the first day, we were walking. He was going to something that I was going to in Des Moines, and I hadn't had a story come out since Jordan. I'd written two, but he didn't know that, and he looked over at me and goes, you know, there's a lot of pressure on you too. I'm like, well what are you talking about? He goes, well, you just had this story that everybody liked, and so, what if this story's not any good? People are going to think it's over. I looked at him. I'm like, are you trying to get in my head? He got this huge grin on his face and then walked out of the hotel, and I'm like, well that's the quintessential Dan Gable moment.

Was there anything that surprised you about Dan Gable or anything in the reporting process that you didn't expect going in?

It took me several days, but it was definitely still during the initial reporting, when I figured out the central arc of the story, which is, any loss brings back every loss for him, because watching wrestling with Dan Gable the first night, I was struck. There's something weird about this, and some poking and prodding and it quickly became apparent that that's what was going on.

Did you know the backstory of Gable and his sister before you went there?

I did, and it was interesting because he brought it up first. That's the thing I was worried about; how do you bring it up? It's one of those things that people know, but he doesn't talk about much, and when he does talk about it, if you go back and read all these stories, it's almost the same quotes. He talks about it in a way that seems like he is reading from his own script. The scene in the sauna, in the next to last section, happened, and I was blown away.

When you go into interviews and you know there's a tragic back-story that you feel like they're not going to want you to ask about, how do you get over that and ultimately ask?

You just gotta ask it. That's the job. It's a question of timing. It was interesting because I knew that when he found out, when he'd gotten the phone call about the guy who killed his sister being dead, this guy named Mike Duroe was with him when he got the phone call, and I knew that, and we were in the sauna with Mike, so I thought, I wonder if this is going to come up? I had cardboard and a pencil because the notebooks weren't working in the sauna. A notebook and a pen weren't working, so I tore a cardboard box into squares and then took a pencil so I could take notes, but it's funny because that pencil was so damn loud on the cardboard in these quiet moments of him baring his soul. I was trying to wait a couple of beats and write as he was saying the next thing so it wouldn't be like this silence of the sauna.

Can you talk a little bit about your relationship with your editor at ESPN, Jay Lovinger? I'm always interested to hear successful writers talk about their relationship with their editors.

The conversations get shorter and shorter because we know each other so well that it's almost shorthand. In the beginning, I would file a story and then he would send me back an edit that had big thoughts in all capital letters. Then I would try to fix that, and he would send back one with questions, and then I would do that, and he would send back an actual edit. Now I file it, and he calls and tries to explain what he thinks the problem is. It's all on the phone. I'll take notes and then do a new draft, and then, we'll do an edit. We'll go through and ask questions, and we go back and forth.

For Gable, we edited that in person. Every now and then for a stor that we think is really good, I'll fly out to New York, and we'll do it at his house. We did that for Gable.

With the Michael Jordan story, the first thought I had when I read it was, how did you ever get the access to Jordan?

I think I chased him for a year and a half, and I was going to do the story either way. Basically, I paid to get the last eighteen months of his flight logs to try to figure out everywhere he went because I was going to stalk him. We were doing it no matter what, for the story to run on his fiftieth birthday, and I was ready to do it no matter what. I was in England doing British Open stuff when I had the first conversation with his publicist, and then we talked, and then I sent an email to his agent that was blunt, and they were into it because they knew I was going to do it anyway, and he had to talk to somebody about turning fifty.

They said yes, but I had already agreed to be at LSU for the One Day, One Game issue in November, and that's the weekend they wanted to do it. I wrote Jordan back and said no. I thought it was dead frankly. I thought it was over, and two months later, they came back and said okay we're going to do this. It was basically like can you be in Charlotte in three days? The answer was yes.

What was it like interviewing and being around someone like Jordan?

I don't think he ever felt like he gave up control. When the story came out, I know he asked the people around him, "How did he find all this stuff out?" There's always a moment in a profile where they're feeling you out, and it doesn't matter what access you agreed to beforehand, that's totally meaningless. They're going to decide in the room, and with him it was, I started talking about how Mickey Mantle always thought he was going to die young. Jordan got this look on his face, and it was like, you could tell he was deciding whether or not to be honest, and then, he got open, and all the people around him got open. The inner circle takes their cues from the person in charge, and once he's open, everybody was open.

There's a line early in the story that I like. It's a couple sentences. "There's a palpable simmering whenever you're around Jordan, as if Air Jordan is still in there, churning, trying to escape. It must be strange to be locked in combat with the ghost of your former self." Is that the main thing you took away from spending time with him, that he's constantly in this inner battle?

I think more than that it's that he's still trying to figure out what to do after you've been Michael Jordan and the cost of his ambitions. Dealing with the loss of a kid from Wilmington, North Carolina, named Mike Jordan and still struggling with the death of his father and trying to figure out what he does now and what it means and why.

Can you talk about how you focused the story?

I wanted it to have some of that short story structure. I caught him during the two weeks where he was between homes for the first time since his rookie year in Chicago. I caught him in this weird period of transition, and the gravitational pull of that transition is what made the story work. It was him at a vulnerable moment.

What was it like to sit and watch a basketball game with Jordan?

He's intense. I don't know what the appropriate example is, but it was clear watching that he couldn't not watch. I'd been with him so long that it was comfortable. This is going to sound weird, but I was focused.

How do you get these people who tend to be closed off to talk about their worst days to you?

I offer a lot of information about myself during interviews. Always, it reminds the people that you're not part of some faceless borg trying to mine their personal lives for profit. It reminds them that you're a real person. I think that helps.

What is your book _Pappyland: A Story of Family, Fine Bourbon, and the Things That Last_ about?

It's a weird hybrid of a book. It's part narrative nonfiction story about bourbon in Kentucky and part first-person travelogue meditation on these ideas of family and inheritance and home.

We've talked about your reporting on Dan Gable and Michael Jordan, where you're writing deeply about other people. You write deeply

about Julian Van Winkle as well. What was it like to write about your-self in the same deep way?

I'll be honest with you; I'm pretty uncomfortable this week too. It's not my favorite feeling in the world. You sit down in your basement, and you write this thing, and you forget that anybody is ever going to read it. When I started this draft, I thought there was no way Penguin was going to go for it, so there was a certain amount of freedom. I can tell other people's stories, and I'm in a lot of my stories, but it's often as a tour guide not as a character.

You write in chapter 10 that "I've always been happiest when dreaming of escape." With this book, you are diving into Julian, into every-thing that's happened with him, but I also feel like you dive deep into yourself.

I am working out some shit in public that maybe I should have done in private. I think the combination of this book coming out, and these past seven months of COVID means I've been at home the longest I've ever been at one point since I was eighteen years old, and it's weird.

Talking about this book, and to have done all of this, and then be forced to be still is odd. We knew we were going to have another child in our house. I love our neighborhood and our neighbors. We live right by the square in Oxford. I don't want to move from our neighborhood, and so I took my office at home, and I turned it into a playroom for the girls, and I bought some land and a little cabin outside of town. That's my office. I am staring at a horse field right now. It's totally silent. It all feels still. To answer your question, I feel like I'm sorting some of it out.

People who write memoirs are always trying to sort things out in public.

It is a weird thing to do. But once you put it like that, this is a weird, insecure, narcissistic thing to do. Jay Lovinger always used to say writers have a weird mixture of arrogance and insecurity.

Sarah Weinman

Sarah Weinman is the author of *The Real Lolita: A Lost Girl, an Unthinkable Crime, and a Scandalous Masterpiece*, named a Best Book of 2018 by NPR, BuzzFeed, the *National Post, Literary Hub*, the *San Francisco Chronicle*, and Vulture. It also won the Arthur Ellis Award for Excellence in Crime Writing. Weinman is the crime fiction columnist for the *New York Times Book Review*. Weinman has also edited several true crime anthologies, including *Unspeakable Acts: True Tales of Crime, Murder, Deceit & Obsession*. She has also written for the *New York Times, Vanity Fair*, the *Washington Post*, and other publications.

The Real Lolita is about the case that inspired Vladimir Nabokov's novel *Lolita*. Weinman said there were clues that Dolores Haze, the prepubescent girl in Nabokov's book, was based on the 1948 kidnapping of a girl named Sally Horner. Weinman wrote a long-form piece for the Canadian magazine *Hazlitt* but wanted to do more on Horner and how Nabokov used her story to create his own. "I felt nine thousand words wasn't enough to cover the full spectrum of what I wanted to in writing about Sally's kidnapping and how it intersected with *Lolita*," Weinman says, later adding: "I've figured out when a story fits more as a long-form piece and when the long-form piece is actually constrained in that there's much more to be discovered, investigated, and written about." She researched several of the people involved with Sally Horner. One of them was Ruth Janisch, who helped engineer Sally's rescue. Weinman says that in the *Hazlitt* piece, she represented Janisch as more of a cardboard heroine than anything. But after talking to two of Janisch's daughters, she learned that she was a much more complicated figure than local newspaper articles had shown her to be. "Getting a sense of what the family dynamics were, how fraught, complicated, and in many ways damaging, made Ruth a much more three-dimensional figure who did a lot of terrible things, but this one decent thing she wanted to define her life," she says.

Weinman was a National Magazine Award finalist for Reporting in 2020 for her story, "Before, and After, the Jogger"—about the survivors of the real Central Park Five attacker—which ran in *New York*.

We spoke in December 2018, primarily about *The Real Lolita*.

You've edited several books of true crime writing, but *The Real Lolita* is the first book you authored. What's the book about?

The short answer is that it's about the real case that inspired Vladimir Nabokov's novel *Lolita*, published in America sixty years ago. I'd been looking for my next crime story and spend a lot of late nights on the internet looking at some combination of Wikipedia entries about unsolved cases or missing people, Reddit threads, and true crime–related message boards. All of that converged into one specific rabbit hole that led me to this 2005 article in the *Times* literary supplement titled "What Happened to Sally Horner?" It wasn't the first time I'd read that piece, but this time it stuck.

Why do you think it stuck?

I paid attention to what this particular writer, a Nabokov scholar named Alexander Dolinin, was arguing: That *Lolita*—which is of course about a middle-aged man's illicit obsessive desire for a prepubescent girl named Dolores Haze—suggested that Nabokov knew about this 1948 kidnapping of Sally Horner. That there were clues, some of them in evidence, some of them buried. In *Lolita* the novel, there's a line late in the book where Humbert Humbert, the middle-aged man in question, thinks, "Had I done to Dolly perhaps what Frank La Salle, a 50-year-old mechanic, had done to 11-year-old Sally Horner?"

This line didn't jump out at sixteen when I first read it. But seeing it in the context of this essay made me wonder, had anybody reported out Horner's kidnapping as a crime story? That's what I set out to do.

What did you learn?

I learned that Horner was taken from Camden, New Jersey, where she grew up, on to Atlantic City, then Baltimore, Dallas, and finally San Jose, where she was rescued after a twenty-one-month, cross-country nightmare. The more I learned, the more I felt compelled to figure out what news information was still accessible, what court documents I could find, were there people still alive who remember Sally that I might be able to talk to.

The initial result was a long-form piece published by Canadian magazine called *Hazlitt*, but I knew pretty quickly that I had a lot more to say, especially not just about what happened to Sally but how her life and case intersected with Nabokov's writing of *Lolita*. So that became the book.

At what point did you realize there was a solid connection between Horner and *Lolita*—when did you realize that was book worthy?

When I read that initial *Times* literary supplement piece published in 2005 in mid- to late 2013. I worked on the long-form story in March 2014, and it was published in November. I spent several months gathering information, sending a bunch of FOIA requests, collecting court documents, and reporting what I could find at the time. There were appeals court files that landed in my inbox almost in this serendipitous manner.

I've figured out when a story fits more as a long-form piece and when the long-form piece is actually constrained in that there's much more to be discovered, investigated, and written about. That's what I felt with Sally's story. I knew if I had more time, patience, and resources that I could answer all of the lingering questions that I couldn't quite within a long-form story.

Ultimately, the piece that ran was just shy of nine thousand words. I felt nine thousand words wasn't enough to cover the full spectrum of what I wanted to in writing about Sally's kidnapping and how it intersected with *Lolita*.

What's an example of one of those lingering questions that you felt like you wanted to find the answer to, but you couldn't in the shorter piece?

A month before I filed the story was when I learned of Ruth Janisch's existence. Janisch helped engineer Sally's rescue. I'm reading through papers at the Camden County Historical Society Library, and only then and there, I learned there was somebody that Sally had confided in—but I didn't know the person's name or what the connection was. Suddenly, not only did I have a name, but there were quotes.

In the original *Hazlitt* piece, I represented her as a more cardboard heroine who engineered Sally's rescue. Months later, once I realized that I still wanted to do some reporting, I decided to see if there were any children of Janisch who might still be alive. I found her youngest daughter and spoke with her first. In the midst of that initial conversation, it became clear to me that Janisch was a much more complicated figure than the newspaper articles had represented her to be.

Speaking with her youngest daughter led me to an older daughter who was pseudonymously referred to as Rachel in the book. Getting a sense of what the family dynamics were, how fraught, complicated, and in many ways damaging, made Ruth a much more three-dimensional figure who did a lot of terrible things, but this one decent thing she wanted to define her life. Of course, that one decent thing was helping bring Sally home.

There are several different types of reporting in your book: historical true crime reporting regarding Sally, literary archival, and interviewing. Is there one type of reporting that you enjoy more than others?

The similarities are looking for answers to questions. I love archival work. There's nothing quite like sitting in a library, university, or some institution, looking at people's letters, manuscript pages, or ephemera. I remember going through Nabokov's archives. Nabokov has two main archives; the original one is at the Library of Congress in Washington, D.C., but the bulk of his papers are at the New York Public Library in the Berg Collection, this magical place. At the time that I was doing research there, you weren't allowed to bring in phones or laptops. It felt like I was hermetically sealed off from the world.

I was looking through a folder that was marked as miscellaneous material. I've learned those are the folders that I am most interested in looking through, because often they aren't well cataloged, but they contain some treasures. In this instance, the miscellaneous folder contained all sorts of clippings and ephemera related to the publication of *Lolita*. Even in the midst of all this, there was nothing at all except for that note card in the LOC archives relating to Sally Horner. Because I knew there had been at least some correspondence, I found it intriguing that there was no trace evidence.

Research isn't as much about what you find as it is about what you don't find. It's putting together conclusions and analysis based on what you have but also what you don't. In doing so, you have to make informed guesses and speculation.

As you were working on this book, what were some of the bigger challenges when it came to reporting and writing?

So many—because I was writing about a story that began seventy years ago. There were sources who died. When I started reporting the story, Sally's brother-in-law was still alive, so I was lucky to speak with him once by telephone, but by the time I began the book, he had passed. Sally's best friend in the last year of her life, who was known as Carol Starts at the time; I was able to track her down, but she passed in 2017 and didn't live to see the book's publication.

Those are the more emotional regrets that I have, that people that I talked to who would have appreciated knowing the book was published were not around to see it.

From a reporting standpoint, though, information disappears. I remember one rainy day in May of 2017, I was in Philadelphia doing some research. I took the Patco, which is a connecting train between Philadelphia and Camden, and decided to see if I present myself in person, if someone will find me documents. I went to one courthouse, then an appeals courthouse, then the police station, then the prosecutor's office. I asked people who would stare at me with blank expressions, like: You expect us to find documents from 1950? I said, "It's worth a shot, right?" I have subsequently realized that sometimes you shake a tree and things emerge but never on your schedule; it's always on the documents' schedules. I had a book deadline, and I didn't want to push because I might not have a trove of documents that would lead me to a few choice details. I would have to write around them.

Were you worried about writing around the things you didn't know for certain?

Another pitfall: What happens when a nonfiction writer-reporter ventures into speculative waters. I didn't want to at first. I had turned in the first draft of the book, and my editors were incredibly helpful, but one of their repeated notes was: Okay, we have Sally's story and Nabokov's story, but one of the ways you can bridge these two narratives is by bringing yourself into it. I protested because I thought, "Well, this is going to make things more complicated." They stressed that, I wasn't writing a memoir, but the reader needs to know what I didn't know because that gives greater authority on the details I do. Once that rattled around, I rewrote certain chapters more effortlessly.

Do you have any examples?

I'm thinking of the chapter where Sally spent a few months in Baltimore. I had a bunch of details that weren't adding up as a cohesive narrative. It's almost like I would throw up a bunch of dice, they'd land, and the numbers wouldn't check out. It didn't coalesce. When I rewrote it, the first line I thought of, I'm going to paraphrase here: here's the point in the story when I tell you what happened to Sally Horner and Frank La Salle in Baltimore. Frankly, I didn't learn all that much. What I wanted to do with the speculative aspects was keep them as limited as possible and to details that were verifiable.

While I couldn't know what Sally was doing at a given point, because I knew more or less the street she lived on, the fact that there was a diner at the end of the road, the school that she went to, the timeframe that she was present . . . I could extrapolate and go: Well, let me see if I can find a comparable memoir of somebody who was a student at a Catholic school in Baltimore around the same time. What might they be able to tell me? That's how I was able to, within reason, be like: Here's a good guess as to what a typical day Sally might have had in Baltimore was like.

That was the limit to which I was comfortable speculating. I wasn't going to intuit her thoughts and feelings and figure out which people she may have interacted with. If I listed names, it's because I found them in records or court documents. Otherwise, that was my brick wall that I deliberately wanted to run up against.

I think it worked well. What makes it work is the transparency.

If somebody came forward and said, "I knew Sally in Baltimore and this was what happened," I would not just be happy, but I'd welcome that knowledge. Even though *The Real Lolita* is published as a hardcover, I still feel this feeling that there could be more. When the paperback is out next fall, I will update it based on information that has since come through. Not a huge amount, but things here and there. Ultimately my goal is to tell the most accurate story possible. I want it to come as close to the truth about what happened to Sally Horner as I can possibly report out.

The main philosophical quandary of any nonfiction writer is that we have facts, but we're constructing a narrative story, and we're beholden to the way our particular brains work. Somebody else might have approached this story in a different way because they're not me. They wouldn't necessarily make the associations and connections that I do. They wouldn't necessarily seek out some of the information sources and people that I did.

My Sally Horner, so to speak, is as accurate a reflection of the information that I had on hand. But it's also why I never want to forget that Sally had family. She had people who loved her; people she loved; people who remember her. Even though it was important for me to tell her story in the best way that I knew how, I also wanted to make sure that I was, within reason, doing right by her relatives. They're the ones who have to live with this unimaginable loss all these decades later.

I have done historical archival research for narrative nonfiction stories, and the hardest thing, for me, is bringing the writing to life. What was your process like when you sat down with this research and had to start writing?

This is where having cut my teeth writing a lot of fiction is helpful. Obviously, fiction is 100 percent imagination, and nonfiction is supposed to be 100 percent truth. In reality, when writing fiction or nonfiction to entertain and to engage the reader, writers employ a lot of the same techniques. It was important that *The Real Lolita* read fast. I wanted it to have the sense of being a suspense thriller. Pacing was important, as was creating indelible characters as best as I could. I wanted the sentences to reflect that these were living, breathing people. I feel like the techniques between fiction and nonfiction do help one another.

The fact that I published short stories from my early twenties onward helped me as a journalist. I'm presuming nonfiction and all the techniques that I've learned from long-form reporting and books will eventually help when I next approach fiction.

It isn't that fiction and nonfiction blur. It's that the techniques can be similar. Ultimately, I'm telling stories. In this case, these are true stories. But the way we tell stories and the way we approach narrative all have the same aim: Is the reader going to put this down? Is the reader going to care? Is there going to be an emotional connection? All of those are central questions no matter what side of the fiction/nonfiction divide you are on.

Did you learn anything about yourself as a writer or a reporter while doing this project?

I learned I could write a nonfiction book. Learning how to write a nonfiction book was itself a tremendous experience. I also learned that it's difficult, but important, to get people to tell their deepest, darkest secrets. It's important to have as much empathy, understanding, and as much care as you can. It requires a lot of finesse, preparation, and background conversations.

It is important to know when to push, when to pull back, and when to let sources guide you with respect to their own emotions, feelings, not to rush them, and to respect the information they want to convey. They do want to tell you stuff, and they do want to connect, but journalists can't necessarily impose their own opinions or perspectives right away. So much of reporting is listening and waiting—silence before people break it. Getting to experience those things firsthand, I already know that will make me a better journalist on the next project.

How does, say, editing a book of crime fiction compare to writing a full-length, reporting-heavy nonfiction book?

One of the reasons I wanted to do the paperback anthology was to get a sense of what book publication was like but at a more modest level where I could advocate for writers who are not me. I was already starting to do some long-form reporting but didn't have a project that was book length. I was passionately interested, and still am, in midcentury crime fiction by women. At the time that I started on what became *Troubled Daughters* in 2011, there was a gap that had not been adequately discussed or articulated. We knew a lot about hard-boiled fiction by men, and we knew a lot about golden age, cozy crime fiction by women, but there was this in-between group of suspense writers about whom people didn't think about or take seriously as a group. Reading their work was so informative, especially with respect to reading more contemporary suspense fiction by women.

Serendipitously, *Gone Girl* came out as I was working on this project, so I had a hook where I could say: here are the grandmothers of *Gone Girl*. *Troubled Daughters* was published, and it sold well, which led me to a conversation with the then publisher of the Library of America. They invited me to edit this two-volume set, a project they'd been thinking about off and on for some time. It was the right project for me, and it was wonderful to read all these older novels and figure out which should be part of the modern canon. It still amazes me that I got to do this.

I also learned a lot about book publishing. I've had this publishing reporter day job for a long time, and I'm well versed in how the book publishing trade works. That said, when it came time to write *The Real Lolita*, I had to put all that aside and found that, when you're writing, you are alone with the page. It doesn't matter what you might know about how the business works or if you're the coolest person, you still have to produce the best book you possibly can. The only way you're going to do it is to sit down in front of your screen and type as needed and revise as needed.

Did you think from an early age you were always going to be a writer?

I like to say it was through a series of happy accidents. Let's say I was not the writer in the family. I have an older brother who still lives in Toronto, and he was a longtime writer and reporter for *Maclean's*, which is the equivalent of *Time* magazine in Canada. When I went to university, and later graduate school, I was pursuing science. I moved to New York in August of 2001 to attend John Jay College of Criminal Justice's forensic science program. I'd always had an interest in crime though.

Being a child in the eighties in Canada, there were formative crimes happening. When I was a teenage girl, the major event, crime-wise, were the killings by Paul Bernardo and his wife, Karla Homolka, of teenage girls who were a little older than I was. It felt like a resonance to be a teenage girl at that time in the early nineties.

All of that influenced what I wanted to study and pursue. I saved up, spent a year working, and saved up tuition money. I applied, got in, moved, then 9/11 happened. My 9/11 experience was distant, but I had a particular window because of classmates who were working at the office of [the] chief medical examiner processing remains and working on the ground. The following summer, I did an internship at the me's office in their investigations unit, and there were still people assigned to help process human remains. I learned a lot from being in that particular internship environment.

How did you get into writing?

While I was at grad school, I was also working one day a week at a wonderful mystery bookshop called Partners & Crime in Greenwich Village. That was my first exposure to the book business; I met authors, editors, and agents but quickly learned that I didn't want to own a bookstore. The margins were low and the stress was high. I built an initial library of contemporary crime fiction, which I'd been reading since college.

Eventually, when I'd returned to my hometown in Ottawa, I'd finished the coursework of my graduate school and had a thesis to write—including a lot of downtime. This was 2003, there weren't that many blogs, and none devoted to crime fiction. I started one with a fanciful title, and I wish I remembered why I picked it, but it was called "Confessions of an Idiosyncratic Mind." It lasted about seven years, and it became a virtual water cooler for the crime fiction community. I'd attend conventions and go to book events. Essentially, this blog led me to my first book reviewing assignments, which led to columns, which, as I grew more restless and ambitious, led me to pursue short-form reporting as a publishing reporter and eventually more long-form pieces.

You mentioned that you started writing fiction at one point. Were those crime-related stories as well?

The vast majority of short fiction that I've published either appears in *Ellery Queen's Mystery Magazine*, its sister publication, *Alfred Hitchcock's Mystery Magazine*, or various crime-related anthologies.

Crime is such a roomy genre that pretty much can encompass any idea in any form and any theme you could imagine. Crime is everything: It's society; it's philosophy. I don't think I'm going to run out of stories to pursue, whether fiction or nonfiction, that don't have some criminal element to them. We can't understand the way the world works without understanding how crime plays into that.

Matt Tullis, in memoriam

HE WANTED TO know about writers. He wanted to know about where they worked and what the view was like, if they had a window; what brand of pens they used; what shape of notebook. He wanted to know if they were habitual or had superstitions. He was in search of peculiarities that might've aided them in what they wrote. If they listened to music while writing or carried around a backpack on assignment, it said something about individuality, about preference. He asked if they recorded interviews with a digital recorder or if they just used an app on their phone. The kind of computer or laptop a writer preferred seemed to him like an important detail about the words writers conjured from their fingertips, as well as asking them to describe if there was anything special about the room in their house where they did the typing. Matt was an attentive listener, his students in the feature writing classes he taught through the years remembered, so he was perfect for a project like this, and though he was a journalist with his own ambitions and ideas about method, or craft, he would've taken down notes and absorbed the advice that forms this book without any kind of disagreement or pretensions. He needed to know if other writers came back from reporting trips and had to decompress, if they drove there or if they flew, if they transcribed their own interviews or handed the grunt work off to someone else because of the deadline. Who were their influences; what were they reading? How did they come up with their ideas? Seeking answers not merely for his own edification but because he was using the conversations with a book like this in mind: the different points of view, the different work ethics, the different ways of approaching a subject, the various methods of both discretion and persuasion, the writerly obsessions and the behaviors that were hard for writers to explain to other people but worthy of Matt trying to get them to. So many journalists opened up to him with a thousand tips and tactics that it was difficult for him to digest, to remember it all, or whittle it saliently into parts of his own process, which he'd actually learned firsthand through experience as a newspaper reporter and professor and advisor and eventually long-form writer of nonfiction and memoir. These interviews, these anecdotes are not just a way to preserve the authors here, and their ideas, but his own life story as well. He wanted deeper insights into the levels of decorum depending on the story subject, how close writers sometimes could get with the people about whom they wrote, the range of sensitivities and depth and time spent required to approach any kind of omniscience, and the empathy, to borrow a word he considered kind of a long-form journalism catchall, involved with the intensities of immersive reporting in general. He wanted to know it all, hence this book.

HE WAS HABITUAL. In order to write he needed a desk lamp and a jar for pencils and pens, a file folder box on the left side of the desk and a three-tray organizer on the right, a wicker basket to both camouflage and store his power cords, Zoe the Golden Retriever and Border Collie mix at his feet. He almost refused to write anywhere else but at that desk; it was small and wooden and about the length of his outstretched arms. He needed the window shades open at 6 AM to get his reading in and to try and start typing before anyone else in the house was up (if they did rise early to come downstairs, he might say, looking over his shoulder, "What are you doing awake?"). He needed a cup of coffee, black, in the same blue American Press Institute mug, of course, brewed and finished around the same time each day. And a power nap at 2 PM, the last few years he rarely missed thirty minutes of sleep before getting back to the afternoon, perhaps a superstition of his own from when he was a kid in the hospital with acute lymphoblastic leukemia, getting injections all over his body and spinal taps and brain scans, in dire need of rest. His wife, Alyssa, a fifth-grade teacher, observed him down the hallway when he was working from home during COVID, saw firsthand the mysteries of his routine, him conducting an interview, him looking at his notes, him crossing his arms in different ways on the desk, him picking books from the shelf for motivation, him clacking away or speaking into the mic, sometimes Matt just sitting there and looking out the window for a while, engrossed—she preferred to leave him be. When he was folding laundry he listened to music, she could hear the Ohio musician Chris Castle so often that it had to be his preferred background noise while doing anything, be it the dishes or cooking. He had a blue Akron Marathon water bottle on the desk, it always needed a refill. The Akron Marathon's sponsor for years was Akron Children's Hospital, where Matt spent much of 1991 being treated for cancer. He finished the marathon three times while raising money for the Leukemia and Lymphoma Society through Team in Training. Each time he crossed the finish line, the hospital loomed behind him in the commemorative picture.

The gray swivel chair in his office, his preference that clips be printed out so he could hold them and leaf through the pages, his own scrawl in the margins and sticky notes on the borders, his radio mic adjusted chin level for interviews. He worked from a MacBook laptop at home, Mac desktop in his office at Fairfield University, the laptop screen open and the computer balanced on a hardbound Oxford dictionary on the desk. He used yellow Sharpie Hi-Liters to shade in particular sentences and paragraphs, a long white legal pad so he could jot at the desk while someone else was talking. Though he didn't wear them always in order to be able to see, he had a pair of reading glasses on the desk often sitting on a printed page of interview questions, double-spaced. He took a green and gray LL Bean backpack on the road and to work, with multiple Uni-Ball

VisionElite pens in case he lost one. He once used a digital recorder but retired it in preference of his phone. Though no one had been with him during his reporting, to watch his own process, to make note of it and include it in a book, it wasn't difficult to guess by listening to his podcast or sitting in on a class that his own way of doing things—his own style of interviewing or hanging around—must've been self-deprecating, sweetly curious, focused and sensitive and disarming, and almost laconically patient. Like some of the writers he admired, he also bought those long rectangular and white NEWS Professional Reporters notebooks and wrote notes into them both while he was on assignment and interviewing his childhood doctors and friends and family as part of his memoir, *Running with Ghosts*, about surviving childhood cancer and a way for him to honor the tattoo on his forearm, which is the title of this book, a way for him to memorialize the stories of his childhood friends in the pediatric hospital that weren't so fortunate as him.

His office at Fairfield was a picture of similar order to the one in his house. Twelve framed stories he'd written for the *Columbus Dispatch*, about a horseshoe champion and a basketball player who was the son of Matt's cancer doctor, a series on each zoo in Ohio, and some narrative obituaries, six frames to a row, hung together on one of the walls. A Harry Caray sticker above his computer and beneath a neat shelf of books and magazines. Some signed baseballs and framed sports cards. A large signed poster (and a humorous conversation piece) of the football player Bubby Brister. A collage of pictures of his wife and two children below a coat hanger draped with dozens of press passes, to the Cleveland Cavaliers versus the Toronto Raptors, Trans-Siberian Orchestra VIP, a credential from the PGA Tour, a Board of Advisors placard that read "Matthew Tullis, MFA, Assistant Professor of English and Digital Journalism."

One of the reasons he asked other writers about it is because he had his own view from his desk, at home—a panorama of six acres in southwestern Connecticut, one of the best parts about the Tullis family living in the middle of nowhere. During the summer, say, if he needed to stand and stretch, to get up and pace around in the middle of a thought, or break the infinitum of staring at words—or maybe just a little inspiration—he could zone out into the trees, which occluded the entire view at full bloom, woods so thick and colorful he couldn't even see the road or a trace of civilization or even, really, the sky. Which he loved. He used a leaf blower to clear a trail out there where he or Alyssa or the kids could walk easily from the house and into the wild. The large bay window framed nearly the entire wall in front of him, in the home office that was essentially just a living room off the main entryway in the New England–style house with a sectional couch behind his desk chair. Alyssa helped him build and push IKEA shelves against all the walls in the room except the one with the window, both because he wasn't great with written directions—"I'm a writer, the only thing I'm good at is building sentences," he'd said to Alyssa—and he owned a million books and had nowhere else to put them. Books first ordered by him into the categories of nonfiction and fiction and then changed on a whim (it took forever to rearrange them) to alphabetical order, his own book the only one with the cover proudly facing outward. His favorite time of the year was when the library had its used book sale. He kept buying books as though the office shelves stretched forever, was influenced by every kind of writer in any kind of genre—Alyssa even received some books in the mail after his funeral like they were some kind of last message to be decoded; he'd ordered several of them before he passed.

Below the books, Zoe refused to leave the vacant office, sitting there at the end of the past year and into the beginning of this one, in front of the footrest and beside his desk like she was waiting on him to come back home.

MATT WAS ALMOST done with this book, his second, when he passed at forty-six years old. Some of the interviews were conducted at home and at Fairfield, recently, and in a sound booth in the J-school of Ashland University years ago, in Ohio, where he also majored in journalism and English as an undergrad and wrote sports for the *Collegian* and DJ'd for the radio station, WRDL. The preceding pages are a culmination of both hours spent in front of a microphone and on Zoom, talking to journalists and authors during the past ten years, and what turned out to be an entire professional career in discourse about the processes of the people who wrote stories he enjoyed and from which he wanted to learn. Matt was the kind of person who traveled a few hours just to meet some of these writers, to put a face to a name. Driving just so he could listen and speak with them in person, at events and in classrooms, like that of his friend and journalist Jim Sheeler at Case Western University. Matt, sitting with students, leaning in the back of the room, like he still had much to learn and was just another undergrad, using the opportunity to ask even more questions or to take the writer out to dinner where he might talk about what he was working on, himself, and solicit their advice and buy them a beer.

Late in 2022 Alyssa sat at his desk and looked through his computer at the Word files to help finish this book, feeling like a detective after he was gone. She started at the beginning of Matt's podcast, *Gangrey: The Podcast*, going through a hundred episodes at first just in order to learn more about him and to hear his voice again. "Then I got interested in the processes," she says. "The different writers were talking to him about how they go about it. How they did was so intriguing to him, how they interacted with the people they were interviewing. I think that's something that was really important for him and to get across to his students. I really feel like it reiterates to me about what was important to him as a journalist and a professor. The questions he asked, 'What made you come up with this idea?' The main thing that comes across, he was very much interested in the connection the reporter made with whoever they were interviewing."

Some of the documents were half-finished interviews or ideas about who to talk to next, and story ideas that he never got to see to fruition, excited to his last day when he had an operation on his brain that this book had been picked up by the University of Georgia Press and would become real. "I would describe this book to other people," Alyssa says. "It's like a textbook of narrative journalism, and Matt would say, 'No, no, no—it's much more than that.'"

THE MOURNERS DROVE a few blocks from O'Bryan's Pub to the campus of Ashland University, where they snuck into the journalism school around midnight, a Saturday night, in late October 2022, let into the locked building by someone with a key, a person who turned out to be sympathetic to their objective when they described what they wanted to do, someone who also knew and remembered Matt Tullis. The punctuation on an evening spent eating and drinking and raising glasses to hours of stories about their friend—these former coworkers, old students who now were married and had their own jobs in journalism, still thinking about his advice—at his favorite spot, where he liked to walk after the day was finished and have a drink himself. O'Bryan's, with decent food and moderately priced alcohol and a calming dimness of overhead lighting, him sitting in a booth in a corner, the place where on the last day of class anyone who'd been one of Matt's students and was over twenty-one and wanted to go, he would take them.

They weren't exactly mourners, per se. As the evening went on it seemed a little less crippling that he was actually gone, that they had kind of brought him back to life for a short while, at least, and the journalism school was right there, where he used to always, always be. It was sort of mutually decided to visit where he worked, to trace his path up the concrete steps into the rooms and floors he spent years inhabiting as a teacher, as a reporter, as lurker in the hallways in between classes, as advisor running the student paper and telling the *Collegian* staff we are doing important journalism here. Matt, who not only oversaw the paper but picked it up from the printer and from his car distributed the copies around campus himself, someone who was obsessed with what turned out to be an unending conversation until he passed away, "Did you read this?, Did you see how she began this story?," always arming younger writers with incessant bits of information and support, "Just sit down and try it," "Any type of writing improves your writing, it's like flexing a muscle." Talking about stories so much that he almost jokingly buried the topic into the ground.

They went through the back of the old building and made their way kind of rowdily upstairs to the second floor where his office used to be, where the old magic happened; it was now a utility closet, with layers of dust and old cardboard boxes in opposition to how lively a room it had been: Matt sitting beneath a bulletin board with stories printed out haphazardly and ideas for the paper written here and there and magazines flayed over the desk, before he became more organized later on. They lingered in the office a few minutes, where Matt defended his wardrobe choice of black button-down short-sleeve shirt with sparkly silver pinstripes one day more than a decade ago, where Matt encouraged students individually or in groups to visit and chat, to shoot around ideas. Matt with his laptop open, Matt arguing about the eighties hair band Savatage so much it was hard to figure out if he was joking when he said, "This is real music," Matt buzzing on coffee and the adrenaline of having written his first big piece for SB Nation Longform about horseshoes (but "not really about horseshoes", if anyone asked), never believing that he could do this kind of journalism until he hosted a panel of long-form writers in 2012 and they encouraged him to try. It turned out to be an example of one of the lasting lessons he tried to impart upon his students, that stories never go the way you think they're going to: "Feet of Clay, Heart of Iron" was supposed to be about a man expected to win the horseshoe competition but who essentially choked, Matt had to figure out what to do with it and turned out a piece about a guy who'd lost his grip on the sport at which he was the best.

They went to the room where he used to teach feature writing, eight students in an old computer lab with Matt in front of them and asking they address him not as professor but as Matt, where he preferred to sit on one of the tabletops with his legs dangling casually off the floor instead of standing at the head of class—the tables now vacant there, the lectern pushed to the side. His old voice an echo for the students that night: He wanted to know about an assigned feature story, "What did the subject look like? What was their attitude like? What did they say? What did they do?" Matt walking around and emphasizing a point, making sure the day's lesson was more of a conversation than a lecture, handing back in drafts like the interviews on his desk in Connecticut for this book, marked up with his handwriting and purposefully printed out so he could hold them in his hands.

"He always said, 'Find another angle,'" one of the former students who was there, Glenn Battishill, remembers. "Come early, work hard, stay later. That's a big thing for him I use every day. Sometimes when I write stories, I think, I've got enough. But would Matt think I have enough? Would Matt make one more call to this person? He appreciated a sense of gravity of stories: Put your heart into this. Tell this story as seriously as you can. These stories deserve to be told. Also: he told us over and over, never leave a meeting early."

They looked for traces of him in hallways and around corners. In the sound booth where he'd essentially begun this book, it actually remained pretty much how it used to be, when he started doing the podcast, the microphone still there, in fact the one he'd chosen and used. They went in this passageway between his office and a classroom that sometimes only he used, that wasn't for students, kind of like a secret entrance. They were looking for him, yes, where he used to hang stories on the wall or have meetings, as they made their way through the old building that chilly evening just after the funeral, with the downtown of the small city all orange and white with cobwebs in shop windows and the campus dressed in the garlands of Halloween. Most of the people who organized and then gathered at the bar knew Matt from a time of prosperity, when he would've been hitting his stride as a young professor, advocating for the power of journalism, of the story—and above creativity, or risk taking, or ambition, imploring students to tell the truth. They found it impossible not to remember him, in his thirties, with his head shaved, with his backpack, with his rectangular glasses, chewing on a pen tip, lithe from running, snarky and affirming, poring over proofs, the childhood cancer scars in the form of moles on his face and nose. Those years he and Alyssa lived in a duplex in Ashland with a three-year-old and six-year-old, and he drove to work and invited students to come over and carry the classroom discourse to the dinner table, though there was really no room for them, dinner being cheap pizza. He gave students his cell number and told them to text with questions, no matter the time. It was Matt that came up with the idea for awards for the paper, the Ozzies, trophies in the shape of an eagle inspired by the statues in front of the J-school, the entire paper hanging out at his house and staying up all night.

They took their time in the *Collegian* offices, looking at the old papers, the old stories, the microphone, and the radio wall. One last glance into the storage closet, into the classrooms, they had to turn the lights off as they left, rooms redecorated and shifted around to a point where Matt might've not recognized anything about them had he reappeared. The longer they stayed in the building, the longer they talked about him, it almost seemed like he could.

—Justin Heckert, February 2023